The Black Muslims in America

by C. Eric Lincoln

Foreword by Gordon W. Allport

Beacon Press   Boston

Published simultaneously in Canada by
S. J. Reginald Saunders and Co., Ltd., Toronto

Library of Congress catalog card number: 61–5881

Printed in the United States of America

January, 1963

This book originated as a dissertation submitted in partial fulfillment of the requirements for the degree of Doctor of Philosophy in the Graduate School of Boston University

ACKNOWLEDGMENTS

The author wishes to acknowledge with thanks use of material from the following sources: E. D. Beynon, "The Voodoo Cult Among Negro Migrants in Detroit," *American Journal of Sociology* (July 1937-May 1938); A. E. Fauset, "Moorish Temple Science in America," in J. M. Yinger's *Religion, Society, and the Individual*, Macmillan; E. Hoffer, *The True Believer*, New American Library; Mike Wallace and Louis Lomax, "The Hate That Hate Produced," *Newsbeat* (WNTA-TV); *Sepia*, November 1959.

Preface

In the autumn of 1956, I was teaching courses in religion and philosophy at Clark College in Atlanta, Georgia. This study of the Black Muslims began when I read the following appraisal of Christianity in a term paper submitted to me by a senior student:

The Christian religion is incompatible with the Negro's aspirations for dignity and equality in America. It has hindered where it might have helped; it has been evasive when it was morally bound to be forthright; it has separated believers on the basis of color although it has declared its mission to be a universal brotherhood under Jesus Christ. Christian love is the white man's love for himself and for his race. For the man who is not white, Islam is the hope for justice and equality in the world we must build tomorrow.

Inquiry revealed that the writer, a sensitive and gifted young man, had come under the influence of the local Muslim minister, as had a few other students at the college. Despite their Christian backgrounds, and despite the fact that they were even then attending a church-related college, these young men had despaired of Christianity as a way of life capable of affording them the respect and dignity they sought and deserved.

I did not share those sentiments, and I do not share them today; but the challenge to study the alternative proposed in the term paper was irresistible.

This study of the Black Muslims has been an interesting and fascinating adventure, full of surprises and of social and religious inconformities. I soon discovered, for example, that these were no ordinary Moslems, nor did they wish to be taken as such. To distinguish themselves from the small Moslem enclaves that have existed in a few American cities for generations, they chose the spelling "Muslim" rather than the more familiar "Moslem." Further, these Muslims emphasize that they are "Black Men," *black* as the antithesis of white. They do not subscribe to the familiar Moslem doctrine that a common submission to Allah erases and transcends all racial awareness. On the contrary, they do not conceive the white man as capable of being a Muslim. "By nature he is incapable!"

The racial emphases peculiar to this rapidly growing, Chicago-centered movement suggested the descriptive phrase "Black Muslims," which I coined in 1956 and which has been widely used since to designate this group. Theretofore they had been variously known as the "Temple People," "the Muhammadans," "the Muslims," "the Voodoo Cult" and "the Nation of Islam."[1]

The study of the Black Muslims has taken me to many cities across the country, and it has provided unusual opportunities for me to sense directly the several pulses of America's Negro community, which is now making a determined struggle for a creative and meaningful existence. To most Negroes the teachings of the Black Muslim leader, Elijah Muhammad, are intellectually repugnant, but one is uncomfortably conscious of an emotional ambivalence towards the attraction and the power of a doctrine which promises an "escape into freedom" after so many years and so many forms of bondage. The rational self rebels against racism in any form and from any quarter, but the emotional self resists the contemplation of a reversal of fortune only with great effort.

This study is in no sense complete. At best it presents a partial perspective of the dark and serious problems of racial tension—problems which confront responsible men in this country and throughout the world. We need more studies about the voiceless people who want to be heard in the councils of the world. We need more action in terms of the truths that are already known. We shall have to hurry, I think, if we hope to pass on to our children a world in which there is reasonable hope for creative survival.

Many individuals and institutions have lent encouragement or support to the study during the years it was in progress. It would be impossible to name them all, but I wish to express my thanks and appreciation to every person who has in any way participated in bringing this piece of research to its present stage. First of all, I would express my thanks to Albert and Jessie Danielsen of Wellesley Hills, Massachusetts, whose comfortable home and warm friendship have provided a haven of refuge at periods when the day to day pressures have demanded respite.

I am particularly indebted to Professor Gordon Allport of Harvard University and to Professor Harold Isaacs of the Center for International Relations at the Massachusetts Institute of Technology for their encouragement and advice at critical periods of research and writing.

Dr. Kenneth Benne, Director of the Boston University Human Relations Center, and Mr. Frank Hurwitz, Executive Secretary of the Center, not only placed the facilities of the Center at my disposal but also relieved me of the normal responsibilities incident to being a Human Relations Fellow, thus permitting me to give full time to research on the Black Muslims. Professor Robert Chin at the Center has been of invaluable help and encouragement in helping to structure the research and in criticizing my methods of procedure and investigation.

I wish also to express my thanks to Mr. Elijah Muhammad, the "Spiritual Head of the Muslims in the West," for his cooperation in certain phases of the study. I am especially indebted to Minister Malcolm X of New York City and to Minister Louis X of Boston for the unusual degree of cooperation I have received from them during the course of the investigation. While we have not always agreed on certain premises incident to the Movement, these gentlemen have always welcomed me with courtesy, respect and a spirit of cooperation.

The *Pittsburgh Courier* made its files available to me, an important courtesy for which I am very grateful indeed.

To President James P. Brawley and Dean A. A. McPheeters of Clark College, I would express my appreciation for their continued encouragement, and for the extended leave of absence which made it possible for me to complete the research, the dissertation and this manuscript before returning to my post as Professor of Social Philosophy at Clark.

It would be difficult indeed for me to adequately express my gratitude to Dean Walter G. Muelder and Associate Professor Paul Deats, Jr., of the Boston University School of Theology. Nominally the professors directing my graduate studies, they have in fact been friends and counselors through three long and crucial years. I cannot hope to repay them for their guidance and confidence—and for their abiding friendship, which has always been a dimension external to the professor-student relationship.

I wish to express my indebtedness to Miss Sylvia Lafargue, Miss Hester W. Price and Mrs. Bertha S. Mintz, whose expert typing turned my original notes into an acceptable manuscript.

This has been an expensive undertaking, and it could not have been accomplished without generous support from several sources. The initial investigation was unsupported; but three years of study and research at Boston University were supported by grants and fellowships from the John Hay Whitney Foundation, The Crusade Scholarships of the Methodist Church, the Lilly Foundation, the Boston University Human Relations Center, the Society for the Psychological Study of Social Issues, and the Anti-Defamation League of B'nai B'rith.

Professor Lyman V. Cady, head of the Department of Religion and Philosophy during my graduate studies at Fisk University, very graciously interrupted his summer vacation to read portions of the manuscript and to make suggestions for its improvement; so also did Alex Haley, who has himself been an observer and interpreter of the Movement, and Dr. J. T. Wright, former director of the Staten Island Mental Health Association. All three are wise and perceptive friends and critics. Whatever inadequacies may persist in this study can but reflect my own inability to employ effectively the prudent judgments available to me.

Finally, it should be acknowledged that the real sacrifice making this study possible has been borne by those most dear to me, who have had to carry on in my absence longer than it was reasonable to ask. I only hope that in some way this effort has been worth their patience and deprivation.

C. ERIC LINCOLN

Boston, Massachusetts
December 1960

Contents

Preface   iii

Foreword by Gordon W. Allport   ix

1. The Verdict Is "Guilty"—The Sentence Is "Death"   3
   The End of the Second-Class Ride 6   The Stranger in Detroit 10
   Economic and Political Power 17   The Believers . . . 21
   . . . And Why They Become Believers 27

2. The Dynamics of Black Nationalism   33
   I. Bitter Soil and Bitter Fruits 34
        Group Consciousness 34   Avoidance 35   Acceptance 38
        Aggression 39
   II. Black Nationalism, U.S.A. 41
        Stereotype and Identity 41   Black Nationalism 43   Black
        Nationalism and Social Class 46

3. Black Nationalism: The Minor Leagues   50
   Religious Nationalism: The Moorish Science Temples 51
   Political Nationalism: The Garvey Movement 56   Preparing
   the Way for Allah 66

4. The Faith and the Future   67
   I. Doctrines and Mythology 68
        The Plight of the So-Called Negroes 68   The Coming of
        Allah 72   The Original Man 75   The White Man and
        Christianity 76
   II. Muslim Morality 80
   III. The Goals of the Movement 84
        The United Front of Black Men 84   Racial Separation 87
        Economic Separation 90   Some Good Earth 94

5. Reaching for the Masses   98
   I. The Nature of a Mass Movement 98
        The Importance of Mass Membership 98   The True Be-
        liever 99   Leadership in the Mass Movement 101   The
        Instruments of Unification 103

II. The Black Muslims as a Mass Movement 106
Reaching for the Masses 106   Lures for the True Be-
liever 108   Recruitment 111   Visit to a Temple 115
Schools and the Center 126   Mr. Muhammad Speaks 129

6. Tensions: Outside the Movement   135
I. The Negro Community 135
Individual Negro Leadership 135   The Negro Press 141
Institutional Negro Leadership 145   The Negro Christian
Churches 155   The Negro Man in the Street 159
II. The Jewish Community 165
III. The American Islamic Community 169
IV. The White Community 172

7. Tensions: Inside the Movement   179
I. The Concentration of Power 180
The Long Road from Sandersville 180   Malcolm X:
First Plenipotentiary 189   Near the Center 192   Trouble
on the Horizon 194
II. The Secret Army 199
III. The Search for Respectability 204
Violence and the Christian Tradition 204   The Race
Issue 208

8. The Black Muslims and Orthodox Islam   210
A Legitimate Religion? 212   A Moslem Sect? 218   The Political Implications 223

9. The Meaning for America   230
I. The Spectrum of Negro Protest 227
A Vestige of Faith 227   Group Identification: The Cor-
porate Response 229
II. Separatist Organizations 234
III. Integrative Organizations 238
IV. The Black Muslim Movement 246
The Edge of the Spectrum 246   Function and Dysfunc-
tion 248
V. The Deeper Cause 253

Notes   257

Index   270

Foreword

One century after the Emancipation Proclamation we are still trying in our country to repair the moral ravages of slavery. Our progress is slow and sluggish. It is this sluggishness that has given rise to the melodramatic Black Muslim Movement.

Dr. C. Eric Lincoln gives us a clear, moving, balanced account of the origins and rationale of this movement. His book makes fascinating reading. It is also one of the best technical case studies in the whole literature of social science. From it we learn that while the tenets of this strange Moslem sect are fantastic and unbelievable, yet at the same time the movement as a whole makes good sense and has functional value for its numerous adherents. Oppression evolves a logic of its own. An ideology, though wierd, often means more than it says.

The Black Muslim believes that the day of the white man has passed—or soon will. Peaceful integration is not the Negro's goal, for "why integrate with a dying man?" What the Negro requires is a new morale, economic self-sufficiency, a high code of personal morals, and a return to the pristine glory of his race. He needs to free himself from all remnants of slave mentality and from Christianity which has too long kept him doped in subservience to the white man. These are the underlying propositions upon which the movement rests. It has a Nietzschean flavor. But since abstractions require concrete symbolization in order to motivate, Elijah Muhammad, the leader, has evolved a heady array of myths, rituals, styles of greeting, to provide the effective scaffolding of imagery needed by his less educated followers. The tie to Islam is, of course, an historical monstrosity, but this fact does not trouble minds innocent of theological antiquity.

The entire movement rests upon an absolute and inflexible dichotomy of white–Negro, or, more accurately, white–non-white. White is evil; non-white is good. Here are a few key phrases: "There is no white man a Muslim can trust." If you say the movement rests on hate, it is "the hate that hate produced." Even the impartial reader concludes that much Elijah Muhammad says about the white man is "true enough to be embarrassing."

Thus the reader himself easily slips into a spurious black-white frame of mind. Like the Black Muslim he may find himself exalting race, "man's most dangerous myth," to the position of a final fixed truth.

Biologically speaking, color is a trivial fact. It leads none the less to coarse and dangerous misclassifications when it is applied to relationships within the human family. Some white men say that non-whites (all of them) are inferior. They are, of course, wrong. The only true statement would be, that in *some* respects *some* of them are inferior, *many* are not. Similarly, the Black Muslim says "the white man" is responsible for all the disprivilege suffered by the non-white. The truth is that *some* white men under *some* conditions are responsible for *some* of the disadvantages of colored people. Overgeneralization is the very essence of prejudice. Hence such dogmas as these follow the line of bigotry rather than logic.

Most of us believe that improvement in group relations will come about when—by education and exhortation, by law and law-enforcement—fewer and fewer whites are led to behave in ways injurious to non-whites. But the Black Muslim does not agree. For him the case is closed: it is non-white *versus* white. All people are fatally typed by skin color forever. Human beings are not mixtures of good and bad, wise and stupid, friendly and un-friendly, just and unjust, trustworthy and untrustworthy. Rather they are white and non-white, the one group, by its essence, incarnates evil qualities, the other virtues. This erroneous slicing marks the thought of all racists—of Hitler, of the White Citizens Council, of the Black Muslims.

Why do I feel it necessary here to refute the haunting irrele-vancy of race? I confess it is because in reading these pages I found myself at times carried away by the persuasiveness of Elijah Muhammad and his ministers. I succumbed to Dr. Lin-coln's deeply understanding and sympathetic account. Even though he writes as a social scientist his penetration of the topic forces me to wrestle with both the pros and cons of the case.

The author properly notes the ambiguity with which the leaders shroud the ultimate objectives of the movement. Its implications for the future are in a sense frightening, even though for the present one must admit there are gains for its devotees in heightened morality, economic improvement, and in hopeful outlook.

Further developments will bear close watching—by government authorities and also by social scientists. Will the sect continue to spread or will it wane? Will the fantastic legends on which it is based lose their appeal as the educational level of Negroes rises? Or, to the contrary, will educated Negroes find it possible to subscribe to an absurd ideology as did many German intellectuals under Hitler? And what other changes will occur over time? It is not enough to dismiss the movement as a lurid anomaly. It has deep roots in protest and is puzzling in portent.

Many of us live with false but cozy illusions concerning our relationships with other racial, ethnic, and national groups. We are not aware that a present battle rages between enlightened and fanatic solutions of our family problems. The situation in the United States, in South Africa, in Asia shows this to be the case. By deepening our insight Dr. Lincoln strengthens the hand of enlightenment. For only if we face the realities of race relations with accurate knowledge can we hope to find a sensible issue out of our predicament. We do well, therefore, to ponder closely the case of the Black Muslims.

GORDON W. ALLPORT

The Black Muslims in America

To

Cecil Eric

and

Joyce Elaine

1   The Verdict Is "Guilty"—
The Sentence Is "Death"

A slightly-built, light-skinned Negro paused casually before twelve grave-faced Negro men and women sitting in a jury box at Boston's John Hancock Hall. There was an air of gentle friendliness about him, and he hardly looked the part of a prosecuting attorney. Slowly he turned and looked at a red-faced, tow-haired white man slumped disconsolately in the dock and flanked by two grim and alert Negro policemen. The prosecutor's eyes hardened. His jaw stiffened, and the veins stood out clearly about his temples. His right arm shot out like a rapier and froze—the index finger pointing at the figure in the dock like a javelin momentarily suspended in flight. The white man cringed in his chair and was hauled erect by the officers. Some two thousand Negroes in the audience sat petrified with the novelty and daring of it as the young Bostonian delivered his indictment against the white man on behalf of the Black Nation of Islam:

I charge the white man with being the greatest liar on earth! I charge the white man with being the greatest drunkard on earth. . . . I charge the white man with being the greatest gambler on earth. I charge the white man, ladies and gentlemen of the jury, with being the greatest peace-breaker on earth. I charge the white man with being the greatest adulterer on earth. I charge the white man with being the greatest robber on earth. I charge the white man with being the greatest deceiver on earth. I charge the white man with being the greatest trouble-maker on earth. So, therefore, ladies and gentlemen of the jury, I ask you, bring back a verdict of guilty as charged![1]

The foreman polled the jury in the box. Within seconds he rose to read the verdict:

"We find the defendant guilty—as charged."

The sentence pronounced was "death," and the frightened defendant was dragged away, loudly protesting his innocence and enumerating all he had "done for the Nigra people."

3

The audience thundered its approval of the play. Its repeated ovations required several curtain calls by the players.

What was behind it all? Who were these people clamoring for the death of the white man? They were, for the most part, Black Muslims—followers of Elijah Muhammad, "Spiritual Head of the Muslims in the West." The drama they had just witnessed was written and produced by members of the Movement,[2] and it has been staged in many of the major cities across America.[3]

The Black Muslims are probably America's fastest growing racist sect—100,000 militant "Black Men" who look forward to the day when the white man in America will be "treated as he ought to be treated." The Movement is growing rapidly, and it is nationwide; in December 1960, there were sixty-nine temples or missions in twenty-seven states, from California to Massachusetts and Florida. Under the leadership of Elijah Muhammad, who has been hailed by thousands inside and outside the Movement as "the most fearless Black Man in America," the Black Muslims are demanding—and getting—a hearing from a significant element of the Negro community. Their ultimate demand—that Black Men be allowed to set up a separate state within the United States, occupying as much as one-fifth of the nation's territory—commands little or no attention among non-Muslim Negroes. But the lashing indictment of the white man that supports the demand, strikes a responsive, if reluctant, chord in many Negro hearts.

The Black Muslims are neither pacifists nor aggressors. They pay zealous attention to the requirements of the letter of law regarding peace and order. They engage in no "sit-ins," test no segregation statutes, participate in no "marches on Washington" or anywhere else. But they do believe in keeping the scores even, and they have warned all America that "an eye for an eye and a tooth for a tooth" is the only effective way to settle racial differences. Minister Malcolm X of the New York temple explained in a Boston address:

We are never aggressors. We will not attack *anyone*. We strive for peaceful relationships with everyone. BUT—[we teach our people that] if anyone attacks you, *lay down your life!* Every Muslim is taught never to [initiate a] fight. Respect another man's rights whether he is white, black, brown, yellow or what-not! Respect him as a man. "Do unto others as you would have them do unto you!" Never be the aggressor, never look for trouble. *But if any man molests you, may Allah bless you!*[4]

Although tense situations involving the Muslims and the civil authorities have occasionally developed, little violence has been associated with the Movement in recent times. Nevertheless, the Muslim image is such that an eventual eruption of violence is not unanticipated. Police in many communities maintain constant alerts. In Los Angeles, for example, the news media which co-operate with the local police avoid publicizing the Movement, yet the Los Angeles police openly worry about "what it's going to take to light the fuse."[5] The leaders of the sect are under constant surveillance by the FBI, and most of their important meetings are probably monitored by informers.

Despite these precautions, the expectation of an eventual racial clash is widespread among observers who know the Movement firsthand, whether as officers charged with the maintenance of public order or as Negro youth who visit the Muslim temples for a vicarious swing at "white oppression." The belief that the Muslims plan some kind of overt attack against the Black Man's oppressors, or that they will retaliate in kind if attacked by the white man, is widely held by the youth of the "Black Ghetto"— that is, the slum sections of the large cities, where most Negroes are compelled to live. The perspective of a New York youth is typical, if somewhat picturesque:

Man, I don't care what those [Muslim] cats say *out loud*—that's just a hype they're putting down for The Man [i.e., the white man]. Let me tell you—they've got some stuff for The Man even the Mau Mau didn't have! If he tries to crowd *them* like he's been used to doing the rest of us all the time, they're going to lay it on him from here to Little Rock! I grew up with some of the cats in that temple—went to school with them; ran around with them. Man, those cats have changed. They ain't for no light playing. Those cats are for real, and you'd better believe it![6]

How did it all begin? What is the meaning of the Black Muslim Movement? What kind of people belong to it, and just what are its aims? All observers agree that its membership is increasing, yet most Negro leaders insist that the Muslim membership "should reach its peak shortly."[7]   Meanwhile, the Muslims continue to found new temples, and Elijah Muhammad continues to draw thousands to his rallies. Why do they come? What are they after?

To answer these questions, we shall have to look at the socio-logical drama of contemporary America, especially at the American Negro's increasing dissatisfaction with the "bit" role he has been permitted to play. As one Muslim minister put it: "We've just had a 'walk-on' part. We've been nothing but background scenery for everybody else. Now we've got something to say, and we're going to say it loud enough for the whole world to hear."

The End of the Second-Class Ride

How different [was the tolerant spirit of the medieval Western Christian] from the spirit in which the white-skinned Western Protestant of modern times regards his black-skinned convert. The convert may have found spiritual salvation in the White Man's faith; he may have acquired the White Man's culture and learnt to speak his language with the tongue of an angel; he may have become an adept in the White Man's economic technique, and yet it profits him nothing so long as he has not changed his skin.[8]

Thus observes Professor Arnold Toynbee: in Western Protestant societies, at least, the first credential for acceptance is a white skin. A man who happens to be born with a different skin color cannot hope to be accepted, whatever his spiritual or intellectual merit.

This observation, from the perspective of world history, is on solid sociological ground. In his famous "Yankee City" studies, W. Lloyd Warner writes:

The ethnic group carries a divergent set of cultural traits which are evaluated by the host as inferior. . . . The racial groups are divergent biologically rather than culturally. . . . Such physical attributes as dark skin, the epicanthic fold, or kinky hair become symbols of status and automatically consign their possessors to inferior status. . . . The cultural traits of the ethnic group, which have become symbols of inferior status, can be and are changed in time; but the physical traits which have become symbols of inferior status are permanent.[9]

The data of sociology derive, of course, from observable human relationships. Every intelligent Negro experiences a feeling of quarantine when he ponders his future and the avenues of creative existence open to him. Malcolm X, the "angriest Muslim," protests loudly and at length: "When you say 'Negro,' you're trapped right there. Makes no difference who you are nor how many degrees you have from Harvard; if you're a Negro, you're trapped. If you're black, the doors close." And the Muslims are not unique in these sentiments. No less distinguished a person than Dr. Anna Hedgman, former administrative aide to the Federal Security Administration and an administrative assistant to New York's Mayor Wagner, complained bitterly to a television audience: "I don't know why white people are so absolutely wound up on this business, but [you] have to be white. If you could manage it, you ought to be white with blue eyes and blond hair." America, she charged, "has so bottled up the Negro" as to render him completely frustrated and defiant.[10]

The "school case" decision which the United States Supreme Court handed down in May 1954 was instrumental in focusing extraordinary attention upon this major racial dichotomy in the American society. It is unlikely that any single event since the Emancipation Proclamation of 1863 has produced so disturbing an effect, or has been so portentous of the possibility of extensive social change.[11] People throughout the world acclaimed the new promise of broadened opportunity for the expression of human creativity implicit in the decision and were encouraged by it.[12] Yet, in practice, the shift from "segregation" to "integration" has not been spectacular, even in education.

There have been other scattered but hopeful indices of change in Negro-white relations since 1954. Much encouragement for change has come from the courts. Segregated seating in interstate transportation no longer has legal sanction, and in a few areas Negro citizens now enjoy the unrestricted use of parks, beaches and other public recreational facilities. These and similar legal advances have given impetus and encouragement to improvements in some private institutions which, by their nature, cannot be the subject of litigation aimed at desegregation. This has been particularly true of some churches and church-related schools, which

have admitted Negroes although under no legal compulsion to
do so.

In the economic sphere, the picture is less bright. Race remains a determining criterion for employment throughout the
South and generally elsewhere in the country, and job restriction is
a formidable barrier to the Negro citizen's fulfillment of his creative potential. In spite of federal executive orders and state and
municipal legislation,[13] discrimination in employment remains the
rule rather than the exception.[14]

In political affairs, Negro-white relations have not perceptibly
improved. On the contrary, in many parts of the South there has
been a general *strengthening* of traditional methods to restrict
Negro voting or to exclude it altogether. In Fayette County in
west Tennessee, for example, Negroes were "starved out" for
wanting to vote. For months it was impossible for Negro citizens
to buy oil or gasoline for their tractors and other machinery. Bank
credit for crop loans—indispensable in this rural county—had
been stopped. No Negro could buy food or household necessities
in the local white stores, and wholesale houses refused to supply
Negro businesses.[15] Why? Because 450 Negroes insisted on
registering to vote, as did 3,000 white citizens. Negroes constitute
a majority in the county, but they have never been permitted even
a single voice in its government.

It is against this backdrop that one must come to grips with
the Black Muslim Movement. The lynchings, the danger of being
killed while under arrest,[16] the unevenness and uncertainty of
justice in the courts, the continuing problem of simply finding a
decent place to live—all are contributory to the making of a
Muslim and to the propagation of a mass movement of protest.

Perhaps the nearest parallel to the Black Muslim Movement
was the Garvey movement of the post-World War I era. The
social conditions which made Garveyism possible were similar to
those obtaining at the present time, if not quite the same. We
have had "Little Rock" and "Clinton, Tennessee," though there
has been no wholesale murder of Negroes such as occurred during
the infamous "Red Summer" of 1919. There have been improvements in the Negro's total status since Garvey's day—a little here,
a little there. There have been some breaches in the high, white

wall of segregation. But for Negroes in general, and for the Black Muslims in particular, these isolated improvements in the Negro's total status are not enough. The tradition of disprivilege and the continuing formidable opposition to first-class citizenship are the discouraging elements that contribute most to the "Muslim mood."

Yet we cannot dismiss the Black Muslim Movement as simply another reaction against the traditional expressions of American race-consciousness. The history of the Negro in America is per se a history of race-consciousness and its consequences,[17] but American history has not heretofore produced an archetype of the Black Muslim Movement.

The new and most challenging factor, of course, is the expansion of the American Negro's horizon from the national to the international scene. World War II saw the practical end of European colonialism, and the rapid demise of colonialistic philosophy has been a significant feature of postwar international relations. The determination to be free is the characteristic mood of the hundreds of millions of people whose destinies have not for centuries been self-determined; and for the most part, the colonial powers have seen and heeded the signs of the times. In an address before the United Nations, as the world community welcomed the newly independent Cameroons into membership, French delegate Armand Berard called pointed attention to the fact that "independence need not come as the result of conquest and violence."[18] Seventeen African states achieved more or less peaceful independence in 1960. "Everywhere the Dark Continent is emerging into the news spotlight. It is demanding attention—and getting it. Some observers are calling 1960 'Africa Year.'"[19]

The emergence of Africa is a vitally significant factor in the aggressive impatience of the American Negro. Most of the colonial peoples of the past three centuries have been non-white and under white domination, and American Negroes have understandably felt some identification with them. The independence of India, Indonesia, the Philippines and other non-white Asian nations stirred applause, though little hope, in the breasts of America's largest minority. With Africa, the parallel strikes painfully close. Many Negroes for whom Africa seemed as remote as the planet Jupiter now find themselves exhilarated and encouraged by the emergence of black national states in the once "dark" continent. But they also find themselves strangely threatened, for the African may leave his American brother behind as the only remaining symbol of racial inferiority, of the socially and politically *declassé* "Black Man," left in the world.

There is a feeling among American Negroes that the non-white world is waiting—waiting to see if they are fit to be counted as men. There is a new determination in the Negro community to "go first class, whatever the cost." For most, "first class" means an unqualified enjoyment of all the rights and duties of citizenship. For others, "first class" means political and social autonomy—a national state for the "Black Man" in America.

The Stranger in Detroit

Sometime in the midsummer of 1930, an amiable but faintly mysterious peddler suddenly appeared in the Negro community of Detroit. He was thought to be an Arab,[20] although his racial and national identity still remains undocumented. He was welcomed into the homes of the culture-hungry Negroes, who were eager to purchase his silks and artifacts, which he claimed were like those the Negro people wore in their homeland across the sea.

He came first to our houses selling raincoats, and then afterwards, silks. In this way he could get into the people's houses, for every woman was eager to see the nice things the peddlers had for sale. He told us that the silks he carried were the same kind that our people used in their home country, and that he was from there. So we asked him to tell us about our own country.[21]

His customers were so anxious to learn of their own past and the country from which they came that the peddler soon began holding meetings from house to house throughout the community.

At first, the "prophet," as he came to be known, confined his teachings to a recitation of his experiences in foreign lands, admonitions against certain foods and suggestions for improving his listeners' physical health. He was kind, friendly, unassuming and patient.

. . . he would eat whatever we had on the table, but after the meal he began to talk. "Now don't eat this food, it is poison for you. The people in your own country do not eat it. Since they eat the right kind of food they have the best health all the time. If you would just live like the people in your home country, you would never be sick any more." So we all wanted him to tell us about ourselves and about our home country and about how we could be free from rheumatism, aches, and pains.[22]

He also used the Bible as a textbook to teach them about their true religion—not Christianity, but the religion of the Black Men of Asia and Africa. He used the Bible because it was the only religious book his followers knew. It was not the proper book for the Black Nation; but, carefully interpreted, it could be made to serve until they were introduced to the Holy Qur'an (or Quran).

Eventually the stranger's teachings took the form of increasingly bitter denouncements against the white race; and as his prestige grew, he "began to attack the teachings of the Bible in such a way as to shock his hearers and bring them to an emotional crisis."[23] People experienced sudden conversions and became his followers.

Up to that day I always went to the Baptist church. After I heard the sermon from the prophet, I was turned around completely. When I went home and heard that dinner was ready, I said: "I don't want to eat dinner. I just want to go back to the meeting." I wouldn't eat any meals but I [went] back that night, and I went to every meeting after that.[24]

Before long, the house-to-house meetings were inadequate to accommodate all those who wished to hear the prophet. The solution was obvious: they hired a hall, which they named the Temple of Islam. Thus the movement which has become known as the Black Muslims was born.

No one knew very much about the founder of this first temple. Usually he referred to himself as Mr. Farrad Mohammad or Mr. F. Mohammad Ali. He was also known as Professor Ford, Mr. Wali Farrad and W. D. Fard. One of his earliest converts recalls that, on one occasion, the prophet said:

My name is W. D. Fard, and I come from the Holy City of Mecca. More about myself I will not tell you yet, for the time has not yet come. I am your brother. You have not yet seen me in my royal robes.[25]

Inevitably, there was a proliferation of legends about so mysterious a figure. One such legend is that Fard was a Jamaican Negro whose father was a Syrian Moslem. Another describes him as a Palestinian Arab who had participated in various racial agitations in India, South Africa and London before moving on to Detroit. Some of his followers believed him to be the son of wealthy parents of the tribe of Koreish—the tribe of Mohammed, founder of classical Islam.[26] Others say that he was educated at a London university in preparation for a diplomatic career in the service of the kingdom of Hejaz, but that he sacrificed his personal future "to bring 'freedom, justice, and equality' to the 'black men in the wilderness of North America, surrounded and robbed completely by the Cave Man.' "[27] Fard announced himself to the Detroit police as "the Supreme Ruler of the Universe," and at least some of his followers seem to have considered him divine. At the other extreme, a Chicago newspaper investigating the Black Muslim Movement refers to Fard as "a Turkish-born Nazi agent [who] worked for Hitler in World War II."[28]

Fard described himself to his followers as having been sent to wake his "uncle"—that is, the Black Nation—to the full range of the Black Man's possibilities in a world temporarily dominated by the "blue-eyed devils." The illiterate Negroes who heard his heady talk were awed by his apparent fearlessness (as were to be the hundred thousand others and more who pledged themselves to follow his successor a generation later). They became increasingly alert to the subtle discriminations they faced in the North. For the North was no Promised Land: it was the South all over again, with the worst features of racial prejudice thinly camouflaged by "sweet talk about equality."

The fact that the country was in the throes of the great Depression did not help the situation. The starving, overcrowded Negroes living in the slums of Detroit (as in other Northern cities) became increasingly bitter toward the whites who seemed to control their lives. Policemen, who are the ever-present reminder of the white man's power; white workers, who displaced the Negroes as jobs became more scarce or who retained their jobs as thousands of Negroes were being laid off; even the welfare workers, who insulted the Negroes and made them wait long

hours before passing out the pitiful supplies of flour and lard—
all these became the symbolic targets of a virulent hatred of the
white man growing in the breasts of Fard's Black Nation. One
extreme example:

An Asiatic trend among Negro dole recipients of the Elmwood district, noted at the time as a passing whim . . . came back with horror
to two women welfare workers on learning that the fanatical [Black
Muslim] Robert Harris had intended them for human sacrifice as
infidels. . . . Harris stated to the police that each of these was a "no-
good Christian," and that they would have been sacrificed if he knew
where he could have found them.[29]

At first the contact between the Negroes and Fard was casual
and informal. After a temple had been secured, however, the
house-to-house meetings were discontinued, and a tightly knit
organization replaced the informal gatherings. Members were
examined before acceptance and were then registered, and a
hierarchy was established. At this point, some of the followers
of the late Noble Drew Ali began to pledge themselves to Fard.

Fard continued to teach his followers about the deceptive
character of the white man and to help them relive, at least in
fantasy, the glorious history of Black Afro-Asia. An unusually
resourceful teacher, he was able to utilize such varied literature
as the writings of Joseph F. "Judge" Rutherford, then leader of
the Jehovah's Witnesses, Van Loon's *Story of Mankind,* Breasted's
The Conquest of Civilization, the Quran, the Bible and certain of
the literature of Freemasonry to bring his people to "a knowledge
of self." Some of the illiterate were taught to read so that they
could learn firsthand about the past greatness of their race. All
were encouraged to purchase radios so that they could hear the
addresses of Rutherford and of Frank Norris, the Baptist funda-
mentalist.

The white man's words were not to be taken literally, for he
was considered incapable of telling the truth. His writings were
symbolic and needed interpretation, and this was Fard's mission
to his "uncle" in the West. So, having taught his followers to
read, he then interpreted for them what they read—interpreted it
in the name of the one true God, "whose right and proper name
is Allah." Thus, he explained, the white man served as a tool in

the hands of Allah through which the Black Man could learn the secrets of his own past and prepare himself for the role history would demand of him.

To supplement the "symbolic" literature of the white man, Fard himself wrote two manuals for the Movement. *The Secret Ritual of the Nation of Islam* was (and still is) transmitted orally; it is memorized verbatim by the students at the Movement's parochial schools and has become an oral tradition. *Teaching for the Lost Found Nation of Islam in a Mathematical Way,* though it was printed and given to registered Muslims, was written in Fard's own "symbolic language" and required his interpretation.

Within three years, Fard had developed an organization so effective that he was able to withdraw almost entirely from active leadership. He had not only set up the temple and established its ritual and worship but also founded a University of Islam (actually, a combined elementary and secondary school), dedicated to "higher mathematics," astronomy and the "ending of the spook civilization." He had created the Muslim Girls Training Class, which taught young Muslim women the principles of home economics and how to be a proper wife and mother. Finally, "fear of trouble with unbelievers, especially with the police, led to the founding of the Fruit of Islam—a military organization for the men who were drilled by captains and taught tactics and the use of firearms." [30] A Minister of Islam was now appointed to run the entire organization, aided by a staff of assistant ministers. Each of these men was selected and trained personally by Fard, who gradually stopped his public appearances and eventually disappeared from view.

One of the earliest officers in the Movement under Fard was Elijah Muhammad, who was born Elijah Poole. Poole and his family migrated from Georgia in the 1920s; and after Fard's appearance, several of them were soon identified with the Nation of Islam. An interesting mishap occurred at the time of Poole's initiation into the Movement. Under Fard, each proselyte was required to write a letter asking for his "original" (Islamic) name; when he received this name, the "slave name" given his ancestors by the white man was discarded. When the three Poole brothers applied for names, they neglected to mention that they were blood brothers, and "despite his omniscience, the prophet gave [them] the surnames of Sharrieff, Karriem and Muhammad." When the mistake became apparent, Fard explained that he had "divine knowledge" of the proper names of the three brothers.[31]

Elijah Muhammad devoted himself wholeheartedly to Fard and to the Movement. Though opposed by moderates in the hierarchy, he became Fard's most trusted lieutenant. At his initiation he had been given the "original" surname Karriem, but Fard now acknowledged his higher status by renaming him Elijah Muhammad. When a chief Minister of Islam was named to preside over the organization, Fard chose Muhammad, and the choice proved a wise one. Elijah Muhammad was almost singlehandedly responsible for the deification of Fard and for the perpetuation of his teachings in the early years after Fard disappeared.

The Prophet's disappearance occurred in about June 1934, shortly after Muhammad was named Minister of Islam, and he vanished as mysteriously as he had arrived. Even the police seem to have been baffled. A report that he was last seen "aboard a ship bound for Europe" is unsubstantiated; so also are reports that he met with foul play at the hands of either the Detroit police or some of his dissident followers. It is certain that many of those who heard Fard were openly hostile to his anti-white diatribes and resented his attacks on the Christian church.[32] But any link between these antipathies and his strange disappearance remains in the realm of undocumented conjecture.

Some of Muhammad's critics hint darkly at the coincidence of Fard's disappearance at the moment of Muhammad's rise to power. But Muhammad's rise was neither sudden nor unchallenged, and Fard himself had had to struggle to retain leadership after the Movement began to grow. Muhammad simply cast his lot on the side that eventually prevailed.

The very nature of the Prophet's teachings made schism and factionalism inevitable. Quite early in the life of the Movement, Abdul Muhammad, another of Fard's trusted officers, withdrew and organized a competing temple. Fard had consistently taught that his followers were not Americans and that they owed no allegiance to the American flag. It was stupid, he argued, to pledge allegiance to a flag that offered no protection against "the

depravities of the white devils [who] by their tricknology . . .
keep our peoples illiterate to use as tools and slaves." Abdul
Muhammad's splinter group, in contrast, was founded on the
principle of complete loyalty to the American Constitution and to
the nation's flag. This splinter group, however, did not survive.

As early as 1932 the Communist party attempted to infiltrate
the Black Muslim organization and take it over. It was followed
by the Japanese, who sought to establish a fifth-column beachhead
in the group under the direction of the wily Major Takahashi. The
major tried to persuade the Muslims to swear allegiance to the
Mikado, and he succeeded in splitting off some members of the
Movement.[33] Nor were these the only international interests seeking to cultivate the Muslims. By 1934 even the Ethiopians developed a sudden interest in "the Black Nation in the West"; one
Wyxzewixard S. J. Challouehliczilczese sought to use the Movement to promote various financial schemes in the interest of his
native land. Closer to home, America's "union-busting" interests
did not hesitate to take advantage of the hunger and poverty of
the unsophisticated Negroes in a war against the CIO. All these
efforts failed, but the struggle against them drained much of the
vitality of the Movement.

After Fard's disappearance, the Muslims soon lost their
aggressiveness; and the Movement, to which Fard had drawn
eight thousand adherents, began to decline in size and in power.
Quarrels broke to the surface, and the relatively lethargic moderates drove Elijah Muhammad from Detroit to the Temple No. 2
in Chicago, which had been established as the Southside Mosque
two years earlier. There he set up new headquarters and began
to reshape the Movement under his own highly militant leadership. Fard became identified with the god Allah; having been thus
deified, he was worshipped with prayer and sacrifice. Muhammad,
who had served "Allah," naturally assumed the mantle of
"Prophet," which "Allah" had worn during his mission in Detroit.
Today Muhammad is referred to both as the Prophet and, more
often, as the Messenger of Allah.

The Black Muslims have come far under Muhammad. He
has given them temples and schools, apartment houses and grocery
stores, restaurants and farms. Most important of all, he has given

them a new sense of dignity, a conviction that they are more than the equals of the white man and are destined to rule the earth. "The Messenger," the faithful say reverently, "has taught us knowledge of ourselves; and this is the knowledge that makes it possible for us to obtain freedom, justice and equality in the world, no matter what the white man thinks, no matter what the white man does." This is not a passive belief: Muhammad has promised to "do something for my beautiful Black Nation," and the Muslims are certain that he will. "That's right! That's right!" they say fervently, and swear to lay down their lives if it should be his will.

Economic and Political Power

The Black Muslims are an intensely dedicated, tightly disciplined block of more than 100,000 American Negroes, convinced that they have learned the ultimate truth and ready to make any sacrifice it may demand of them. Theirs is not a "Sunday religion": the Muslim temples hold frequent meetings, and every Muslim is required to attend two (and often more) meetings a week. Nor is it a religion that spares the billfold. The mass of Muslims are from the Negro lower class, with relatively low incomes, and they are encouraged to live respectably and provide for their families. But the men are urged to hold steady jobs; and all Muslims are forbidden to gamble, smoke, drink liquor, overeat, indulge in fripperies or buy on credit. As a result most Muslims enjoy a healthy standard of living and still have enough cash left over to swell the Movement's coffers.

Every Muslim is expected to give a fixed percentage of his income to the Movement each year. In 1952 this percentage was set at one-third of all earnings; but the figure is probably not always so high. In addition, the temples collect contributions for a variety of funds, many for local purposes and at least six for the use of the national headquarters at Temple No. 2 in Chicago. Of the six known national funds, four are earmarked for real estate, public relations, official travel and new cars; one is an annual collection on the anniversary of Fard's birthday, February 26th, with no purpose designated; and one is a discretionary fund, the "No. 2 Treasury and Central Point Fund," for Muhammad to use as he sees fit. The increase in the total funds available to the Movement is suggested by the increase in its real estate holdings in Chicago in the last six years—from an estimated $150,000 in 1954 to an estimated $500,000 at the end of 1960.

But the Muslims' power to influence the general American community is significant, not only because of their increasing membership and financial resources, but also because they can be mobilized to act in unswerving unison on any matter designated by the leadership. They will, for example, vote as Muhammad tells them to vote and buy where he tells them to buy. A Muslim bloc, therefore, even in a large city, may be the determining factor in the balance of political and economic power.

It is already said in Harlem that Malcolm X, minister of the large Temple 7 and Muhammad's chief lieutenant, is in a position to decide the election of U. S. Representative Adam Clayton Powell's successor, when and if Powell decides to retire. Whether or not this is true, the deference shown Malcolm X by numerous political figures in New York City is impressive. Even more impressive—and far more sinister—as evidence of the Muslims' political weight is the fact that Fidel Castro, during his dramatic sojourn in Harlem in the autumn of 1960, invited Malcolm X to a private conference which lasted some two hours. Malcolm had earlier been invited, along with other important American Negroes, to visit Castro in Cuba. That the invitation was not accepted—or that acceptance was delayed—can be attributed in part to Muhammad's distaste for communism as a white ideology and in part to his doubt whether Castro is a Black Man (as he seems intent upon proving) or a "blue-eyed devil" hiding behind a slogan and a sword.

Muhammad has not yet seen fit to use the undeniable power of the Black Muslim vote as a lever to prise concessions from the white or the non-Muslim Negro community. From the start, Muslims have generally preferred not to vote at all. This has been due partly to their self-identification with Afro-Asia, partly to their belief that America is already corrupt and doomed, and partly to their sense of futility in electing any white man to office. Malcolm X notes that "Roosevelt promised, Truman promised, Eisenhower promised. Negroes are still knocking on the door begging for civil rights. . . . Do you mean to tell me that in a powerful country like this, a so-called *Christian* country, that a handful of men from the South can prevent the North, the West, the Central States and the East from giving Negroes the rights the Constitution says they already have? No! I don't believe that and neither do you. No white man really wants the Black Man to have his rights, or he'd have them. The United States does everything else it wants to do."[34]

The Muslims have also refrained from voting in an effort to keep their strength a secret. "If you don't vote, nobody knows what you can accomplish when you do," and so far there has been no issue worth a real display of strength. In an address following the 1960 political conventions, Muhammad admonished some seven thousand Negroes at a New York meeting simply to "go to the polls with your eyes and ears open, and remember that it is not necessary for you to go seeking justice for anyone but yourselves. . . . The white people of America already have their freedom, justice and equal rights."[35]

The time may come, however, when more than an undefined "justice" will be at stake. The Muslim leadership may one day feel ready to issue specific demands on local, state and national political bodies. Then, even at the national level, they can expect to be heard with respect. Recent elections seem to have demonstrated that a party, to win, must control the large industrial cities of the North, in which the Negro vote is potentially pivotal. But Negroes do not vote as a bloc; they split their votes between the two major parties. Anyone who could amass and "deliver" a significant number of Negro votes in these cities, therefore, would lead from strength in dealing with the national party organizations. It is precisely in these cities that the Black Muslim Movement is now flourishing. And, "You can be sure of one thing," says Malcolm X. "Every single Muslim man and woman will vote the way Mr. Muhammad tells him to vote."

The Black Muslims' political power is ominous but, for the moment, latent. It is reckoned with seriously at the local and state level in many states, but Muhammad is not seeking political alignments even there, and he is unlikely to attempt a national power-play for some years to come. The Muslims' economic power, on the other hand, is already being brought to bear against the white community. There is as yet no organized boycott of white merchants, but every Muslim is expected to "buy black"—that is, to trade with his own kind in preference to "spending your money where you can't work and can't sit down." Muslims have only contempt for the Negro sit-in movement, in which Black Men are "going out of their way to force the white man to let them spend more money with him," rather than contribute to the establishment of businesses run by and for Black Men.

The Muslims demand an entirely separate black economy, arguing that not until the Negro is economically independent will he be, in any real sense, free. The total annual income of the American Negro, they point out, is more than $20 billion—greater than the total income of Canada and greater than that of several European states. Such a purchasing power, if spent among Negro businessmen and invested in Negro enterprises, would earn the respect of every nation in the world. The Muslims concede that the white man has, for the moment, an edge on technical and commercial know-how. The Black Man must learn whatever the white man can teach him and then outstrip the white man in productivity and trade.

As the Negro community develops its own business and industrial plant, the Muslims' pressure for economic separation is virtually certain to increase. In the not too distant future, this may well take the form of an official boycott against white merchants in the Negro ghettos. In a related move, the Muslims might picket the downtown stores so as to discourage Negroes from entering and shopping there. Such a maneuver would be so explosive that white store-owners and policemen might yearn for the good old days of the tension that accompanied the student sit-ins. Store-owners cannot be expected to take calmly the probable loss of much of their patronage; but the Muslims are neither "passive" nor "loving" toward white men, and any violence on the part of whites would certainly be met with violence. "If it ever happens," said one police official darkly, "that's when we're going to have hell on our hands."

The Believers . . .

Who are these "faithful," these true believers, these Black Muslims?

Most simply, a Black Muslim is an American Negro who is a follower of Elijah Muhammad, "Spiritual Leader of the Lost-Found Nation in the West." Black Muslims are distinguished from orthodox Moslems not in the mere spelling of the word (strictly speaking, either form is correct), but in their belief that their leader, the Honorable Elijah Muhammad, is the Messenger of Allah, directly commissioned by Allah himself, who came in person (under the name of Fard) to wake the sleeping Black Nation and rid them of the white man's age-old domination.

A survey taken in Detroit during the early years of the Movement (1930–1934) showed that the overwhelming majority of Muslims—all but half a dozen or so of the two hundred families interviewed—were recent migrants from the rural South. The majority had come to industrial Detroit from small communities in Virgina, South Carolina, Georgia, Alabama and Mississippi. Investigations by the Wayne County Prosecutor's office indicated the same origin.[36]

Those attracted to the early Movement were not only recent migrants, but they had typically visited their old homes in the South one or more times before becoming Muslims. The limited freedom they had experienced in the North made them acutely conscious of the extreme subordination of the Negro in the South —a realization which sharpened their hostilities and increased their sense of frustration.

Through these visits they had become more conscious of race discrimination on the part of the Caucasians. After their brief sojourn in the North they tended to reinterpret with sinister implications incidents of race contact in the South. They began to realize that lynchings and the indignities of the Jim Crow system were perpetuated by Caucasians who worshipped the same God as they did and worshipped Him in the same way.[37]

Finally, most of those who joined the early temples were, one can fairly assume, functionally illiterate.

In 1959 the pattern of membership remained generally the same, but the disproportion of recent, rural migrants did not appear so extreme. Several factors may be responsible. In the first place, the proportion of Negroes in the North and East is now much greater than it was in the depression years 1930–1934, and they have been there longer. The Muslims can thus proselytize a more established population. Secondly, although there is a continuing stream of migrants from the South, many of the current migrants are from Southern cities and towns, or at least have had some urban experience before pushing on to the North. Again, the Black Muslim Movement is no longer limited to the industrial cities of the North. Its temples are scattered from New England to San Diego and from San Francisco to Miami.[38] At least a dozen cities in the South have temples or missions.

Thus, while the vast majority of Muslims still belong to the most disprivileged class, they are no longer necessarily recent, rural migrants from the South, nor are they functionally illiterate. A recent poll taken of 460 Muslims in Atlanta, Chicago, Boston and New York[39] revealed that more than half had lived in their present city longer than five years. Fifteen per cent had lived in the city for at least ten years, and 5½ per cent were born there. Forty-six per cent of the group sampled claimed to have had at least a sixth-grade education, and only 2 per cent admitted to less than a fourth-grade education.

But we must not lean too heavily upon this sampling. Muslims are extremely wary about giving *any* information about themselves or the Movement unless such information is of obvious propaganda value. The typical Muslim will talk freely about the teachings of the Messenger or the treacheries of the white man, but he will seldom provide information subject to statistical analysis. If he does not evade factual questions entirely, the Muslim brother politely refers them to his minister, who in turn invokes Elijah Muhammad.

Critical observation and informal interviews have, therefore, been the best tools available for determining the constituency of the Movement. My observations and experiences with Muslims in several cities suggest the following:

1. The membership is young. Up to 80 per cent of a typical congregation is between the ages of seventeen and thirty-five. This pattern has been noted again and again in temples across the country. In the newer temples, youth is even more pronounced; in some, fully three-quarters of the membership is under thirty years of age. About the same proportion of the ministers are under thirty-five; the youngest is only twenty-three.

The reason for such a concentration of youth is clear. This is an activist movement, and the appeal is *directed* to youth. Large, young families are eagerly sought, and least attention is paid to older people reared as Christians. Older people have a certain security in their familiar religious orientation, and they do not readily shift to a position so unfamiliar and radical as that preached by the Muslims.

The older people who do belong to the movement, especially in the Northern cities, are for the most part ex-Garveyites or ex-Moorish Science Moslems, or they have belonged to some of the more esoteric cults flourishing in Harlem, Detroit or Chicago. Many of these older "nationalists" consider Muhammad a natural successor to both Garvey and Noble Drew Ali, and they have had little difficulty in making the transition. Muhammad himself professes "a very high opinion" of both Garvey and Noble Drew Ali; he refers to them as "fine Muslims" and calls upon their sympathizers to "follow me and cooperate in our work because we are only trying to finish up what those before us started."[40]

2. *The membership is predominantly male.* Unlike the typical Christian church, the Muslim temples attract many more men than women, and men assume the full management of temple affairs. Women are honored, and they perform important functions within a defined role; they are not in any sense considered mere "property," as has sometimes been the case in classical Islam. However, they do not constitute the organizational foundation through which the Movement functions, either in service or in finance. They work alongside the men in the various business enterprises owned by the temples, and they share in the affairs of the temples themselves, but almost always in roles not in conflict with the male assumption of primary responsibility.

3. *The membership is essentially lower class.* A generation ago Erdman Beynon could report:

At the time of their first contact with the prophet, practically all of the members of the cult were recipients of public welfare, unemployed, and living in the most deteriorated areas of Negro settlement in Detroit.[41]

That was in the early 1930s—the worst of the depression years. By 1937, however, Beynon observed:

At the present time, there is no known case of unemployment among these people. Practically all of them are working in the automobile and other factories. They live no longer in the slum section . . . but rent homes in some of the best economic areas in which Negroes have settled. They tend to purchase more expensive furniture, automobiles, and clothes than do their neighbors even in these areas of higher-class residence.[42]

The socio-economic pattern today is a fusion of these two trends. Muslims are fully employed, yet they live and meet in the most deteriorated areas of the slums.

Recruitment for the Movement is still predominantly from among low-income groups at the lower end of the educational scale. It has attracted a few intellectuals, an increasing number of college students and a scattering of business and professional men; but a majority of the membership of any given temple is composed of domestic and factory workers, common laborers and the like.[43] An increasing number of the men, however, are skilled and semiskilled craftsmen; the businesses owned by the group are usually housed in buildings renovated by the Muslims themselves —from the plumbing to the electric signs that mark the entrances. The Muslims are justifiably proud of the "technicians" who operate their sound and recording equipment, and of their expert stenographers and secretaries. They have a corps of excellent photographers, who make film records of every important event; the photographic mural on the wall of their Temple 7 Restaurant in New York is a display of their professional skill.

Many Muslims have come into the movement from various levels of extralegal activity. Some are ex-convicts—or even convicts, for at least three temples are behind prison walls. Some have come into the Movement as dope addicts and alcoholics, or from careers as pimps and prostitutes, pool sharks and gamblers. But all who remain in the Movement are rehabilitated and put to work. The members' claim that they are able to secure work much more easily than other Negroes[44] appears valid. There are no idle Muslims; and delinquency, juvenile or adult, is almost unheard of.

Today's Muslims, however, do not generally live in the better residential areas available to Negroes. Where Negroes of middle- and upper-class status have developed—or moved into—residential areas consistent with their new prosperity, Muslims have not followed, for the Movement continues to emphasize its affiliation with the working class. There are exceptions: Elijah Muhammad lives in a nineteen-room mansion in a quiet neighborhood near the University of Chicago. But the Messenger has an unusually large family (seven children); his offices occupy part of the building; and several rooms are set aside for the use of his many guests—ministers called to Chicago for consultation and, often, visitors from abroad. Even in this mansion there is no ostentation in furnishings or appointments, and few of Muhammad's ministers and followers have elected to abandon the slums.

The Muslim leaders tend to live and to build their temples and businesses in the areas from which they draw their major support—the heart of the Black Ghetto. This ghetto houses the most dissident and disinherited, the people who wake up to society's kick in the teeth each morning and fall exhausted with a parting kick each night. These are the people who are ready for revolution—any kind of revolution—and Muhammad astutely builds his temples in their midst. Furthermore, in the segregated Black Ghetto, the illusion of a "Black Nation" within a surrounding and hostile "white nation" takes on a semblance of reality. The only whites around are the hated shopkeepers who "suck my people blind." These white tradesmen are ready-made symbols—representatives of the impersonal white oppressor who has "penned us up like sheep, the better to drink our blood."

4. *The membership is almost wholly American Negro.* The Garvey movement was built around a hard core of West Indians, who, sharing his nationality and cultural experiences, were most readily attracted to his program. American Negroes gave Garvey little attention until he had already attracted a large following of West Indian immigrants.[45] But the Muslim leadership has not especially welcomed the West Indians in this country, possibly because the West Indian habit of making distinctions among

Negroes in terms of color could jeopardize the Muslim appeal for a "United Black Front."

There may have been some Japanese "advisors" connected with the Movement in its early days, when Major Takahashi was active in Detroit. The Muslims consider all non-whites to be Black Men, whatever their skin color, and it is worth noting that Muhammad was indicted for pro-Japanese sympathies in the first year of World War II.[46] But no significant Oriental influence is apparent in the Movement today.

At one time, Muhammad's chief minister was a Haitian, Theodore Rozier. More recently, a number of Arab nationals have been associated with the movement in teaching or advisory capacities. Shaikh Diab, a Palestinian Arab, for example, taught Arabic at the (Chicago) University of Islam—a combined elementary and secondary school—for several years. A number of Egyptian nationals are friendly to the Movement and its leadership, but whether they hold membership in the temples is not known. A Nigerian graduate student also teaches at the (Chicago) University of Islam, and foreign students from all parts of Asia and Africa frequently attend the local temples, which are found in nearly all cities having large universities.

These foreign contacts are highly prized, yet the Movement itself remains distinctively "Black American." Other Moslems have been welcomed as visitors, but they have not been encouraged to seek membership.

5. *Finally, the membership is predominantly ex-Christian.* American Negroes have always been a religious people; and until very recent times, "religion" has for them meant Protestant Christianity. Except for the Moorish-Americans and a few hundred ex-cultists of varying past proclivities, almost all of the Muslims seem to be drawn from Protestant families or traditions, although there are significant numbers of ex-Catholics in the Movement. Many Muslims have come from revivalistic sects, but a substantial number have held active membership in the established denominations, and some of the Muslim ministers are former Christian preachers.

The younger Muslims, especially those under twenty, have usually had no strong Christian convictions, but almost without exception they come from Christian homes. All too often, their conversion reflects a serious inadequacy in their religious environment. One parent whose son had "gone Muslim" turned to his minister in anguish. "Now," said the minister, "he expects me to save his son from the Muslims when I haven't a single handle to grab him by. The parents come here four or five times a year, and the boy doesn't come at all. No wonder the Muslims got him; he was looking for something."

. . . And Why They Become Believers

The fundamental attraction of the Black Muslim Movement is its passion for group solidarity, its exaggerated sense of consciousness-of-kind. What matters above all is that men acknowledge themselves as black or white, and that all black men work together to accomplish their group aims. These aims have been summed up by a Muslim minister as:

To get the white man's foot off my neck, his hand out of my pocket and his carcass off my back. To sleep in my own bed without fear, and to look straight into his cold blue eyes and call him a liar every time he parts his lips.[47]

The ultimate appeal of the Movement, therefore, is the chance to become identified with a power strong enough to overcome the domination of the white man—and perhaps even to subordinate him in turn.

In this context, although the Black Muslims call their Movement a religion, religious values are of secondary importance. They are not part of the Movement's basic appeal, except to the extent that they foster and strengthen the sense of group solidarity.

The Muslims make no secret of the fact that they count themselves a part of the growing alliance of non-white peoples, which they expect eventually to inundate the white race, washing away the hated supremacy that that race has so long enjoyed. Almost fifteen years ago, Dr. Buell Gallagher warned about orthodox Islam:

There are signs that the Pan-Islamic movement may harden into a new political nationalism, based on race, which may replace the Islam of an international and interracial brotherhood. This Pan-Islamic spirit which appears about to come to full fruition in a union of the entire Muslim world against the rest of the globe is one of tomorrow's imponderables. . . .[48]

Gallagher did not refer to, or even contemplate, the Black Muslims; yet his words are pertinent to them. The Muslims are not recognized by orthodox Moslems in this country, but they consider themselves Moslems and are apparently so considered by the many Moslem countries in Africa and the Middle East who have welcomed and honored their leaders. Certainly, to the extent that the Pan-Islamic goal is a power structure forged out of anti-white sentiment, these goals are shared by the Black Muslims in America.

The anti-Christian tone of much of the Muslim teaching also has a strong attraction for some Negroes. Occasionally this attraction is personal, as with the youth rebelling against a parental authority which has been symbolized by enforced church attendance. But increasing numbers of Negroes are disillusioned by the continuation of racial segregation in the church and are coming to identify the church with social apathy and racial subordination. To these disaffected Christians the Muslims make a shrewd appeal. On the one hand, aware that the Christian tradition rejects hatred, they proclaim a positive slogan: "Not anti-white, just pro-black. We're so pro-black we havn't time to be anti *anything!*" But at the same time, they insist on the close link between the Christian church and white supremacy.

Your Christian countries, if I am correct, are the countries of Europe and North and South America. Predominantly, this is where you find Christianity, or at least people who represent themselves as Christians. Whether they practice what Jesus taught is something we won't go into. The Christian world is what we usually call the Western world. . . . The colonization of the dark people in the rest of the world was done by Christian powers. The number one problem that most people face in the world today is how to get freedom from Christians. Wherever you find non-white people today they are trying to get back their freedom from people who represent themselves as Christians, and if you ask these [subject] people their picture of a Christian, they will tell you "a white man—a Slavemaster."[49]

The appeal works—with individuals and with groups. One minister in Richmond, Virginia, discouraged by his denomination's posture on the racial issues in that state, led his entire congregation out of the Christian church and into the local Muslim temple, where he eventually became the new Muslim minister. His congregation is said to have doubled since in numbers and vitality.

Because Christianity is "the white man's religion," the repudiation of Christianity is an overt act of aggression against the white man. To be identified with a movement that openly rejects the fundamental values of the powerful majority is to increase vastly one's self-esteem and one's stature among one's peers. This social incentive to defiance is not limited to the Muslims; among Negro intellectuals generally, a deviation from the white man's ways of doing things has come to be called "independent thinking" and reaps its rewards. The difference between the intellectual and the Muslim is simply one of degree: the intellectual's defiance is carefully calculated; the Muslim's is wholehearted and absolute. Thus the intellectual will not become a Muslim, but he will embrace Bahai. Both men are repudiating an identity to which they are hypersensitive in the presence of the white man, and both are chiding Christianity for its racism. But the intellectual astutely remains within the orbit of the white man's culture, while the Muslims set themselves completely adrift.

The challenge of an ascetic ideal, balanced by the absence of social barriers to affiliation and service, have brought thousands under the banner of Muhammad. [Probably in no other religious organization are alcoholics, ex-convicts, pimps, prostitutes and narcotic addicts welcomed so sincerely.] The Christian church is, in most instances, careful to take none to its bosom until they are cleansed. The Muslims welcome the most unregenerate and then set about to rehabilitate them. They have stern rules of conduct, but no man is condemned for what he was—only for what he refuses to be.

They say a man should never be condemned or tried twice for the same crime once he has paid the penalty. Yet, when a man goes to prison and pays his debt to society, when he comes out he is still looked upon as a criminal. . . . Well, Mr. Muhammad has succeeded there where Western Christianity has failed. When a man becomes a Muslim, it doesn't make any difference what he was [doing] before as long as he has stopped doing this. He is looked upon with honor and respect and is not judged for what he was doing yesterday. And this, I think, explains why we have so many men who were in prison following Mr. Muhammad today.[50]

The stress upon—and the outward manifestation of—fraternal responsibility is a strong attraction for many Negroes, whose social and civil insecurity is often extreme. The Negro has often been characterized as a ready "joiner," and more often than not this characterization has been justified. He is compelled to join in order to escape the isolation and sense of helplessness he experiences as a social outcast. He joins for recreation (when public recreation is not available to him) and for security against sickness and want. He joins for consolation and companionship—the attempt at flight of an earthbound Negro in a white man's world.

All these elements are present, to some degree, in the appeal of Muslim membership. But the appeal goes deeper: every Muslim holds himself ready to die for his brother, and more especially for his sister.[51] This extreme solidarity attracts not only those in search of security but also those in search of a *cause*—a focus for the free-floating hostility that racial oppression always breeds. In 1958 a Muslim was arrested in New York City (on a false identification, as it turned out). Within an hour, several hundred of his brothers turned up at the precinct station in a quiet show of fraternal solidarity to insist that "justice be done." They waited patiently and quietly until the wrongly accused man was released; then they took him away with them. Membership in the local temple immediately spiraled. Their show of solidarity had won what the Negro community interpreted as an important victory.

The intensity of this sense of unity makes unnecessary the usual trappings of organizations which emphasize group solidarity. It is unrealistic (though at least one Negro leader has done so) to dismiss the Movement as "another mutual admiration cult—another opportunity for people who aren't going anywhere to hang out the signs to prove it." The usual "signs" of social status associated with Negro organizations are fanciful titles and flamboyant uniforms. Among the Black Muslims, however, there are no phony "doctors" or specious "saints," no uniforms and no prestige offices. The only titles are those given to Muhammad and to the hierarchy of the secret military organization, the Fruit of Islam. To be called a "brother" or a "sister" is the highest compliment a

Muslim can be paid, for (as Minister Louis X of Boston puts it) "we were brothers before we were ministers." Christians, of course, also call each other "brother" and "sister" at times, but one senses that the Muslims are appealing to something beyond ordinary religious courtesy.

Another aspect of the Movement that has strong appeal-value is its emphasis upon youth and masculinity. The ministers are young and personable; some have been entertainers or have otherwise had public followings. All Muslim men are clean-shaven, close-cropped and well-dressed in conservative clothes whenever they appear in public. Inside the temples there is a constant movement of young men with military bearing; they move quietly but with an unexaggerated dignity and the inescapable suggestion of latent force. They wear no uniforms or insignia except for a small star-and-crescent button in their lapels. Polite and self-assured, they seem alert to the demands of the present and confident of the future. Their attitude toward Christian Negroes is not quite one of condescension, nor yet one of toleration. It is more a kind of patient amazement that intelligent people could be unimpressed with the Messenger's dicta or could still find it possible to want to live in the world of the white man.

These are the "Young Blacks" who will usher in the Black Nation of Islam. "We are not looking for crumbs," says Malcolm X:

In America today, where the so-called Negro is concerned, you have a high degree of dissatisfaction. It is hard for me to believe that the white man, as intelligent as he is, cannot realize the degree of dissatisfaction in the minds of the young generation of Black Men. The old generation forgets. . . . It is on its way out. . . . What you [whites] have to know now is what the man is thinking [whom] you will have to deal with in the future.[52]

A surprising number of young people are attracted by the Muslims' redefinition of the roles men and women should play in the home and in the religious life of the sect. There is a strong emphasis on the equality of individuals irrespective of sex, but each sex is assigned a role considered proper to itself. The trend in our larger society today seems to be toward blurring the distinct line between the traditional social roles of men and women. The

Muslims, on the other hand, claim to have restored the woman to a place of dignity and respect, while restoring to the man his traditional responsibilities as head of the family. Muslim women seem to welcome the security and protection implicit in this arrangement, and the men seem to exhibit a deeper sense of responsibility than is common to others of the working class. Children seem to profit the most, for among Muslim children, delinquency is unheard of.

Finally, the Negro-oriented parochial schools maintained by the Muslims in Detroit and Chicago have attracted some followers. If, as is planned, the Muslims establish schools in most of the larger cities where they have temples, their numbers will probably increase proportionately. One Chicago domestic, who was not a Muslim, was asked whether she sent her children to the Muslim school in her neighborhood. "Well, no, sir," she replied with some hesitation. "But my husband, he's been talking about it. Whatever *he* says. They teach the children how to behave up there, and they teach them something about ourselves, too—all about what the colored people have done in the world, not just the white. You ought to know something about your own people, don't you think? Especially if you're going to live in a free country."

Few if any children of the middle- or upper-class Negro families attend the Muslim schools, for not many of their parents are in the Movement. Yet there is a widespread sympathy for the Muslim curriculum emphasis on the history of the Negro in America and on the black African civilizations of the pre-Colonial era. This is often expressed obliquely by resentment of the completely white-oriented training given to almost all Negro children. Said one Nashville intellectual: "They grow up, and they don't know *who* the hell they are. They aren't white, and white rejects them. But white is all they know about. And you talk about adjustment! It's a wonder any of us survive!"

2 The Dynamics of Black Nationalism

The Black Muslims are not an isolated phenomenon. They are rooted in the whole structure of racial tension. In New York City alone, a score or more organizations operate in the name of black solidarity. Their central theme is always the glorification of black civilization and the deprecation of the white man's culture, which, whenever it has been adopted by the black man, has reduced him to impotence and ignominy.

In the South, where resentment of the white man has until recently been less overt, black nationalism has expressed itself in lodges and fraternal societies, in which tens of thousands of Negroes learn various "ancient rites" of supposed Afro-Asian origin. Every Negro community in the South has its multitude of legends illustrating the Negro's superior physical strength, sexual prowess and moral integrity. "Mr. Charlie" is never a match for the cunning of "Ol' John." And "Miss Ann," though she is "as good a ol' white woman" as can be found anywhere, remains in the mind of the Southern Negro a *white* woman and, therefore, a legitimate target for the petty machinations of her Negro servant, "Annie Mae."

Most Negroes do not, of course, spend most of their time "thinking black." But no part of Negro life is wholly free of this glorification. A defensive kind of black nationalism finds occasional expression in the quarrels of Negro children everywhere. "Black is honest," they cry out, and "the blacker the berry, the sweeter the juice." Even the Negro churches are often tinged with nationalism. An obscure African slave who rescued the prophet Jeremiah from a cistern into which he had been thrown by his enemies is exalted as a symbol of righteousness and fearlessness in the service of God. And the biblical promise that Ethiopia shall soon "stretch out her hands" is taken as a divine pledge that black sovereignty will be restored.

From the soil of repression and hostility grow bitter fruits, and black nationalism is one of the most bitter. It feeds on the prejudices, stereotypes and discriminations which tend to characterize relations between whites and blacks in America. It accepts the white man's allegation that there are "inherent differences" between people who have different colored skins. But it inverts the values: it worships what it cannot change. It forges a weapon of vengeance for the Black Man out of the very attributes for which he is held to be inferior.

The Black Muslims have made a science of black nationalism. They have made *black* the ideal, the ultimate value; they have proclaimed the Black Man to be the primogenitor of all civilization, the Chosen of Allah, "the rightful ruler of the Planet Earth." And their extreme racist doctrine has attracted more than a hundred thousand adherents—a vivid warning of the deep resentment American Negroes harbor for their status in our society and of the futility they feel about the likelihood of a genuine and peaceful change.

I. BITTER SOIL AND BITTER FRUITS

Group Consciousness

An interesting phenomenon is found in every society in which several discrete groups live side-by-side. This phenomenon is known as *consciousness of kind,* that state of mind in which a man is vividly aware of himself as a member of a group different from other groups—as a Negro, a white man, an Irish Catholic, an Anglo-Saxon Protestant, a Jew.

Consciousness of kind usually operates as a defense mechanism for a minority group which is seeking to preserve its identity or its most cherished values. But group consciousness may also be aroused in a *majority* group when a minority is seeking to merge with and lose itself in the larger, more powerful or otherwise pre-eminent group. In such a case, the majority may feel that some of its prized values are threatened: its social status, racial purity, religious cohesion—or even its economic security or physical survival. Majority group consciousness is an almost instinctive defense against such a real or imagined threat.

The group consciousness of a minority is, of course, increased by acts of discrimination directed against it by an effective majority. An effective majority need not be a numerical majority: 11,000 Europeans constitute an effective majority in the African state of Uganda, which they share with 6½ million Africans and about 75,000 Asians; and 20,000 Europeans are an effective majority in Tanganyika, a country of 8½ million blacks.

An effective majority, whatever its size, holds the main concentration of power. Its power may be *actual,* as in the military superiority of a contingent of soldiers armed with modern weapons and garrisoned in a native village; it may be *potential,* as when a pair of patrolmen walk the streets of a tough neighborhood; or it may be *imaginary,* as is the power of the cult of priests or magicians in a primitive society. When it enjoys actual power backed by a massive numerical superiority—as does the white majority in the United States—the group consciousness of the minority can be very sharp indeed.

For any minority group, faced with a constant environment of prejudice and discrimination, three basic types of response are possible. These responses are *avoidance, acceptance* and *aggression.*

Avoidance

Group consciousness is a form of consolation derived from a shared sense of discrimination; it is often expressed in ambivalence and self-hatred. Such an acrid consolation is not for every taste. Many individuals would rather not be identified with a minority; they would prefer not to have a personal awareness of its existence or its claim on them as members. Such persons may seek to avoid entirely their identification with their group.

Avoidance may also be motivated by a haunting concern for personal security, physical or psychological. In this case, while acknowledging themselves as members of a group, individuals may seek to avoid the *meaning* of that identity in a wider context. Many Negroes, for example, avoid contact with whites by doing business with Negro businesses wherever possible; if they find it necessary to deal with white businesses, they order goods and pay their bills by mail. In this way, they minimize the likelihood of being insulted or otherwise humiliated by whites. Such avoidance also reduces the possibility of an inadvertent breach of the highly complex "etiquette" of race relations. In many parts of the South, a Negro who violates the etiquette requirements imposed by the whites may readily incur physical harm or even death.

For those individuals who wish to avoid their identification with a minority group, the most complete form of avoidance is to withdraw entirely by "passing" into the dominant group. But such passing is often hindered by distinctive names, accents or other cultural habits associated with the minority group. Racial minorities such as Negroes encounter a far more immediate obstacle: their distinctive color or "visibility," which is an unrelenting barrier to total acceptability. Thousands of fair-skinned Negroes do pass as white, however, and some dark-skinned Negroes pass as Filipinos, Spaniards, Italians or Mexicans.

In some Southern cities, light-skinned Negroes often pass in order to shop at certain stores or to use such facilities as libraries, toilets, theaters and hotels. In Memphis, one family of light-skinned Negroes regularly attends white churches. "This way," they explain, "we get to hear speakers not otherwise available to us, and the children have a chance to hear the great music and see the pageants performed on festival occasions." In Boston, at least two Negro businessmen passing as white operate businesses in white neighborhoods and because of their locations, cater almost exclusively to whites. In Birmingham, a fair-skinned Negro lunches occasionally at the best downtown hotels "just to look at the other side from time to time." In New Jersey, a Negro passing as white and married to a white woman holds a major executive position in a nationally-known drug firm. Such examples could be multiplied a thousandfold.

A second kind of avoidance is often exhibited by upper-class members of the Negro minority, especially those in the business or professional groups who are not dependent upon the white majority for a livelihood. These individuals often seek to insulate themselves from contact with lower-class Negroes as well as from the whites, and they do not identify themselves with the common problems of their group. They become a society unto themselves, "asking the white man for nothing" and sharing nothing with the Negroes from whom they derive their status and wealth. They form themselves into tight little cliques, which play at being part of the white society from which they are excluded.

For those individuals who wish to avoid the social *meaning* of their minority-group status, avoidance may take the form of developing towns or communities composed principally of members of their own group. Even when such residential segregation is initiated and enforced by the dominant group, minority-group members may actually *prefer* to live in the ghettos, rather than contend with the constant harrassment incident to living in the larger community. But no ghetto, forced or voluntary, can really ward off the consequences of prejudice and discrimination; and the mere fact of its existence is a constant reminder of the lack of a more healthful and harmonious relationship.

Finally, avoidance may take the form of escape from feelings of inferiority and futility while maintaining contact with the dominant group. Those who choose this path attempt to obliterate the meaning of their minority-group status by emphasizing and enhancing their status as individuals. The result may be clearly beneficial—a determined self-improvement in order to meet the approved values of the dominant group in such areas as education and professional skill.

The other extreme, however, is an escape into a world of make-believe, where fantasies of wealth, power or position in "society" shut out the realities of a humiliating and frustrating day-to-day existence. Negroes of wealth and education, whose only barrier to unrestricted participation in the complete life of the community is that fact that they *are* Negroes, probably constitute the largest single class of social neurotics. Often their relationship to their white social counterparts is tenuous and marginal, but they can no longer find a place acceptable to their heightened sense of personal worth among the Negro classes out of which they rose. In their frustration, the creative talent which pushed them to the top and set them off from the masses is too often crudely dissipated.

Acceptance

Some minority-group members feel that it is sensible to accept what cannot be changed or avoided: "You don't like it, but what can you do?" This attitude of conscious resignation or futility is the most common form of acceptance, but it is not the whole story. At the other extreme is the wholehearted acceptance of disparate social conditions characteristic of a caste society such as pre-Gandhian India. In such a society every group—high or low, favored or scorned—is felt to have a divinely ordained place in the sun. Social discrimination is no more than obedience to the divine order of the universe, and resentment against it would be as unthinkable as resentment of God. This attitude comes naturally, of course, to many white men in America; but there is some evidence that it was also widely held among American Negroes several decades ago, and vestiges of this kind of adjustment behavior are probably retained among the present "folk Negroes" of isolated rural areas and among certain family servants who identify closely with their employers.

Few Negroes today exhibit this wholehearted acceptance of discrimination and special privilege, but many will consciously defer in specific situations in which inferiority is implied. Many Negroes ride Jim-Crow busses, for example, when no other means of transportation is available; and a Negro servant may accept the epithet "boy" or "girl" because to reject it would mean the loss of employment and the possibility of livelihood. But, in both instances, the individuals involved may categorically reject the whole status pattern and its implications. They reason simply, "We've got to live if we're going to fight!"

These outward accommodations to specific situations of discrimination or prejudice are often misinterpreted as a wholehearted acceptance of inferior role or status. Such an assumption is, of course, illogical, and it can only be made by a mind which brings to the situation a serious misconception of Negro intelligence. No healthy mind assumes that another healthy mind will welcome an inferior status or its degrading concomitants.

Prejudice has been called "the refuge of a sick mind" and "a method of transferring our sickness to others." Certainly the Negro who *welcomes* the kind of social subordination imposed upon him in our country may be considered to be quite ill. No more can be said for those who practice it.

Aggression

Aggression is an act or a pattern of behavior which aims to discomfort, injure or destroy a person or his values. As an individual response among American Negroes, it may express itself in very different forms. To be a "race man"—that is, a professional champion of the in-group, speaking or writing in its defense, or agitating for its rights—is a common expression of direct aggression, especially among the upper classes but increasingly among all classes. Boycott; inefficiency and sloppy work done for white employers; ostentation, such as expensive automobiles or homes; refusal to observe the customary forms of etiquette—all these are direct means of expressing personal hostility. Some physical attacks also take place. Negroes seldom initiate physical attacks against whites, but there is less hesitation now to return violence for violence, whatever the cost.

Literature, art and humor are readily available vehicles of direct aggression, and they are widely used as such. The Negro press is well known for its explicit posture against prejudice and discrimination, but countless individual Negro poets and novelists have also used their talents to express their resentment of and hostility toward the white man.

Not all aggression, however, is overt and outspoken. Silence or absolute immobility may also be aggressive, as, for example, when a Negro fails to respond to what he considers a degrading epithet or refuses to yield his seat on a public bus or trolley to a white person.

Even certain postures of meekness and deference may be

expressions of aggression, as with the apparent humility and self-effacement often displayed in situations of great dependence or where intimidation is present. The suffering then experienced is accepted as a means to ultimate victory, for from the suffering, power is derived. Again, meekness is a Christian virtue, and through its expression the humble Negro asserts his moral superiority to the arrogant white. Aggressive meekness is also a common device for ridiculing the white man; while he egoistically accepts the meek behavior at face value, the Negro may be laughing at him secretly for his gullibility.

So sensitive are white men to any challenge to their position that even a *possibility* that aggression *might* be expressed is considered dangerous. In 1957 a Negro in North Carolina was arrested and charged with "assault" because he *looked* at a white woman; and in Georgia, a year later, a parade featuring a high school band and the usual corps of majorettes was stopped and disbanded because Negroes joined other citizens in standing along the street to watch. In the southern part of the United States and in South Africa, even a suspicion that a Negro might want to strike back can cost the Negro his freedom or his life.

But aggression can also be misdirected. Hurt and angry, yet too frightened to act against his powerful tormentor, the Negro sometimes thrashes about, seeking a target for his hostility. Often unconsciously, he displaces his aggression onto other minority groups—Jews, for example—which cannot retaliate so effectively. All too often, the aggression is simply inverted: Negroes turn their rage against other Negroes or against themselves. The result is sporadic intra-group violence and a general splintering of group solidarity, a disastrous development in a world unsympathetic to the dignity of powerless individuals or groups.

Even responsible and controlled aggression, as a response to offenses against one's human dignity, is a dangerous undertaking, and it is shrouded in moral and ethical ambivalence. Many individuals prefer the paths of avoidance and acceptance. In every minority, however, there will always be men who are willing to confront directly the source of their oppression and who will seek to remove, moderate, deflect or destroy it.

II. BLACK NATIONALISM, U. S. A.

Stereotype and Identity

Aggression as an actual and continuing expression of Negro protest has long been underestimated in America. An image of the Negro as casual, passive and content with his lot was fabricated during the days of slavery. Manifestly absurd, it was accepted as fact and has persisted into modern times. Such a picture has done little to prepare Americans to live together in peace and mutual respect.

Historians have contributed to the confusion by stereotyping the Negro slave as a docile, devoted, contented servant, or else by ignoring him altogether. The Negro's active protests to the condition of slavery imposed upon him by a comparatively infinite power do not commonly appear in America's textbooks. Knowledge of the numerous slave revolts and insurrections, for example, is available only to the scholar who has the facilities for laborious research.

The problem is intensified by the racial segregation which prevents knowledgeable contact between whites and educated Negroes. Incredible as it seems, many Americans are surprised to learn that Negroes love and hate, accept and reject, with all the intensity of feeling common to human nature. Or perhaps it is not so incredible: he who would systematically degrade his fellow man must defend himself against reprisals. Since this cannot be done empirically, one way to gain a comforting sense of invulnerability is to pretend that the problem does not exist. If the Negro does not feel *anything,* his docility can be taken for granted.

Aggressive leaders will arise, however. Since they threaten the protective fantasy, the most militant of them must be discounted and isolated from the Negro masses. By dismissing them as "Communists" or "radicals" (or whatever is beyond the pale at any given moment), we can keep our fantasy of the contented Negro pure. But the Negro is not contented, and he will be heard. If his moderate leaders are dismissed as radical, then movements which are *in fact* radical will become more and more extreme, if only to get on ground where the white man will acknowledge their existence.

We are mired in complacency. The majority of unsuspecting whites are still shocked with disbelief and chagrin by the Negro's occasional public repudiation of the stereotype of good-natured, uncomplaining docility, which they have always accepted as true. When the Negro they thought they "knew" so well steps out of the role in which he has been cast, it seems to many like an act of treason. For example, when Marcus Garvey announced in 1920 that "the white man need expect no more Negro blood shed on his behalf" and that "the dying to be done by the black man in the future . . . will be done to make himself free," the speech was sufficiently alarming to be cited as sedition.[1] And when, forty years later, Negroes insisted upon being served at the lunch counters of stores which readily accepted their money in every other department, no less a person than ex-President Harry Truman—a man who had done much during his administration to remove racial barriers—cried out in outrage.

It is incredible that such expressions "against the system" should be viewed with surprise. It would be logically more surprising if resentment and hostility were *not* felt by a people who conceive themselves as oppressed and who can identify their oppressors. But this is precisely the tragedy of America, that she is oblivious of the smoldering resentments of millions for whom the American Creed is often a mockery. This "ignorance about the Negro is not, it must be stressed, just lack of interest and knowledge. It is a tense and high-strung restriction and distortion of knowledge, and it indicates much deeper dislocations within the minds of Southern whites"[2]—and, to a lesser extent, of the entire white community.

This "convenient ignorance"[3] on the part of whites compounds the frustrations of the Negro minority, which now more than ever before is determined to be heard—or at least seen. The conspicuous consumption; the overemphasis on titles; the preoccupation with such values as academic degrees, foreign travel and unique professional appointments; and the increasing activity of organized protest—all these add up to an open rejection of racial anonymity and the traditional stereotype. Many of these activities are also, of course, valuable in themselves. They are like the "double duty dollar"—the money a Negro spends with a business which employs Negroes, thus (1) buying goods for himself and (2) helping to provide jobs for others of his race.

Every important aspect of the Negro's behavior is likely to have a race angle, though he himself is not always conscious of that fact.

To the Negro himself, the Negro problem is all-important. A Negro probably seldom talks to a white man . . . without consciousness of this problem. Even in a mixed white and Negro group of closest friends in Northern intellectual circles, and probably even in an all-Negro group, the Negro problem constantly looms in the background. It steers the jokes and allusions if it is not one of the dominant topics of conversation.

The Negro leader, the Negro social scientist, the Negro man of arts and letters is likely to view all social, economic, political, indeed, even aesthetic and philosophical issues from the Negro angle. What is more, he is expected to do so. He would seem entirely out of place if he spoke simply as a member of a community, a citizen of America. . . . In the existing American civilization he can attain some degree of distinction, but always as a representative of "his people," not as an ordinary American. . . . The Negro genius is imprisoned in the Negro problem.[4]

Black Nationalism

Under the circumstances confronting him, the Negro is required to be "Negro" before—and sometimes to the exclusion of—anything else. At some point, therefore, he will inevitably be tempted to glorify that from which he cannot escape. He may repudiate the white man's stereotype, turn his eyes from the painful reality and substitute for them an idealized self-image. Drawing on the political parallel, in which each state considers itself distinct from and superior to its neighbors, this attitude has come to be known as *black nationalism*.

It would be absurd to say, of course, that all Negro race pride is only a rationalized form of acceptance. It is often a simple and spontaneous awareness of one's human dignity. Such, for example, was the pride of Denmark Vesey, an ex-slave who engineered an elaborate insurrection in Charleston in 1822:

Even whilst walking through the streets in company with another, he was not idle; for if his companion bowed to a white person he would rebuke him, and observe that all men were born equal, and that he was surprised that any one would degrade himself by such conduct; that he would never cringe to the whites, nor ought any one who had the feelings of a man. When answered, "We are slaves," he would sarcastically and indignantly reply, "You deserve to remain slaves."[5]

Vesey was hanged, along with thirty-four confederates, for leading the insurrection; but he died as he had lived, with courage and conviction, acknowledging no man his inherent superior.

Black nationalism is more than courage and rebellion; it is a way of life. It is an implicit rejection of the "alien" white culture and an explicit rejection of the symbols of that culture, balanced by an exaggerated and undiluted pride in "black" culture. It involves a drastic reappraisal not only of present realities but also of the past and future. The black nationalist revises history (or corrects it, as he would say) to establish that today's black men are descended from glorious ancestors, from powerful and enlightened rulers and conquerors. This reconstruction of history may reach ridiculous extremes; and it can never be accepted by white men, who, to bolster their own security, must perceive history as a record of *white* men's achievements. But a proud history is essential to the black nationalist's self-respect. Essential, too, is the certainty of a brilliant future, in which the inherent superiority of his race will triumph and he will again rule the world.

In any technical sense, of course, it is inaccurate for American Negroes to adopt a black nationalist position. The term implies that they are—politically, culturally, ethnically or racially— a distinct group. But this is emphatically not true. Politically they are Americans, as American as one can be (with the sole exception of the American Indian). Culturally they are merged into the American mainstream; as Lloyd Warner observes, they are "culturally more like the white 'old American' than [are] any other sub-groups in America."[6] Nor are they ethnically separated from other Americans, holding allegiance to an earlier shared culture. On the contrary:

The conspicuous feature of the Negro in America is *that his aboriginal culture was smashed.* . . . The importance of this basic fact for the

Negro in America cannot be overestimated. It means in effect that the old types of social organization and all their derivations could not continue, but a new type of emergent adjustment derived from the new conditions would have to be established.[7]

Nor, finally, are they racially distinct. "Race" is at best a nebulous term.[8] There are no pure races, and it would be especially inappropriate to apply the term to the American Negro, who is at once African and Anglo-Saxon, Indian and French, Portuguese, Spanish, German and Italian—a composite of every major "racial stock"[9] and every nationality of Western Europe.[10]

W. E. B. DuBois observes that a common suffering, rather than a common biology or ethnic identity, has been the important factor uniting the Negro in what is usually referred to as "nationalism."

The so-called American Negro group . . . while it is in no sense absolutely set off physically from its fellow Americans, has nevertheless a strong, hereditary cultural unity born of slavery, of common suffering, prolonged proscription, and curtailment of political and civil rights. . . . Prolonged policies of segregation and discrimination have involuntarily welded the mass almost into a nation within a nation. . . .[11]

The "nationalism" of the American Negro is not voluntary, prompted by a desire to set himself apart in order to preserve some cultural values. It is, rather, a defensive response to external forces—hostile forces which threaten his creative existence. It is a unity born of the wish not to conserve but to *escape* a set of conditions.

Black nationalism seizes the conditions of disprivilege and turns them to advantage as a tool for eliminating the disprivilege. It challenges the supercilious attitude of the majority group by glorifying the unique symbols of the blacks—symbols which the whites consider repugnant. Some sociologists have labeled this behavior "negritude":

. . . an exaltation of African-Negro specificity, a "kind of highly elaborated counterracism." . . . It involves a "particularly intense racial awareness," not uncoupled to political activity and demands. It is a term descriptive, also, of an appreciation of a new black unity experienced by its adherents, a consciousness of sharing in a past and in the making of the future. . . .[12]

Nationalism is ordinarily political; it refers to common values arising out of the existence of a state. Black nationalism addresses itself not to an existent state but to a state of mind.[13] But if there is no past or present black nation, what is to prevent the projection of a Black Nation of the future?

To the extent that it is couched in political terms—and this varies from movement to movement—black nationalism envisions and works toward the creation of such a state. In the creed of some movements, this political goal is relatively insignificant, a potentiality which the black man may or may not choose to realize. For the Black Muslims, however, the goal of a Black Nation is of consuming importance. The Muslims do not rest content with any concept of black nationalism that is not expressed in concrete economic and political terms.

Black Nationalism and Social Class

In the American Negro groups of highest and lowest status, hardly anyone wants to be a Negro. Upper-class Negroes seek to identify themselves with the white society; lower-class Negroes prefer to identify themselves with any group *except* the whites in order to escape the danger and humiliation that all Negroes incur. Only middle-class Negroes are generally willing to acknowledge themselves as Negroes and, at the same time, to seek an accommodation with the white society. Black nationalism, therefore, with its repudiation of both Negro identity and white culture, sinks its roots deepest in the lower class.

Upper-class Negroes are rarely "Negro" by choice. Those who have obvious strains of white ancestry are often at great pains to dissociate themselves from those who do not, and they are remarkably oblivious of the implications of their whiteness. Darker Negroes of the upper class must content themselves with pointed references to their "Indian ancestry" lest they be mistaken for full-blooded Negroes—an intolerable possibility.

The Negro of the upper class is largely committed to the idea that America's racial dilemma will be resolved when the Negro loses his distinctiveness, social and biological. He would prefer to become so thoroughly assimilated into the American mainstream as to be *biologically* indistinct, for his new status could not then be revoked or qualified in a future crisis. In short, the ultimate security in living among a white majority is to be white. But this security is almost impossible to achieve in view of the general disdain for miscegenation. The barrier is circular: unqualified social acceptance is the only gateway to racial anonymity, which in turn is the only gateway to unqualified social acceptance.

For the time being, therefore, the upper-class Negro is settling for that degree of assimilation which will make him *socially* indistinct from those whites who are his counterpart in terms of education, affluence and refinement. He tends to venerate everything that is "white" and "Western." In spite of the inconvenience of his color, he sees himself as part of this tradition; and he resents as irrational and unjust the social custom which emphasizes his black skin while overlooking the fact that his ancestry is partly European and his culture totally Western.

The members of the growing Negro middle class are least concerned about disestablishing themselves as Negroes. They ridicule the upper class as "neurotic sub-marginals" who make themselves ridiculous in trying to attract the white man's attention. Nor can they see the importance of having white ancestry, since almost all American Negroes share this qualification to some degree. Besides, white ancestry is not a criterion of the white man's judgment when he erects barriers to set himself apart from all others. Segregation is directed at a *class,* not at members within it; and all Negroes, whatever their names, ancestry or skin color, belong by definition to the segregated class.

The Negro middle class is somewhat ambivalent about black nationalism. The black nationalists' emphasis on a united struggle against subordination has a certain appeal, but the rejection of Negro identity and the search for cultural roots in Afro-Asian traditions has little or no appeal. The middle-class Negro feels no need to be either "Asiatic" or "European." He accepts the designation "American Negro" with no particular sense of opprobrium, and often with a certain pride, for he thus identifies himself with America's most important minority—a minority which has distinguished itself, in a brief span of history, by an achievement of progress unequaled by *either* "Europeans" or "Asiatics."

The self-image of the Negro middle class is one of ability and militancy, uncontaminated by either sycophancy or hatred for the white man. The middle-class Negro is not obsessed with status pretensions, as is the upper class, nor does he suffer the abject despair of the Negro masses. As a result, he seldom displays the kind of insecurity that needs to search for ancestral pegs upon which to hang a claim for present status and acceptance.

The main appeal of all black nationalist movements, then, is to the Negro lower class. Here the Negro's resentment is crystallized and open. He has long despaired of the white man's justice and of the trustworthiness of the "acceptable" Negro leaders who court the white man's favor. Moreover, he is already at the bottom of the ladder, so his economic and social position is not vulnerable. An indiscreet word, an admission of hostility or an identification with "radical" or "extremist" groups can cost him nothing. What has he to lose if the demagogues of black nationalism fan his resentment into hatred, openly expressed in defiance of all white men and their compliant Negro "friends"?

The lower-class Negro lives in a no man's land between two alien worlds, both of which he spurns. Unlike his upper-class brother, he has no conscious desire to be white or even "like the whites," whom he identifies with most of his misfortunes. But neither will he accept the implications of being "Negro"—a white man's word, which he sees as an epithet of contempt. The black race has a rich cultural heritage, extending thousands of years into the past; but the black men who were torn from their homes and shipped to the New World in chains were carefully isolated from that heritage. The history of the "Negro" begins in the torments and degradation of slavery in America. Unlike his better-educated brothers, the lower class Negro is not generally aware that his ancestors served their new nation with distinction and that the term can be accepted with confidence—indeed, with pride. He is agonizingly aware of what "Negro" implies to most Americans, its humiliating connotations of white supremacy.

The lower-class Negro is ripe for the lure of black nationalism. He is proud to rediscover himself as a Black Man, linked to the great and venerable civilizations of the "single black continent" of Afro-Asia. He is grateful for a mystique, especially one dignified as a religion, that rationalizes his resentment and hatred as spiritual virtues in a cosmic war of good against evil. And he is jubilant at his new vision of the future—a future not of racial equality, for which he believes the white man has shown himself unfit, but of black supremacy. For "black," to the black nationalist, is a quality and symbol of all that is glorious, triumphant and divine.

Many counterpressures exist, of course, to restrain the lower-class Negro from active participation in black nationalist movements. The Christian church is still powerful, though its magic has been seriously eroded. Personal friendships with white men, where they exist, make the absolute generalizations of black nationalism difficult to accept. Some Negroes, like some white men, find a certain comfort and security in being considered inferior; they cling to the status in which all their personal failures are overlooked, since nothing much is expected of them. Others have experienced so rarely the feeling of superiority that they can scarcely imagine it as a way of life.

Above all, the lower-class Negro is a decent and responsible human being, loath to give his life over to hatred and vengeance. He will not do so unless forced to the wall by a smug and callous white society. The future of black nationalism, therefore, will ultimately be decided not by the demagogues but by ourselves.

3 Black Nationalism:
The Minor Leagues

All black nationalist movements have in common three characteristics: a disparagement of the white man and his culture, a repudiation of Negro identity and an appropriation of "Asiatic" culture symbols. Within this framework, however, they take shape in a remarkable variety of creeds and organizations. The smallest groups range in temperament from the innocuous United African Nationalist Movement, with its New York City street-corner harangues, to the criminally trained, marijuana-smoking Ras Tafarians, who are known to have murdered at least six people: two British soldiers, a Chinese shopkeeper and three of their own number whose devotion to the cult had begun to flag.

The more influential black nationalist movements also seize upon varying interests as focal points for group identification or as vehicles of counteraggression against the white majority. One favorite focus is religion; another is political or politico-economic goals. The former has no immediate concern with a national state; the latter makes the creation of a state central to its appeal. These two emphases are perhaps best represented in the Moorish Science Temple movement of Noble Drew Ali and the Universal Negro Improvement Association of Marcus Garvey, both of which flourished about the time of World War I.

The Moorish Science movement was essentially religious; Garvey's UNIA was primarily political. The *raison d'être* of both was to devise some means of escaping the implications of being a Negro in a white-dominated society. Noble Drew sought a psychic escape: by changing their names and the symbols of their culture, his Moors hoped to change their social fortunes. For Garvey, the logical solution was to remove all American Negroes to an independent African state. Both men had substantial followings, but neither did much to change the conditions that were ultimately responsible for whatever measure of success they could claim.

Religious Nationalism: The Moorish Science Temples

About 1913, a forty-seven-year-old North Carolina Negro named Timothy Drew established a "Moorish Science Temple" in Newark, New Jersey.[1] From this seed grew a movement that, at its peak, had established temples in Detroit, Harlem, Chicago, Pittsburgh, Philadelphia and in numerous cities across the South. Membership may have been as high as twenty or thirty thousand during the lifetime of "the Prophet."

Drew never seems to have had a formal education, but at some point he apparently had been exposed to Oriental philosophy. He was particularly impressed by the lack of race consciousness in Oriental religious thought and saw in it a possible answer to the Negro's plight in a color-conscious America. If Negroes could somehow establish an identity with the Oriental peoples, whose religious philosophies either knew nothing of the "curse of Canaan"[2] or else found it irrelevant, they might become less susceptible to the everyday hazards of being "everyday-Negroes" in America.

In pursuing this goal, Drew did not allow himself to be troubled by the inconveniences of history. He simply decreed that, thenceforth, American Negroes were to be known as "Asiatics."

He became obsessed with the idea that salvation for the Negro people lay in the discovery by them of their national origin; i.e., they must know whence they came, and refuse longer to be called Negroes, black folk, colored people, or Ethiopians. They must henceforth call themselves Asiatics, to use the generic term, or, more specifically, Moors, or Moorish Americans.[3]

To document this ethnic transformation, he issued "Nationality and Identification Cards" to his followers. Each card bore the Islamic symbol (the star and crescent), an image of clasped hands, and a numeral "7" in a circle. It announced that the bearer honored "all the Divine Prophets, Jesus, Mohammed, Buddha, and

Confucius" and pronounced upon him "the blessings of the God of our Father, Allah." It identified him as "a Moslem under the Divine Laws of the Holy Koran of Mecca, Love, Truth, Peace, Freedom, and Justice" and concluded with the assurance: "I AM A CITIZEN OF THE UNITED STATES." Each card was validated by the subscription, "NOBLE DREW ALI, THE PROPHET."

Drew's movement spread west from New Jersey to Pittsburgh, Detroit and Chicago, and there were temples in a number of cities across the South. In Chicago the movement rapidly gained momentum and soon became a problem for law enforcement officials. The members of the cult felt an exaggerated sense of security and importance in their new "Asiatic" status, symbolized most openly in the red fezzes which the male members were required to wear at all times. But their social metamorphosis was not accepted by the whites, who saw no reason to relinquish their traditional racial constructs. The Moors' confidence, however, was not diminished. They were certain that the whites (or "Europeans") were soon to be destroyed and that the "Asiatics" would soon be in control.

A number of disturbances developed. The Moors, made conspicuous by their fezzes, walked the streets, treating white folk with open contempt. In various parts of the Middle West they became anathema to the police.

In Chicago, affairs reached the point where members of the cult would accost white people on the streets, and showing their membership cards or the button they wore in their coat lapels, would sing the praises of their prophet, now known as Noble Drew Ali, because he had freed them from the curse of European (white) domination.[4]

The cult members believed that the imminent destruction of the whites was signified by the appearance in the sky of a star within a crescent moon.

As the racial irritations cued by the Moors' aggressive behavior grew worse, Nobel Drew Ali issued a warning to his followers to exercise more restraint. They were cautioned to "stop flashing [their] cards before Europeans" and to avoid making agitating speeches on their jobs. "We did not come to cause confusion," the Prophet observed. "Our work is to uplift the nation."

Despite Drew's sincerity and simple idealism, the Moorish Science movement eventually addressed itself to some new directions not anticipated in its founding philosophy. As is characteristic of mass movements, its growth and expansion began to attract better educated but less scrupulous individuals, who saw it as an irresistible opportunity for private gain and exploitation. Anxious to extend the movement and aware of his own limitations, Noble Drew Ali opened the door to these men; but the "new blood" proved to be costly indeed. The less discriminating followers of the Prophet—like their counterparts in other religious sects—were soon duped into buying various charms, relics, magical potions, pictures and spurious literature concerning their Asiatic heritage. The leaders grew rich off the credulous masses; and when it became apparent that Noble Drew Ali was the chief obstacle to a more complete exploitation, he was shunted aside. Eventually, he was killed.

The responsibility for the death of Noble Drew Ali has never been officially placed. During the struggle for power among the leaders of the cult, one leader was killed. Ali was not in Chicago at the time of the killing, but upon his return he was arrested and charged with murder by police officials, who were at best somewhat weary of his movement. He was never brought to trial, for he died mysteriously shortly after being released on bond. The cause of his death is variously attributed to a "third degree" given him while under arrest or to a subsequent beating administered by his rivals for power within the movement.

After the Prophet's death, the cult split into numerous smaller groups. It is no longer a potent force in the Negro community, though some temples remain active in the industrial cities of the North. Many present-day Moors believe that Noble Drew Ali is reincarnate in their present leaders, and the *Holy Koran* of the Moorish Holy Temple of Science continues to be the sacred book of the various sects. (The *Holy Koran,* not to be confused with the Quran of classical Islam, contains the teachings of the Prophet, along with various other esoteric materials.) Membership continues to be limited to "Asiatics"—that is, to non-Caucasians—who renounce the traditional category and the implications of being "colored" or "Negro." Each new member attaches the

term "el" or "bey" to his name in signification of his Asiatic
status. Initiation fees are usually a dollar; stipulated dues are paid
thereafter.

The cult considers itself Moslem, but it retains many of the
familiar markings of Christianity. Jesus, for example, remains a
prominent figure in the worship services; and hymns, although
revised to appropriate the new teachings, retain the rhythmic chant
forms of the familiar Negro spirituals. Love is taught as the
guiding spirit of the universe: "the fallen sons and daughters of
the Asiatic Nation of North America need to learn to love instead
of hate; and to know of their higher self and lower self."

The Moors believe that "before you can have a God you
must have a nationality" and that Noble Drew Ali, who was a
prophet ordained of God, gave his people the North African state
of Morocco to be their nation. In this connection, they attach
great signification to names:

The name means everything; by taking the Asiatic's name from him
and calling him Negro, black, colored, or Ethiopian, the European
stripped the Moor of his power, his authority, his God, and every
other worthwhile possession.[5]

Conversely, each religion has its proper racial adherents, and
religious faith should not cross racial lines:

Christianity is for the European (paleface); Moslemism is for the
Asiatic (olive-skinned). When each group has its own peculiar religion, there will be peace on earth.

[However], Noble Drew Ali is a kindred personage and spirit to
Confucius, Jesus, Buddha, and Zoroaster.[6]

In the Moors' worship services, there is none of the expres-
sive fervor one associates with the stereotype of the lower-class
Negro church. The services are subdued and quiet. All present
are expected to pay careful attention; but there are few responses
from the congregation, and even these are hardly audible. Meetings begin and end with undeviating punctuality, and the members
are seated separately according to sex. Friday is considered the
Sabbath day, but meetings are held on Wednesday and Sunday
evenings as well. No baptism or communion is observed. The

faithful are required to pray daily at sunrise, noon and sunset, facing Mecca with hands upraised.

Strict personal morality is a keynote of the movement's teachings. The Moors greet their followers with the salutation "Peace!" or "Islam!" As among the Black Muslims, great emphasis is placed upon the husband's responsibility as protector and provider of his family, while women are enjoined to be good homemakers and to obey their husbands. Divorce is discouraged. Monogamy is the only form of marriage recognized, and marriage ceremonies are performed by the "Grand Sheik," or Governor, in charge of the local temple. Most secular entertainments are forbidden, as is the use of cosmetics, alcohol and tobacco. Meat and eggs are taboo. Personal cleanliness is stressed, but men are not expected to shave.

Despite the racial boisterousness of some of its adherents, the Moorish Science movement did not consider itself "radical." On the contrary, the Moors offered themselves as the nucleus around which a world of truth, peace, freedom and justice must be built. Despite their hostility to whites, they stressed obedience and loyalty to the flag of the United States, so long as they were to live in America. For the Moors have two homelands. Noble Drew, the Reincarnation of Mohammed, gave them Morocco as the seat of their Nation. But the dark people of the world are also native to the continent of North America, which is now under European dominion. They have no choice but to submit to the harsh rule of the whites until the whites' time to reign comes to an end.

A few Moorish temples remain scattered among the Negro ghettos today. The congregations believe that they are still led by Noble Drew Ali, with each present Sheik a reincarnation of their revered founder. Many Moors, however, were among the earliest converts to the Black Muslim Movement. They feel quite at home in this new nationalism, which continues them in their familiar "Asiatic" religion without requiring them to love the "Europeans." In fact, they may now look forward to the predicted destruction of their enemies with increased assurance, for Elijah Muhammad, the Messenger—unlike Noble Drew Ali—is not a man to compromise.

Political Nationalism: The Garvey Movement

The name of Marcus Garvey is one of the best known in
recent Negro history, yet it is one that the Negro leadership would
like very much to forget. Few Negroes have elicited such consummate scorn from their fellows as did this belligerent little man,
caricatured by a contemporary as:

A Jamaican of unmixed stock, squat, stocky, fat and sleek, with pro-
truding jaws, and heavy jowls, small bright pig-like eyes and rather
bulldog-like face. Boastful, egotistic, tyrannical, intolerant, cunning,
shifty, smooth and suave, avaricious . . . gifted at self-advertisement,
without shame in self-laudation . . . without regard for veracity, a
lover of pomp and tawdry finery and garish display.[7]

Yet, for all the castigations of his many critics, Garvey
enjoyed the admiration of hundreds of thousands of lower-class
Negroes, who followed him with enthusiasm and money, and who
received from him a new estimate of their worth and their future.
His movement fired the imaginations of a people desperate for a
new hope and a new purpose, however unrealistic. "Its spirit of
race chauvinism had the sympathy of the overwhelming majority
of the Negro people, including those who opposed its objectives.
For this was the potent spirit of race consciousness and race pride
that informed the 'New Negro' " of the 1920s[8]—a period of cultural renaissance and racial militancy among the Negro intellli-
gentsia.

The Garvey movement must inevitably be seen against the
background of the post-World War I era, a crucial and difficult
time for Negroes in the United States. They had helped to win a
war for democracy overseas, only to return to the customary bigotry at home. They had risked death fighting beside the white
man in the trenches of France, only to die in America at the white
man's hand. In the first year after the war, seventy Negroes were
lynched, many of them still in uniform. Fourteen Negroes were
burned publicly by white citizens; eleven of these martyrs were
burned alive.[9] During the "Red Summer" of 1919, there were no
fewer than twenty-five race riots across the country. A riot in the
nation's capital lasted three days; in Chicago, thirty-eight people
were killed and 537 injured during thirteen days of mob rule.[10]

Along with the actual physical violence, there was intimidation everywhere. The Ku Klux Klan had been revived; and New York, Illinois, Indiana, Michigan and several New England states had been added to its traditional roster of Southern states.[11] There was an increasing competition between Negroes and whites for housing and jobs. Despair and militancy were the alternate moods of the Negro veterans who had fought "to make the world safe for democracy." They were disillusioned about the share of democracy America had reserved for them, but they were determined to bid for their rights—loud and clear.

In the summer of 1914, Marcus Garvey had returned home to Jamaica from a visit to London, his mind seething with plans for a new Universal Negro Improvement Association. Ironically, his sense of mission had been triggered by a reading of *Up From Slavery,* the autobiography of Booker T. Washington, who had been despised by many Negroes for his life-pattern of compromise and accommodation.

I read *Up From Slavery* . . . and then my doom . . . of being a race leader dawned upon me. . . . I asked: "Where is the black man's Government? Where is his King and his kingdom? Where is his President, his country, and his ambassador, his army, his navy, his men of big affairs?" I could not find them, and then I declared, "I will help to make them."[12]

And he did. Putting aside Washington's reminiscences of restraint and gratitude for white favors, he originated a movement devoted to extreme black nationalism and self-improvement. As a result, he came to share with Washington the bitter contempt of Negro intellectuals—though for the opposite reason.

The manifesto of the UNIA called attention to "the universal disunity existing among the people of the Negro or African race." It challenged "all people of Negro or African parentage" to subscribe to the UNIA program, which read in part:

To establish a Universal Confraternity among the race; to promote the spirit of race pride and love; to reclaim the fallen of the race . . . to strengthen the imperialism [self-determination] of independent African States . . . to establish Universities, Colleges and Secondary Schools for the further education and culture of the boys and girls of the race to conduct a world-wide commercial and industrial intercourse.[13]

The motto of the Association was: "One God! One Aim! One Destiny!"—a motto which has recently been adopted by the rabid Ras Tafarian cult, which also emanates from Jamaica.

In 1916, Marcus Garvey "came screaming out of the British West Indies onto the American Stage."[14] He landed in New York, where at first little attention was paid to his street-corner speeches. Undaunted, he set out to tour thirty-eight states in order to study conditions of Negro life in America. When he returned to New York a year later, he had formulated certain opinions which were later to shape the largest mass movement in the history of the American Negro. Important among these conclusions was the amazing discovery that the "so-called Negro leaders . . . had no program, but were mere opportunists who were living off their so-called leadership while the poor people were groping in the dark."[15] He seems to have concluded that too much of the leadership was concentrated in the hands of mulattoes and that these "part-white Negroes" could not be trusted.[16] He was exceedingly disturbed that Negro leadership depended so heavily upon white philanthropy—an impossible paradox. He was most contemptuous because this dependent leadership seemed willing "to turn back the clock of progress" at the whim of the white benefactors.

The New York division of the UNIA soon became the headquarters of a world-wide organization. By midsummer of 1919, Garvey claimed to have two million members in thirty branches.[17] His newspaper, *The Negro World,* was printed in French and Spanish, as well as in English, at its peak, it claimed a circulation of more than 200,000, "reaching the mass of Negroes throughout the world." The paper devoted itself mainly to a recapitulation and reinterpretation of the Negro's contribution to history. It recalled "the stirring heroism of such leaders of American slave rebellions as Denmark Vesey, Gabriel Prosser, and Nat Turner. The struggles of Zulu and Hottentot warriors against European rule, the histories of Moorish and Ethiopian empires, and the intrepid exploits of Toussaint L'Ouverture . . . were not neglected in the effort to make Negroes conscious and proud of their racial heritage."[18] Readers were encouraged to speak out on racial matters, and Garvey himself "delighted in references to the greatness of colored civilizations at a time when white men were only barbarians and savages."[19]

At the First International Convention of the UNIA, held in New York in August 1920, no fewer than twenty-five countries were represented. A mammoth parade—led by the African Legion, the Black Cross Nurses and other organizations of the UNIA—wound through Harlem and on to Madison Square Garden, where Garvey set the tone of the month-long convention with an opening address to 25,000 Negroes:

We are the descendants of a suffering people; we are the descendants of a people determined to suffer no longer. . . . We shall now organize the 400,000,000 Negroes of the world into a vast organization to plant the banner of freedom on the great continent of Africa. . . . If Europe is for the Europeans, then Africa shall be for the black peoples of the world. We say it; we mean it. . . .[20]

Later, the UNIA delegates drafted a "Declaration of the Rights of the Negro Peoples of the World," which was adopted on August 13, 1920. The declaration spelled out the Negro's rights in terms of political and judicial equality, racial self-determination and an independent Africa under a Negro government. It alleged that the League of Nations (which had just been organized in Switzerland) "seeks to deprive Negroes of their liberty." The League, it said, is "null and void as far as the Negro is concerned."

The convention also approved a flag for the movement: "red for the blood of the race, nobly shed in the past and dedicated to the future; black to symbolize pride in the color of its skin; and green for the promise of a new and better life in Africa."[21] An order of nobility was created; honorary orders were established; salaries were voted for the leadership; and Garvey was elected Provisional President of the African Republic. Gabriel Johnson, mayor of Monrovia, capital of the free African Republic of Liberia, was named secretary of state in the Provisional Cabinet at a salary of $12,000 a year. So impressed was Johnson that, on his return home, he announced that his office in Garvey's Provisional Government gave him diplomatic precedence over the President of Liberia.

When the convention ended, the Garvey movement had attained world significance. " 'Up, you mighty race,' Garvey thundered, 'you can accomplish what you will,' and the Negro people responded with an enthusiastic determination born of centuries of frustration and despair."[22] They poured a million dollars into the UNIA's Black Star Steamship Line—organized to link the black peoples of the world in commerce and trade, and to transport America's black millions back to their African "home." They gloried in the cooperative possession of grocery stores, laundries, restaurants and hotels. They took an unconcealed pride in staffing the Universal Black Cross Nurses, the Universal African Motor Corps, the Black Eagle Flying Corps and other UNIA auxiliaries with "Black men and women." An unarmed but smartly uniformed Universal African Legion paraded spectacularly through the streets of Harlem, and the admiring Negroes massed along the route whispered knowingly about the liberation of Africa by force of arms. Uncritical Negroes everywhere, and especially the despairing millions in the crowded slums of black America, acclaimed Garvey as the true leader of a new race.

Garvey's political ambitions were never made wholly explicit. The Ku Klux Klan and the fanatical Anglo-Saxon Clubs of that era assumed that he intended to lead all the Negroes in America to Africa; for this reason, they gave him their open support. But Garvey declared, "We do not want all the Negroes [to settle] in Africa. Some are no good here, and naturally will be no good there."[23] His real intentions seem to have been not unlike those of modern Zionism. He wanted to build a state, somewhere in Africa, to which Negroes would come from all over the world, bringing with them a wealth of technical and professional skills. Within a few years, he hoped, the new state would gain such prestige and power that it would be recognized as a symbol of accomplishment and protection for Negroes all over the world. For Garvey was convinced, as is Elijah Muhammad, that the Negro can hope for neither peace nor dignity while he lives in a white society. Like Muhammad, he saw only one solution: the establishment of a separate nation "so strong as to strike fear" into the hearts of the oppressor white race.[24]

But, unlike the Zionists, Garvey did not rest his ambitions here. The eventual liberation of all Africa was never far from his thinking. Presumably his black state, when it became sufficiently powerful, would begin a revolution that would free all Africa, for he spoke mysteriously of the hour of "Africa's Redemption": "It is in the wind. It is coming. One day, like a storm, it will be here." He told a white audience that "you will find ten years from now, or 100 years from now, Garvey was not an idle buffoon but was representing the new vision of the Negro. . . ." In what was perhaps a prophetic warning, he declared: "We say to the white man who now dominates Africa that it is to his interest to clear out of Africa now, because we are coming . . . 400,000,000 strong." And again, "We shall not ask England or France or Italy or Belgium, 'Why are you here?' We shall only command them, 'Get out of here.' "25

Garvey's beachhead on the African continent was to be Liberia, the little country founded on the west coast by American slaves in 1847. The Liberian government had promised to "afford the association every facility legally possible in effectuating in Liberia its industrial, agricultural, and business projects." Specified settlements were laid out by the Liberian government and set aside for colonization, but Liberia's Acting President Edwin Barclay felt it necessary to warn Garvey that "the British and French have enquired. . . . But it is not always advisable nor politic to openly expose our secret intentions. . . . We don't tell them what we think; we only tell them what we like them to hear —what, in fact, they like to hear."26

Garvey's movement was essentially political and social; he did not rest his doctrines and program upon any religious premise. Yet he did not neglect the wellspring of religious fervor—and discontent—in the Negro community. Then as now, many Negroes resented the white man's presumption in depicting God and Jesus as Caucasians, in filling the Christian churches and Bibles with pictures of a white God, a white Savior and an all-white heavenly host. Garvey seized on this resentment and carried it to a logical extreme. Since whatever is white cannot be beneficial to the black man, he pointed out, a white God cannot be the God of the Negro people. This was the God of the white man. The Negro's God must be black.

To promulgate a black religion, Garvey named as Chaplain General of the UNIA a former Episcopal rector, the Reverend

George Alexander McGuire. In the Episcopalian fold, Bishop McGuire had long been a nettlesome critic, first agitating in vain for independent status for the Negro congregations, then organizing an Independent Episcopalian Church. This group followed him into the Garveyite movement and became the nucleus of a new, UNIA-sponsored African Orthodox Church. In his new position, McGuire was ordained a bishop by Archbishop Vilatte of the Syrian Orthodox Church,[27] thus bringing to the African Orthodox Church direct apostolic succession from one of the oldest bodies in Christendom.

Under Garvey's aegis, Bishop McGuire set out to re-order the religious thinking of the vast membership of the UNIA. He established a cathedral and a seminary (named Endich, after an alleged Ethiopian mentioned in the New Testament) for the training of a new order of black priests. The liturgy, based on the Episcopalian ritual, was colorful and impressive. And the new church set high moral demands, seeking "to be true to the principles of Christianity without the shameful hypocrisy of the white churches."[28] But the church was distinguished primarily by its appeal to race consciousness. "Forget the white gods," the bishop demanded. "Erase the white gods from your hearts." By 1924, after four years of his ministry, the Black Madonna and Child had become a standard picture in the homes of the faithful, and the worship of a Black Christ was openly advocated.

In August 1924, at the fourth annual convention of the UNIA, Bishop McGuire issued a public appeal to Negroes "to name the day when all members of the race would tear down and burn any pictures of the white Madonna and the white Christ found in their homes."[29] The Negro clergy was loud in protest, and the Negro press derided the idea of a "black Jesus." But the African Orthodox Church had long since spread its missions through several states and into Canada, Cuba and Haiti. On both fronts, religious and political, Garvey's black nationalism was riding high.

From the start, however, Garvey had not been without his troubles. His movement had been kept under constant surveillance by New York State Assistant District Attorney Edwin P. Kilroe, whose interest bordered on harassment. The federal government was hardly sympathetic to Garvey's international ambitions; and abroad, the various colonial governments viewed him with outright alarm. His newspaper—in its English, French and Spanish editions—had been quickly suppressed throughout the colonial world. In America the newspaper was among several Negro organs cited by the U. S. Department of Justice in a 1919 report on alleged radicalism and sedition among American Negroes. The following year the Lusk Committee, investigating sedition in New York State, cited the *Negro World* as one of the most radical elements of the New Negro press. Both the committee and the Department of Justice portrayed Garvey as a dangerous agitator, inimical to the interests of his own people and of the country as a whole; but neither group was able to substantiate its charges.

Meanwhile, the governments of Great Britain and France became increasingly alarmed over the implications of the Garvey movement and spared no effort to keep it out of Africa—even to the extent of bringing indirect pressure to bear on the Republic of Liberia, which had agreed to provide for the settlement of about a hundred thousand Garvey followers in that country. The UNIA had been enthusiastically welcomed there, and the mayor of Monrovia had accepted a post as secretary of state in Garvey's provisional government. Garvey sent several missions to Liberia, one as late as June 1924, to prepare for the settlement of his followers, who were scheduled to begin arriving in October 1924.

In the summer of 1924, the pressure from the British and French (who governed the territories surrounding Liberia) took effect. The Liberian government, under President Charles D. B. King, sent a diplomatic note to the United States announcing that it was "irrevocably opposed both in principle and fact to the incendiary policy of the Universal Negro Improvement Association, headed by Marcus Garvey." The lands promised to Garvey were leased instead to the Firestone Rubber Corporation, and when the new Garvey mission arrived, the members were arrested for immediate deportation. Thereupon, the Liberian president was lionized by the British for his "courage and statesmanship." The British press hailed him for putting "his foot down very firmly on such misguided movements for the people of his own race, as that sponsored . . . by Marcus Garvey and other agitators." The

French government made him a Chevalier of the French Legion of Honor.[30]

At home, Garvey was encountering increasing resistance within the Negro community. The emerging black bourgeoisie and the Negro intellectuals would have no part of him.[31] Their attempt to mold the public image of Negroes as an intelligent, sophisticated people was undermined by his constant harangues and the spectacle of thousands of his followers parading in flamboyant uniforms through the streets of New York City. At first they simply ignored his movement; but as its notoriety increased, it drew the fire of most of the well-known Negro leaders, including A. Philip Randolph, Chandler Owen and W. E. B. DuBois. DuBois criticized the UNIA as "bombastic and impractical," although he later admitted that competition from Garvey had greatly hampered the development of his own Pan-African Congresses.[32] The NAACP also criticized Garvey's movement, as did the National Urban League.

Nor did Garvey spare his critics. He characterized such leaders as DuBois, James Weldon Johnson and Eugene Kinkle Jones as "weak-kneed and cringing . . . sycophant to the white man." He warned that "the 'Uncle Tom' Negroes must give way to the 'New Negro,' who is seeking his place in the sun."[33]

Thus Garvey's troubles closed down upon him. His own lack of business acumen had kept him embroiled in legal wrangles over the Black Star Line and other commercial ventures of the UNIA.[34] Now the apprehensions of the ruling powers on three continents were joined with those of America's conservative Negro leadership in a demand that the dangerous little Jamaican be cut down to size. The *Messenger* magazine, edited by Chandler Owen and A. Philip Randolph, led the Negro intellectuals in a direct attack. "Garvey must go!" became the rallying cry of many individuals who could agree on no other single issue.

Early in 1922, at the urging of the Negro press, Garvey had been indicted for using the mails to defraud in the promotion of stock in the UNIA's Black Star Steamship Line. But the government's case was weak, and the federal authorities made no move to prosecute. In January 1923, however, the calm was shattered by the murder of James W. H. Eason, an early Garvey admirer who had split with the movement the previous year and was now rumored to have offered himself as a key prosecutuion witness in the mail-fraud case. There was no evidence linking Garvey or the UNIA to the crime, which remains unsolved, but the hostility of the responsible Negro leadership was whetted. Less than a week after the murder, a "Committee of Eight"—all prominent American Negroes, most of them active in the NAACP—sent an open letter to the U. S. Attorney General. The letter condemned Garveyism as a philosophy seeking "to arouse ill-feeling between the races" and urged that he "use his full influence completely to disband and extirpate the vicious movement, and that he vigorously and speedily push the government's case against Marcus Garvey for using the mails to defraud." [35]

Garvey responded with a bitter denunciation of the "good old darkies" who had treacherously sought to curry favor with the white man at the expense of their "fellow Negroes whose only crime has been that of making an effort to improve the condition of the race." [36] But in May the government brought the case to trial and won a conviction. Garvey was fined and sentenced to imprisonment for the maximum term of five years. He remained at liberty for seventeen months while his lawyers vainly appealed the decision, but in February 1925 he was taken to the federal penitentiary at Atlanta, Georgia. In December 1927 his sentence was commuted by President Coolidge; but Garvey had never become an American citizen, and since he had been convicted of a felony, the law required that he be immediately deported. From abroad he labored hard to keep his movement in the United States alive, but it quickly faded, and his death in London in 1940 was scarcely mentioned in the American press.

Garveyism is not dead. William L. Sherrill, once Garvey's representative to the League of Nations, still maintains UNIA headquarters in Detroit and serves as president of the straggling movement. The African Orthodox Church also survives, but its membership has dwindled to less than seven thousand. Various nationalistic cults in America, Africa and Jamaica still celebrate "Garvey Day" each August 1 with appropriate speeches and ceremony. And Garvey's own stature continues to grow as more and more observers concede that, for all his faults, he had a profound awakening effect on the American Negro community. Yet Garveyism lives on not really as a movement but as a symbol—a symbol of the militant Negro nationalism which so many black Americans see as their only alternative to eternal frustration and despair.

Preparing the Way for Allah

By the late 1920s, then, Noble Drew Ali was dead and Marcus Garvey deported. Their movements, shorn of their charismatic leadership, were in rapid decline. But there was no change in the experience that gave rise to both movements—the experience of being black among a white majority. This condition was, if anything, more intolerable than ever, for the Negro masses had been vividly reminded of their human dignity and their proud racial heritage. The failure of the Moorish and Garveyite movements left in the Negro lower class a constrained silence, a vacuum of extremist protest against racial indignities that were soon to be aggravated by the tensions of the Depression. Either America had to come quickly to its senses and live up to its democratic ideals, or a new black nationalist movement would move in to fill that vacuum.

It was just at this time, in the summer of 1930, that Wallace D. Fard appeared in Detroit. Many of those who first came under his spell had been followers of Garvey or Noble Drew. Fard was not alone, of course, in seeking to win over the masses already conditioned to black nationalism, especially those who had flocked to the black, green and crimson banner of the UNIA. Other black nationalist groups were also active, among them the National Movement for the Establishment of a Forty-Ninth State, the National Union of People of African Descent, the Peace Movement of Ethiopia and the United African Nationalist Movement. But none of these groups had a leader with Fard's charisma or his ability to seize on the Moorish and Garveyite passions and transform them into a new force, in which religious and political energies were fused. Fard's movement was destined to become the vanguard of black nationalism and, by solving the problem of succession on which earlier movements had foundered, to give that ancient ambition a fresh permanence and power.

4　The Faith and the Future

The Black Muslims have learned much from Marcus Garvey and Noble Drew Ali. Like those earlier prophets of black nationalism, they capitalize on the lower-class Negro's despair and yearning, and they have developed his race consciousness and his hatred of the white man into a black confession of faith. The Black Man, they teach, has a manifest destiny, and the white man is the personification of the evil that separates the Black Man from his freedom, his moral development and his God. In such a confession, the Moors, the Garveyites and most of the other cults of black nationalism are able to find satisfactory expression. It matters little whether the homeland of the dispersed Black Nation is said to be Asia or Africa. For the black nationalist, Afro-Asia is a single continent, and the Black Man's Zion is where the white man is not.

In elaborating their doctrines, the Black Muslims have achieved what seems to be a paradox: a rigorously high moral standard of personal and group behavior, laced with a consuming and potentially violent racial and religious hatred. For the Muslims, however, this is no paradox. They urge "peace among brothers" but point out that the white man, having scorned brotherhood with non-whites, "can only be a brother to himself." They urge submission to all authority *except* to the authority of the white man, which, they assert, is not legitimate but is simply "imposed by force and maintained by intimidation." The Muslims' social morality is, in short, an in-group morality. They find no mandate, except that of temporary expediency, for peace and submission between whites and blacks. And from this point of view, it is the religion of the Negro Christian that appears as a paradox, if not an outright hypocrisy or madness. For "it is not possible," says Muhammad's chief spokesman, Malcolm X, "for you to love a man whose chief purpose in life is to humiliate you and still be what is considered a normal human being."

I. DOCTRINES AND MYTHOLOGY

Mythologies—and the doctrines they support—are found as the organizing principles of all mass movements, religious and secular. They hold the central position in the most venerable religions and the most specious cults, in social movements as disparate as Fascism and the Townsend Plan, in cultural attitudes ranging from white or black supremacy to the American Creed.

By their very nature, myths are outside the realm of the "true" or the "untrue." They are subject neither to the rules of logic nor to the techniques of scientific investigation. A "religious" myth, in particular, claims for itself an immunity which is not granted to any other kind of information upon whose authority people commit themselves to action.

Like every other mass movement, the Black Muslims have developed for themselves a unique body of myths and doctrines.[1] Much of this material is elaborative and peripheral. Several major themes, however, are stressed by the Muslims, both in their publications and in their public lectures.

The Plight of the So-Called Negroes

Like all other black nationalists, the Muslims do not consider themselves "Negroes." They resent and reject the word and its implications: it is no more than "a label the white man placed on us to make his discrimination more convenient." For this reason, they rarely use the word "Negro" without the qualifier "so-called."

The Muslims prefer to be called "Black Men." Malcolm X explains:

If you call yourself "white," why should I not call myself "black"? Because you have taught me that I am a "Negro"! Now then, if you ask a man his nationality and he says he is German, that means he comes from a nation called Germany. If he says his nationality is French, that means he came from a nation called France. The term he uses to identify himself connects him with a nation, a language, a culture and a flag. Now if he says his nationality is "Negro" he has told you nothing—except possibly that he is not good enough to be "American." . . . If Frenchmen are of France and Germans are of Germany, where is "Negroland"? I'll tell you: it's in the mind of

the white man! . . . You don't call Minnie Minoso a "Negro," and
he's blacker than I am. You call him a Cuban! Nkrumah is an African—a Ghanaian—you don't call him a "Negro." . . . No matter how
light or dark a white man is, he's "white." Same way with us. No
matter how light or how dark we are, we call ourselves "black"—
different shades of black, and we don't feel we have to make apologies
about it![2]

America's so-called Negroes, say the Muslims, have been
kept in mental slavery by the white man, even while their bodies
were free. They have been systematically and diabolically
estranged from their heritage and from themselves. "They have
been educated in ignorance," kept from any knowledge of their
origin, history, true names or religion. Reduced to helplessness
under the domination of the whites, they are now so lost that
they even seek friendship and acceptance from their mortal enemies, rather than from their own people. They are shackled with
the names of the Slavemasters; they are duped by the Slavemaster's religion; they are divided and have no language, flag or
country of their own. Yet they do not even know enough to be
ashamed.

The most unforgivable offense of these so-called Negroes is
that they "are guilty of loving the white race and all that that race
goes for . . . [for] the white race [is] their arch deceiver." Malcolm X sums up the result of centuries of indoctrination by the
white man:

As "Negro Christians" we idolized our Christian Slavemaster, and
lived for the day when his plurality of white gods would allow us to
mingle and mix up with them. We worshipped the false beauty of the
Slavemaster's leprous looking women. . . . We regarded them with
the utmost respect, courtesy and kindness, bowing, and tipping our
hats, showing our teeth. We perfected the art of humility and polite-
ness for their sake . . . but at the same time we treated our own
women as if they were mere animals, with no love, respect or protection. . . .

. . . .

We were supposed to be a part of the "Christian Church," yet we
lived in a bitter world of dejection . . . being rejected by the white
"Christian Church." In large numbers we became victims of drunkenness, drug addiction, reefer smoking . . . in a false and futile attempt

to "escape" the reality and horror of the shameful condition that the Slavemaster's Christian religion had placed us in.

. . . .

Fear ruled us, but not fear of God. We had fear of the Slavemaster, we had no knowledge of truth and we were apparently afraid to let him see us practicing love and unity towards each other.

. . . .

Is it a wonder that the world laughed at us and held us [up] to scorn? We practiced love of others, while hating ourselves . . . patience with others and impatience with our own kind . . . unity with others and disunity with our own kind. We called ourselves "Negro Christians," yet we remained an ignorant, foolish people, despised and REJECTED by the white Christians. We were fools![3]

America's so-called Negroes are the "Lost Nation of Islam in North America." They have now been found, and a Messenger has been sent to prepare them for their day of destiny, for "the judgment of the world has arrived and the gathering together of the people is now going on."[4] The Lost Nation has been as the beggar Lazarus, "the one who was so charmed over the wealth and food of the rich man that he couldn't leave his gate to seek some for himself."[5] But Allah has now found his people, and they must hasten to rise up and be men among men, lest they further disgrace themselves and their God.

The so-called Negroes must be willing to work and to suffer. They must first seek unity among themselves ". . . and then the friendship of others (if there is any friendship in others)." But they must never relent in their striving for a place in the sun:

We must have for our peace and happiness that which other nations have. Allah desires to make the Black Nation the equal or superior of the white race.[6]

If necessary, they must be willing to die for dignity and justice, but they need fear nothing if they will believe in Allah and follow his Messenger.[7] They must never be aggressors, but "it is a Divine Law for us to defend ourselves if attacked."[8] Indeed, if Jesus had permitted Peter and his other disciples to use the sword on the Jews, Jesus might have been more successful in his work. "For it was the sword that put him to death and the Jews remained unbelievers."[9]

The so-called Negroes are "sacred vessels of the Temple of God"; but "America has poured wine into those sacred vessels," corrupting them, and they will now "have to be chastised into the knowledge of Allah, the God of their Salvation." They have been "absolutely deaf, dumb and blind—brainwashed of all self-respect and knowledge of kind by the white Slavemaster." They are now little more than "free slaves," with no land of their own, no justice in the white man's courts, no vote at the white man's polls and no voice in the councils whose edicts they must accept. Yet, led by the Negro clergy, they continue to love their oppressors, while the whites "make fools and Uncle Toms out of our educated professional class of people with a false show of social equality."[10]

"The white man is never going to grant the Negro equal opportunity," says Minister Louis X of Boston, "for the white man knows that the Black Man is by nature a leader. Granted equality, he will automatically assume leadership. Since the white man knows this, he grants symbolic status to a few Uncle Toms and keeps the rest of us available for exploitation."

The Negro in America is "sick," the Muslims say. He has been poisoned to death's door by the spurious teachings of the white man. But the white man is sicker: he has been fatally drugged by his own ego. The white man will never recover, for "he is just like a man on dope. If he kicks it, he'll die, and if he doesn't kick it, it'll kill him." The teachings of Elijah Muhammad are "specifically aimed at those suffering from a particular illness we all know about." They are "designed to rectify the ills of the Black Man in the West."

The Muslim leadership particularly condemns the Negro who, having gained a limited acceptance in the white world, dissociates himself from the Negro masses. Of such a man Malcolm X declares:

No matter how much education he has, everyday things keep reminding him. . . . Makes no difference what he is or how great he is. If he is a physicist, he is a *Negro* physicist. If he is a baseball player, he is a *Negro* baseball player. It's the same if he is in Massachusetts or Mississippi, he can't escape the stigma the white man has saddled him with. . . . They say that only the people who have been tramped upon become Muslims. Well, in that case we should be twenty million strong because there isn't a Negro in America who hasn't been tramped upon! Some are just too busy licking the boots that tramped over them to realize what is taking place.[11]

Negro moderates—those who undertake to defend whites who have shown some liberality in their views—come in for a similar upbraiding:

You have a situation where Negroes are too quick to jump up and shout about what the good white people are doing for them. Well, if Jesse James robbed a bank and his sons came along later and scattered a few coins before the depositors who lost everything they had, some people would want to build a monument to the James boys! . . . So this Negro, he gets elated. He thinks he's making progress when all the time he's catching more hell than any black man on the face of the earth.[12]

The Negro's plight was forced upon him by the white man, but it persists because the Negro has been willing to remain "in a land not his own." It can only be solved by separation. So long as Negroes live among whites, they will be subject to the white man's abuse of power—economic and political. Separation will provide the only realistic opportunity for mutual respect between the races.

But the Muslims are hardly planning to abandon the country to the white man. They emphasize that the white man's home is in Europe and that justice requires a separate "Black Nation here in America," built on "some of the land our fathers and mothers paid for in 300 years of slavery . . . right here in America." Marcus Garvey wanted to found a Black Nation in Africa. Elijah Muhammad thinks America will do.

The Coming of Allah

The so-called Negroes are ignorant and servile, and the behavior they have copied from the white man is shameful. Yet they remain sacred to Allah, who has promised to rescue them from their oppressors. Allah's coming had been predicted for six thousand years, ever since the white race began; at his coming, the white race was to reach its end. "America," says Muhammad, "is the place where Allah will make himself felt."

Allah's incarnation was, of course, the stranger in Detroit, who "came from Arabia in 1930" and "used the name of Wallace D. Fard, often signing it W. D. Fard. In the third year (1933) he signed his name 'W. F. Muhammad,' which stands for Wallace Fard Muhammad. He came alone."[13]

Elijah Muhammad, the Messenger, proclaims his own intimacy with Allah—"I know Allah and I am with him"—but he never presumes to Allah's supreme status. Allah alone is the "Author of Islam," and "it is a perfect insult to Allah" to worship anyone other than him. Allah has found his people and will soon punish the white Slavemasters for the evil they have done. The period of bondage is ended, and "hell is kindling up."

Allah is not, however, a godhead complete in himself. All Black Men represent Allah, or at least participate in him, for all Black Men are divine. A strong Platonic idealism permeates the Black Muslim concept of Allah: Pure Black is equivalent to Absolute Perfection. Again and again the thesis is sounded that *Black* is the primogenitor of all that exists. All colors are but shades of black; white is but the absence of color; hence the white man is incomplete and imperfect. All things that are, are made by man; and only Black Man is truly wise and creative.

Allah is a Black Man, not a spirit or "spook." He is the Supreme Black Man, the Supreme Being among a mighty nation of divine Black Men. This sharp difference from the Christian concept of God was made clear during a television interview of the Muslim leader in 1959.

Mr. Lomax: Now if I have understood your teachings correctly, you teach that all of the members of Islam are God, and that one among you is supreme, and that that one is Allah. Now have I understood you correctly?

Mr. Elijah Muhammad: That's right.

Mr. Lomax: Now, you have on the other hand said that the devil is the white man—that the white man is a doomed race.

Mr. Elijah Muhammad: Yes.

Mr. Lomax: Am I correct there, sir?

Mr. Elijah Muhammad: Yes.[14]

It is Allah who exposed the white man: "He gave us information as to the exact birth of the white race and the name of their God who made them, and how, and the end of their time.

. . . He taught us the truth of how we were made slaves, and how we are kept in slavery by the slavemaster's children." He taught his people to avoid unclean foods, especially pork; and he instructed them in science and astronomy, the civilizations on other planets and the knowledge of self. He taught them the history of the two nations—the black and the white—which dominate the earth and "declared the doom of America for her evils to [Black Men]." That doom is already "past due, and she is number one to be destroyed."[15]

Allah is not unforgiving, and the sins the Lost Nation committed in following and obeying the Slavemasters are not held against them *if they return to their own kind.* Allah's greatest teaching is *"Be Yourself."* He demands that "we must give up our slave names . . . give up all evil doings and practices and do only righteousness or we shall be destroyed from the face of the earth." Of those who submit, Allah will make a "new people" who will participate in "unlimited progress."

The coming of Allah signifies the beginning of justice for the Black Man. Allah came to expose the "great enemy of justice and righteousness" before all the world. His very coming is a judgment upon the behavior of those in power. "If justice had prevailed, there would be no judgment," but the Slavemaster's yoke grows even more oppressive:

With all of your blood . . . given to help keep America for white Americans, you return to meet lawlessness and injustice. You are beaten, raped, lynched, burned . . . and denied justice by the government [which is] defended with [your] life's blood. . . . White lynchers and rapers of our people are judged innocent. . . . You continue like sheep among wolves to go on suffering . . . the government makes it clear to you that it is no defense for us against injustice. . . . The only alternative left is to unite as one on the side of Allah . . . "Fight with those who fight against you," (Holy Quran). "An eye for an eye" (Bible), and fight every injustice against us with every drop of blood that is in us.[16]

Because of the injustices of the Caucasians, "Allah has not come to bring about love and peace between us and the devils, but rather to separate . . . [us] from our open enemies."[17] Allah has further come to bring the "right religion in the right state." He has made it known that Jesus "was only a prophet and not the

equal of Moses and Muhammad, and that his [Jesus'] religion
was Islam, and not the Christianity of the Pope of Rome."[18]

The Original Man

The Original Man is, by declaration of Allah himself, "none
other than Black Man." Black Man is the first and last: creator
of the universe and the primogenitor of all other races—including
the white race, for which Black Man used "a special method of
birth control." White man's history is only six thousand years
long, but Black Man's is coextensive with the creation of the earth.
Original Man includes all non-white people, and his primogeniture
is undeniable: "everywhere the white race has gone on our planet
they have found the Original Man or a sign that he has been there
previously."[19]

The so-called Negro in America is a blood-descendant of the
Original Man. "Who is better knowing of whom we are than God
Himself? He has declared that we are descendants of the Asian
Black Nation and of the tribe of Shabazz,"[20] which "came with
the earth" when a great explosion divided the earth and the moon
"sixty-six trillion years ago." The tribe of Shabazz was first to
explore the planet and discover the choicest places in which to
live, including the Nile Valley and the area which was to become
the Holy City of Mecca in Arabia.

All so-called Negroes are Muslims, whether they know it or
not. It is the task of Elijah Muhammad and his followers to teach
the so-called Negroes that they are of the tribe of Shabazz and,
therefore, "Original." Once they understand this, they will know
themselves to be Muslims, heart and soul. Christ himself was a
Muslim prophet, and several of his parables refer to the so-called
Negroes, especially those of the Lost Sheep, the Prodigal Son and
the Raising of Lazarus. The so-called Negroes are good people
and religiously inclined by nature. In fact, "the Black Man by
nature is divine."[21]

When the whole world knows who the Original Man is—and
only then—wars will cease, for everything depends upon knowing
who is the rightful owner of the earth. Lest there be any possible

confusion, Muhammad addresses himself specifically to the question:

The Original Man, Allah has declared, is none other than the Black Man. He is the first and the last, and maker and owner of the universe; from him come all—brown, yellow, red, and white. . . . The true knowledge of black and white should be enough to awaken the so-called Negroes . . . [and] put them on their feet and on the road to self-independence.[22]

To know the identity of the Original Man is of crucial importance, for the time of "judgment" is approaching and "Allah is now pointing out to the nations of the earth their rightful places."

The White Man and Christianity

It would be difficult, probably impossible, to separate the Black Muslim teachings on Christianity from those on race. A fundamental tenet of the sect is that all Black Men are Muslims by nature and that Christianity is a white man's religion. Thus there is not even a *possibility* of awakened Black Men accepting Christianity. Nor can the white man accept Islam as taught by Muhammad, for the white man is a devil by nature: "Out of the weak of the Black Nation, the present Caucasian race was created."

The "originality" of the Black Nation and the creation of the white race by Yakub, "a black scientist in rebellion against Allah"—this is the central myth of the Black Muslim Movement. It is the fundamental premise upon which rests the whole theory of black supremacy and white degradation. Muhammad explains in patient detail:

Who are the white race? I have repeatedly answered that question in this [column] for nearly the past three years. "Why are they white-skinned?" Answer: Allah (God) said this is due to being grafted from the Original Black Nation, as the Black Man has two germs (two people) in him. One is black and the other brown. The brown germ is weaker than the black germ. The brown germ can be grafted into its last stage, and the last stage is white. A scientist by the name of Yakub discovered this knowledge . . . 6,645 years ago, and was successful in doing this job of grafting after 600 years of following a strict and rigid birth control law.[23]

This experiment in human hybridization was a brilliant scientific accomplishment, but it had one unfortunate side effect. It peopled the world with "blue-eyed devils," who were of comparatively low physical and moral stamina—a reflection of their polar distance from the divine black. Hence white athletes are notoriously poor competitors against black athletes, nor should one wonder at the wholesale atrocities committed by the "civilized" whites. Only the white man could herd millions of his fellows into the gas chambers, set off atomic bombs and run special trains to a lynching at which the women and children are served cokes and ice cream.

In grafting out his creatures' color, Yakub grafted out their very humanity.

The human beast—the serpent, the dragon, the devil, and Satan—all mean one and the same; the people or race known as the white or Caucasian race, sometimes called the European race.[24]

Since by nature they were created liars and murderers, they are the enemies of truth and righteousness, and the enemies of those who seek the truth. . . .[25]

These devils were given six thousand years to rule. The allotted span of their rule was ended in 1914, and their "years of grace" will last no longer than is necessary for the chosen of Allah to be resurrected from the mental death imposed upon them by the white man. This resurrection is the task of Muhammad himself, Messenger of Allah and Spiritual Leader of the Lost-Found Nation in the West. The period of grace was seventy years; forty-six have already elapsed.

During their reign, the devils have "deceived the black nations of the earth, trapped and murdered them by the hundreds of thousands, divided and put black against black, corrupted and committed fornication before your very eyes with your women . . . [and then made] you confess that you love them. . . ."[26]

Four hundred years ago, the white Christians stole the Black Muslims away from their homes and brought them to North America, where the whites were already in the process of systematic genocide against the Indian. The whites enslaved the blacks and ensured their bondage by robbing them of their names (identity), language (cultural continuity) and religion (protection of their God). By robbing them of their true names, the whites both shamed them and effectively "hid" them from their own kind. By making the Black Men accept European names, the whites branded them as property. By requiring them to speak English rather than their native Arabic, the whites cut their slaves off from their cultural heritage and the knowledge of self which is essential to dignity and freedom. Such were the secular bonds of servitude.

But the Christian religion was and is the master stratagem for keeping the so-called Negro enslaved. The whites gave him the "poisoned book" and required him to join the "slave religion," which teaches him to love his oppressor and to pray for them who persecute him. It even teaches him that it is God's will that he be the white man's slave! There is, of course, some truth in the Bible, but it is tangled in the white men's contradictions, for "from the first day [they] received the Divine Scripture they started tampering with its truth to make it to suit themselves. . . ."[27]

The Bible is the graveyard of my poor people. . . .

. . . .

. . . and here I quote another poison addiction of the slavery teaching of the Bible: "Love your enemies, bless them who curse you; pray for those who spitefully use you; him that smiteth thee on one cheek offer the other cheek; him that (robs) taketh away the cloak, forbid not to take (away) thy coat also." . . . The Slavemasters couldn't have found a better teaching for their protection. . . .[28]

The Bible is also held in some suspicion because "it is dedicated to King James (a white man) rather than to God." Moreover, "it makes God guilty of an act of adultery by charging Him with being the father of Mary's baby; again it charges Noah and Lot with drunkenness and Lot begetting children by his daughter. What a poison book!"[29] On the whole, "Christianity is a religion organized and backed by the devils for the purpose of making slaves of black mankind."[30] It "has caused more bloodshed than any other combination of religions. Its sword is never sheathed."[31]

Islam sent several prophets, including Moses and Jesus, to offer Islam to the white men as a religion of brotherhood. But the white man could not accept it, for the white race is evil by nature and cannot love anyone who is not white. "They are ashamed to even call you a brother or sister in their religion, and their very nature rebels against recognizing you!"[32]

They cannot be trusted. The Caucasians are great deceivers. Their nature is against friendship with black people, although they often fool the black people . . . claiming that they are sincere friends. . . .[33]

And: Do not "sweetheart" with white people, your open enemies, for their "sweethearting" with you is not sincere. . . .[34]

The black Christian preacher is the white man's most effective tool for keeping the so-called Negroes pacified and controlled, for he tells convincing lies against nature as well as against God. Throughout nature, God has made provision for every creature to protect itself against its enemies; but the black preacher has taught *his* people to stand still and turn the other cheek. He urges them to fight on foreign battlefields to save the white man from his enemies; but once home again, they must no longer be men. Instead, they must patiently present themselves to be murdered by those they have saved.

Even the Christian God hates his enemies and works to destroy them. This is recorded in the Christian Bible, which all Christians say they accept. "But the black clergy, in trying to ingratiate itself with the whites, will deliver their people up wholesale."[35] Thus, in an unholy and unnatural way, the "Negro clergy class is the white man's right hand over the so-called Negroes,"[36] and the black preacher is the greatest hindrance to their progress and equality.

The so-called Negro clergy, say the Muslims, prostitute themselves to the downtown whites in return for "whatever personal recognition they can get above their followers. North or South it's the same. If a white preacher exchanges pulpits with a so-called Negro minister once a year on Brotherhood Sunday, the black preacher tells his people the millennium is here." And as for their heroics during the recent "sit-ins" staged by Negro students in the South, the black preachers' tactic was simply to "put the children out to expose themselves to the brutality of the uncivilized whites, then . . . rush in and 'lead' after the fight is over." In substantiation, the Muslims cite the following article which appeared in a well-known Negro newspaper:

A shameful display of cowardice and ingratitude was shown last week by certain members of the local clergy. . . . The members took credit for the desegregation of five lunch counters. They neglected to give credit to the students, the persons really responsible. . . . Not one of the ministers sat-in [in] any of the department stores. . . . Brave and persistent activity by the students . . . caused the five lunch counters to be integrated. [But] the ministers, on top secret invitation from the store managers crept downtown to "negotiate." In this, they helped the store ignore the students. Now, after all the hard, dangerous work [had] been done, the ministers have stolen credit for the students' successful work.[37]

The reprehensible behavior of the so-called Negro preachers stems primarily from their desire to be acceptable to the white churches and other religious organizations. Hence the black preacher is far more zealous about adhering to what he has been told are Christian principles than is the white man. The white man does not believe in trying to perfect himself morally, but he wants the Negro to be "past-perfect." As a result, the black preacher is so busy trying to gain the white man's approval by doing what the white man himself has never done, and has no intention of doing, that he has no time to concern himself with the real issues, such as economic justice and the freedom to walk the streets as a man.

II. MUSLIM MORALITY

In their day-to-day living, the Black Muslims are governed by a stringent code of private and social morality. Since they do not look forward to an afterlife, this morality is not related to any doctrine of salvation. It is, quite simply, the style of living appropriate to a divine Black Man in his capacity as true ruler of the planet Earth.

Ritual requirements are inextricably mixed with moral injunctions. The Muslim is expected to pray five times a day—at sunrise, noon, mid-afternoon, sundown and before retiring—and a sixth time if he rises during the night. All prayers are made facing east, toward the Holy City of Mecca. Before each prayer, he must make the proper ablutions: rinsing the mouth, washing the hands, feet and forearms, and so on. Cleanliness of the body, "inside and outside," is essential.

Certain foods, such as pork and corn bread, are forbidden to the Muslim, for "they are a slow death" to those who eat them. Many other foods common to the diet of Negroes, especially in the South, are not to be eaten, since they constitute a "slave diet" and "there are no slaves in Islam." Lamb, chicken, fish and beef are approved, but all foods must be strictly fresh. The hog is considered filthy—"a poison food, hated of Allah"—and was never intended to be eaten except by the white race.[38]

One Muslim minister explained why the eating of pork is prohibited: "The hog is dirty, brutal, quarrelsome, greedy, ugly, foul, a scavenger which thrives on filth. It is a parasite to all other animals. It will even kill and eat its own young. Do you agree? In short, the hog has all the characteristics of a white man!" Asked to explain the analogy implied in the reference to the hog eating its young, he replied, "Didn't they father a million half-blacks during slavery and sell them off like cattle—for money? Aren't they still bastardizing the race today to keep their wives in servants at subsistence wages? This is eating your own young and picking your teeth with the bones!"

Muhammad himself is vociferous in his dislike of pork and those who eat it:

The hog is absolutely shameless. Most animals have a certain amount of shyness, but not the hog or its eater. . . . The hog eater, it is a fact, will go nude in public if allowed. His temper is easily aroused . . . and he will speak the ugliest, vilest, and most filthy language. . . .[39]

Tobacco is also forbidden, and Muslims are admonished against overeating—a habit to which the so-called Negroes are alleged to be particularly susceptible. An overweight Muslim may be penalized by a fine, which continues until he reduces. In general, one meal a day is considered sufficient, for such restraint eliminates physical and mental sluggishness and leaves more time for industry.

Certain temple activities are considered morally binding and lapses can be swiftly punished. The Muslim is required, for example, to attend two (and occasionally more) temple meetings a week. In extraordinary circumstances he may be excused if he secures permission in advance; but members who fail to attend without such permission are summarily suspended. Male Muslims are also expected to "fish for the dead"—that is, to go into the streets in search of potential members. Unsuccessful "fishermen" are penalized.

Sexual morality is defined in ultra-puritanical terms and is said to be strictly enforced. Any philanderer is answerable to the quasi-judicial militia, the FOI. Courtship or marriage outside the group is discouraged, and unremitting pressure is put on non-Muslim spouses to join the Black Nation. Divorce is frowned upon but allowed. No Muslim woman may be alone in a room with any man except her husband; and provocative or revealing dress, including cosmetics, is absolutely forbidden. Any Muslim who participates in an interracial liaison may incur severe punishment, even expulsion, from the Movement. Clear lines are drawn to indicate the behavior and social role appropriate to each sex; and Muslim males are expected to be constantly alert for any show of interest in a Muslim woman on the part of a white man, for whom sex is alleged to be a degrading obsession.

The regeneration of criminals and other fallen persons is a prime concern of the Black Muslims, and they have an enviable record of success. Muhammad claims that his Movement has done more to "clean up the so-called Negroes" than all the churches and social agencies combined. Malcolm X scarcely exaggerated when he declared:

It is a known fact, and sociologists agree that when a man becomes a follower of Mr. Muhammad, no matter how bad his morals or habits were [before], he immediately takes upon himself a pronounced change which everyone admits. He [Muhammad] stops them from being dope addicts. He stops them from being alcoholics, [and alcohol] is a curse on the so-called Negroes. He has taken men who were thieves, who broke the law—men who were in prison—and reformed them so that no more do they steal, no more do they commit crimes against the government. I should like to think that this government would thank Mr. Muhammad for doing what it has failed to do toward rehabilitating men who have been classed as hardened criminals. . . . The psychologists and the penologists—all the sociologists—admit that crime is on the increase, in prison and out. Yet when the Black Man who is a hardened criminal hears the teachings of Mr. Muhammad, immediately he makes an about-face. Where the warden couldn't straighten him out through solitary confinement, as soon as he becomes a Muslim, he begins to become a model prisoner right in that institution, far more so than whites or so-called Negroes who confess Christianity.[40]

Eric Hoffer, however, in his perceptive study of mass movements, comments on this phenomenon from a rather different point of view:

> It sometimes seems that mass movements are custom-made to fit the needs of the criminal—not only for the catharsis of his soul but also for the exercise of his inclinations and talents. . . . There is a tender spot for the criminal and an ardent wooing of him in all mass movements. . . . It is perhaps true that the criminal who embraces a holy cause is more ready to risk his life and go to extremes in its defense than people who are awed by the sanctity of life and property.[41]

Crime, he suggests, is a kind of escape-valve in which "the underground pressure of malcontents and misfits often leaks out." The mass movement draws this scattered energy to itself and harnesses it for its own purposes. Whether this portends an increased hazard for society as a result of the Black Muslims' assiduous rehabilitation, time alone will tell.

But the rank-and-file Muslim is expected to evince general character traits that can only benefit the society as a whole. Men are expected to live soberly and with dignity, to work hard, to devote themselves to their families' welfare and to deal honestly with all men. They are expected to obey all constituted authority —even the usurped and corrupt authority of the white man, until the Black Nation returns to power. Women are especially enjoined not to imitate "the silly and often immoral habits of the white woman," which can only wreck their marriages and their children. While equal in every way to their husbands, they are taught to obey them. Modesty, thrift and service are recommended as their chief concerns.

Above all, self-reliance and a sense of mutual responsibility are the hallmarks of Muslim morality. Muhammad urges his people:

> Put your brains to thinking for self; your feet to walking in the direction of self; your hands to working for self and your children. . . . Stop begging for what others have and help yourself to some of this good earth. . . . We must go for ourselves. . . . This calls for the unity of us all to accomplish it![42]

III. THE GOALS OF THE MOVEMENT

The ends toward which the Muslim organization is directed are the most nebulous points of its entire body of doctrine. This is the area in which the Muslim is almost certain to become vague, mystical, eschatological and evasive under questioning. He may give a misleading impression that the Movement has no well-defined objective or that it lacks the ability to accomplish its goal. But the facts are quite to the contrary. The Muslim knows where he is going, or at least thinks he does, and what appears to be haziness or naivete is only shrewd diplomacy.

Some uncritical observers have tended to dismiss the Movement as "confused and inconsistent" or else as having "improbable" or "fantastic" goals. Muhammad is more often written off as an "illiterate crackpot" or a "self-seeking charlatan" than taken seriously as a "race leader." His followers are frequently categorized by their upper-class critics as "ignorant Southern-type Negroes who don't know any better," and their Movement is dismissed as "just another Harlem-type cult." There are probably elements of truth in all these but they are not the whole truth, and they do not answer any of the really important questions. To ignore the Movement on such grounds would be absurd.

The Black Muslim Movement is alive and growing—at a rate which seriously embarrasses Negro leaders with more moderate programs. It has a vitality unmatched by any other organized movement with a large Negro membership. The pertinent question is *why* this is so. An examination of the goals of the Movement—as they have been stated or implied in its literature and public lectures, and as they may be inferred from careful observation and analysis—may offer some insight regarding the Muslims' ability to attract and hold an important segment of the Negro masses.

The United Front of Black Men

There can be no doubt whatever that Muhammad wants to see "every Black Man in America reunited with his own." This means, of course, that every Negro Christian is the target of the

Movement. At the present time the Movement is predominantly lower-class, and the Muslims are aware that the middle and upper classes will be harder to reach, for these classes are the "satisfied Black Men who think they have the least to gain." Yet Muhammad declares: "We are trying to reach *all* Black Men, those in the colleges and those in the jails. We need leaders at every level to challenge the lies of the white man. We need scholars to search out the truth independently of what the white man has written."[43]

The Muslims' present membership goal is set at a million followers by the end of 1961, five million by 1964. Part of this growth is expected to result from an intensive recruitment drive, part from the increasing disillusion of the Negro middle and upper classes. "By then even the Uncle Toms will know that no matter *who* they put in the White House, the so-called Negroes are right where they were before."

The Muslim ideal is "a United Front of Black Men," who will "take the offensive and carry the fight for justice and freedom to the enemy." Through such a United Front, "the American Negroes will discover themselves, elevate their distinguished men and women . . . give outlets to their talented youth, and assume the contours of a nation."[44] Because he pursues a United Front, Muhammad's attacks against Negro leadership have been mainly retaliatory, and the necessity for such a public display of disunity is distressing to him. During 1960 special attention was given to removing the differences which divide Muslim and Negro leadership. In an address delivered in Detroit in January 1960, Raymond Sharrieff, Supreme Captain of the FOI, announced:

Nineteen sixty marks the beginning of a new era, an era in which our Leader, the Honorable Mr. Elijah Muhammad, plans to unite every stratum of the American Black Man. . . . Even if not a member of our Temple. . . . Religious, economic and political differences are luxuries we American Black Men cannot afford. We must, in the Sixties, sit together and counsel.[45]

Black unity—the "Black Man's one hope for freedom"—is held by the Muslims to be the white man's most haunting fear. And the white man can bring intensely divisive pressures to bear, because the American Negroes, "a nation within a nation," are an "occupied people." The whites control communications, arms and the loyalty of the so-called Negro leadership as thoroughly and effectively as they did during World War II.[46] Operating through "professional Uncle Toms," they have thrown up barriers to black unity; and the divided black people have no way to protect their rights or make themselves heard.

The whites are said to be so desperate that even *talk* of black unity is labeled seditious. Stool pigeons are planted everywhere to spy on their own people: "The same Negroes whose fathers were sold at auction in the town square sell themselves and their people at the white man's dinner table," one Muslim minister declared with disgust. But these traitors are known, and they will be dealt with in due time.

The white man can hire them one against the other for just a few dollars . . . or even a smile. The Negroes must put a stop to the white man's stool pigeons among them . . . if they are ever to become a nation recognized by the nations of the earth.[47]

We have a few who are being paid to keep the enemy well informed of all we say. One day they will be out.[48]

Muhammad warns the Negro community that "the government makes every Negro who opens his mouth in favor of their own kind a promoter of sedition, and labels their teaching as being subversive or un-American." Even " 'divine truth' is un-American if it is on the side of the poor Negroes." But the Negro community should not be panicked into avoiding Muhammad's teachings as seditious, for this accusation is only a white trick to isolate the Muslims and frighten the black masses. "The government is not after me, they are after you to keep you from following me."[49]

Are Muhammad's teachings in fact seditious? No one can say, for his goals—and the ultimate methods he would use to reach them—are never baldly stated. "You are about to become the Head," he tells his followers, "and this should be good news. . . . 25,000,000 people should not be satisfied with anything short of a country for themselves. If you cannot think like a Muslim, it is because you are a coward. . . . The time has come for me to do something for my beautiful nation."[50] His goal sounds *possibly* like secession, and his methods are *apparently* not for cowards, but his only actual commitment is a cryptic promise to "do something." It would not be out of keeping with Muhammad's philosophy for this promise to mask seditious intentions, but an indictment could never be supported on such evidence.

Muhammad is aware of this, and the wily Muslim walks the precipice between sedition and religious license with consummate skill. He speaks knowingly of an impending "Battle of Armageddon" and has promised that Negroes "will soon gain control of New York City—and that 'white rule' in the United States will be overthrown by 1970."[51] Later this is explained to mean that the white nations would destroy each other and that the Black Nation would inherit the spoils. Yet the attitude of such an explanation is hardly consistent with the fervent militancy which characterizes all Muslim doctrine. A return to the Mosaic *lex talionis* is encouraged, for example, as the only possible guarantor of meaningful survival; and Muslims are urged to "fight like 'hell' with those who fight like 'hell' against you, and the world of mankind will respect us as equals."[52]

In a Negro leadership conference held in New York City, Muhammad's chief lieutenant, Malcolm X, reminded his confrères that they must surely "recognize that anyone who can assemble so many well-disciplined young Negroes together as swiftly as we, should never be underestimated as a force to be recognized and reckoned with here in Harlem's community affairs and conferences."[53] The point could not have been lost on the assembled leaders, who could hardly imagine the necessity of swiftly assembling many well-disciplined young men for a *conference*.

Such, then, is the Muslim vision of a United Front of Black Men—a phalanx of American Negroes no longer torn by dissension but standing shoulder to shoulder, ready for battle. The leader and the enemy are known, but everything else is shrouded in mystery: the methods of combat, the terms of surrender and the new way of life to be established after the victory.

Racial Separation

The Black Muslims demand absolute separation of the black and the white races. They are willing to approach this goal by stages—the economic and political links, for example, need not be severed immediately—but all personal relationships between the races must be broken *now*. Economic severance, the next major step, is already under way, and political severance will follow in good time. But only with complete racial separation will the perfect harmony of the universe be restored.

Those so-called Negroes who seek integration with the American white man are, say the Muslims, unrealistic and stupid. The white man is not suddenly going to share with his erstwhile slaves the advantages and privileges he has so long pre-empted. America became the richest and most powerful nation in the world because she harnessed, for more than three hundred years, the free labor of millions of human beings. But she does not have the decency to share her wealth and privileges with "those who worked so long for nothing, and even now receive but a pittance." The so-called Negroes are still "free slaves." Millions of them are not allowed to vote, and few are permitted to hold office. None can wholly escape the implications of color. Ralph Bunche, the most distinguished American Negro on the world scene, refused a sub-Cabinet post in the federal government because he could not live and move in the nation's capital with the freedom accorded to the most illiterate white thug. Even the recognized enemies of the country, so long as they are white, come to America and immediately enjoy the privileges of freedom. To American Negroes—hundreds of thousands of whom have fought and died for their nation—these same privileges are denied.

Again, the Muslims maintain that only the so-called Negro leaders want to integrate. The black masses have no love for the white man and no desire to be in his company. "But for the pseudo-Negro leaders, to be accepted by whites and to be in their company is worth more than heaven itself." These Negroes are forever "begging and licking the white man's boots for [him] to smile and pat [them] on the back."

Finally, the whole scheme of integration is only a stratagem through which the white man hopes to save himself from an inevitable fate. He has sowed the wind, and now he must reap the whirlwind. The ascendancy of the white West is ended. The wheel must turn. When the white man was the undisputed ruler of the earth, who spoke of integration? Now he has seen his empires crumble, his slaves shake off their bonds, his enemies multiply all over the world—"so he is willing to throw his faithful dog the driest bone he has, hoping that dog will once more forget the past and rush out to save his master." But the Negro will still be the loser, for the white man will only "integrate him" where it serves his own advantage, and this will always be at the bottom.

Muhammad urges the Black Man to stand aloof. Why integrate with a dying world?

Today's world is floating in corruption; its complete distintegration is both imminent and inescapable. Any man who integrates with the world must share in its disintegration and destruction. If the Black Man would but listen, he need not be a part of this certain doom.[54]

The Muslims reject the ultimate integration—racial intermarriage—as sternly as any Southern white, and for much the same reasons.

Usually, when the white man says "integrate," he has reservations. He doesn't want to see a black man marry his woman. We all agree on that. Muslims who follow Mr. Muhammad are absolutely against intermarriage. When you say "integration," if you mean that everyone should have equal opportunities economically, that everyone should have the right to socialize with whom they please, that everyone should have the right to all the cultural advantages and things of that sort, well and good. But if [to] integrate means that a Black Man should run out and marry a white woman, or that a white man should run out and get my woman, then I'm against it. *We're absolutely against intermarriage!*[55]

The Muslims are convinced of their "superior racial heritage" and believe that a further admixture of white blood will only weaken the Black Nation physically and morally, as well as increase the loss of face the so-called Negro has already suffered by permitting the white man to bastardize the race. The white race will soon perish, and then even a trace of white blood will automatically consign its possessor to an inferior status.

Muhammad conceives his mission to include the re-purification of the "Lost-Nation-in-the-West"—ideologically, morally and, above all, biologically. Only when this has been done can the black people of America assume their rightful place of dignity and leadership among the triumphant black nations of the world. The United Front of Black Men, therefore, will countenance no interracial dallying. The intelligent Black Man must look beyond today's personal whimsies to the building of the Black Nation of tomorrow.

Economic Separation

The call for a Black Front has important economic overtones, for the Muslims' economic policies are a fundamental aspect of the total Movement. Their basic premise is that the white man's economic dominance gives him the power of life and death over the blacks. "You can't whip a man when he's helping you," says Muhammad; and his oft-quoted aphorism is economically, if not socially or politically, cogent.

Economic security was stressed from the first days of the Movement. As early as 1937 it was observed that:

The prophet taught them that they are descendants of nobles. . . . To show their escape from slavery and their restoration to their original high status, they feel obliged to live in good houses and wear good clothes . . . and are ashamed that they have not been able to purchase better commodities or rent finer homes.[56]

As we have seen, the pendulum has swung back toward the center. The Muslims still prize industriousness and a sense of responsibility, but they shy away from conspicuous consumption. They do not live in the residential sections generally preferred by the Negro business and professional classes, and they do not sport the flashy automobiles usually associated with Negro revivalistic cults. On the contrary, they strongly affirm their identity with the working class. There is a strong emphasis on the equality of the ministers and the "brothers," and all tend to live pretty much alike in terms of housing—in the Black Ghetto—and visible goods.

Thrift is encouraged; and while credit purchasing is not forbidden, Muslims are reminded that "debt is slavery." These counsels have had a clearly salutary effect. Indeed, the more faithful a Muslim is to the teachings of his leaders, the better his economic condition is likely to be.

The ascetic manner of life of the Moslems [Muslims] also has contributed to their economic improvement. No money whatever is spent by them on liquor, tobacco, or pork. Their one meal of the day consists almost entirely of vegetables and fruits. Consequently their expenditure on food is significantly smaller than is that of other Negroes. . . .[57]

Money must not be wasted, and no Muslim is expected to live beyond his means.

Stop wasting your money! Your money was not given to you, so why should you give it away for what you can do without? . . . We could save millions of dollars [for] education . . . land, machines . . . cattle . . . homes and factories. . . . Feed your own stomachs and hire your own scientists from among yourselves. . . .

How can we begin? Stop spending money for tobacco, dope, cigarettes, whiskey, fine clothes, fine automobiles, expensive rugs and carpets, idleness, sport and gambling. Stop . . . living on credit loans . . . seeking the highest priced merchandise. . . . If you must have a car, buy the low-priced car. . . . We must make a better future for ourselves and our children. . . .[58]

Such rigorous self-discipline is not only a virtue in itself but also a step toward the establishment of the Black Nation. Until the economic independence of the Black Nation can be assured, however, some Muslims will find it necessary to work for the white man. There is no shame in that, for all work is honest and even the meanest job can be done with dignity.

The Muslims are urged to be competent and honest in all their dealings, giving a full day's work for the wages received. Muslims are expected to "respect authority, on the job and wherever else it is legitimately exercised." Each working day is to be considered a learning experience against the time when the Black Nation will operate its own factories, farms and other enterprises. But this policy pays immediate dividends as well:

The members of the cult claim they have secured work more easily than have other Negroes. To some extent their claim seems to be justified. . . . Through the Nation of Islam they have gained a new status and a new confidence in themselves. When they meet Caucasians, they rejoice in the knowledge that they themselves are superiors meeting members of an inferior race. Employment managers tend to accept more readily persons whose appearance gives evidence of clean living and self-reliance, than those who show the marks of debauchery, defeat and despair.[59]

As an ideal, the Muslims advocate a complete economic withdrawal from the white community. Their transitional goals seem to hinge on the establishment of black businesses and industries which will reduce interracial contact to a minimum, provide jobs and capital for black workers and entrepreneurs, and offer the sense of group security proper to an "independent" people. To accomplish this end, Muhammad has drawn up an "Economic Blueprint" which is published occasionally in some elements of the Negro press and which is the basic text for Muslim lectures on the economic plight of the so-called Negro. The Blueprint opens with a description of the Black Man in white, Christian America as a Lazarus under the table of the rich, "begging for crumbs" and "entangled in want in the midst of plenty." Lazarus is asleep—"but I go," says Muhammad, "that I may wake him."

The key to the Black Man's economic security consists of five simple propositions:

1. Know thyself and be yourself. Islam makes a true Brother to [every other] Brother. . . . Acknowledge and recognize that you are a member of the Creator's [i.e., the Black] Nation, and act accordingly. . . . Recognize the necessity for unity. . . . This requires action and deeds, not words and lip service.
2. Pool your resources, physically as well as financially.
3. Stop wanton criticism of everything that is black-owned and black-operated.
4. Keep in mind—*Jealousy Destroys From Within.*
5. Observe the operations of the white man. He is successful. He makes no excuses for his failures. He works hard—in a collective manner. You do the same.[60]

Muslims are urged to pool their resources and techniques in merchandising, manufacturing, building, maintenance—any field in which unity and harmony will contribute to efficiency and effectiveness. Those who lack skills or education are urged to ask help from their brothers with more training or experience.

Above all, Muslims are encouraged to "buy black" whenever possible. "The white man spends his money with his own kind, which is natural. You too, must do this. Help to make jobs for your own kind. Take a lesson from the Chinese and Japanese . . . and go all out to support your own kind." Business and professional men must not exploit their black customers or clients; but the black consumer must not hesitate to spend the few extra pennies the black businessman may have to charge in order to meet the competition of the advantaged whites.

The Muslims themselves maintain numerous small businesses and other enterprises. In Chicago they operate department stores, groceries, bakeries, restaurants and various kinds of service establishments. They own large farms in Michigan and near Atlanta, Georgia; and in practically every city with a temple, they have restaurants, barber shops, clothing stores and occasionally other businesses. All are run with efficiency and aplomb.

True Muslims are reminded that if *one* has a bowl of soup, all have soup. "Everywhere, the Negro is exploited by the white man; now, the Black Man must learn to protect his own, using the white man's techniques." By way of demonstration, Muhammad recently bought a large modern apartment building in Chicago, evicted the white tenants, moved in house-hungry Negroes from the South Side ghetto and lowered the rents.

Muhammad believes that much of the American Negro's "sickness" is economic. In February 1960, as a gesture toward strengthening this Lost Nation, he gave free exhibition space to Negro businesses at his Annual Convention, held at the giant Coliseum in Chicago. The three-day convention attracted some fifteen thousand delegates and visitors, and the exhibition was designed to "provide the opportunity for Negro businessmen to promote their businesses in line with Mr. Muhammad's program of Economic Security for the American Negro." There were Asian and African exhibits as well, but the emphasis was on the American Negro's potential for economic independence. The exhibition also represented an open bid by the Muslims for an increasing share of leadership among Negroes—a display of the Muslim potential for inducing the kind of race-consciousness to which Negro business must ordinarily look for survival.

Some Good Earth

It would be hazardous to assume that the Black Muslim Movement is all religion and economics. That these are fundamental aspects of the Movement is not open to serious doubt. But what does Muhammad envisage beyond a well-fed Black Nation under the sign of the Star and Crescent?

When Marcus Garvey began to speak too plainly about the political aspirations of the Universal Negro Improvement Association, his movement was labeled "seditious." Elijah Muhammad, who is not only a student of Garvey but was himself arrested and charged with sedition very early in his Muslim career, has learned the hazards of plain talk in the area of politics. It is doubtful whether any except the top leadership know exactly what the Movement's political aspirations are, or why. The characteristic mood of the Muslim laity is simply a blind faith—a complete confidence in Elijah Muhammad, who "has a plan for all of us" and is considered well-nigh infallible. The Muslim brotherhood have a sense of manifest destiny, an awareness of some kind of impending social cataclysm in which they will figure prominently. They are not certain what this cataclysm will be or when it will take place, but they are unshakably convinced that Messenger Muhammad knows. And they are prepared to lay down their lives at a signal from their leader, if dying will forward the goal he has in mind.

Doubtless the Federal Bureau of Investigation could relax its constant vigilance if Muhammad were more explicit about this goal. Malcolm X alleges that no fewer than fifteen FBI agents are regularly assigned to cover his New York temple alone, and Muhammad complains that the FBI could readily catch "all the lynchers and school-bombers in the South" with a fraction of the agents assigned to cover his personal movements. Responsible Negro leadership and the concerned white community would similarly be obliged if Muhammad's political goals were known. But the Muslims have shown little inclination to announce their ultimate intentions. They revel in the guessing game in which they are "it." Malcolm X often twits his questioners: "Those who say don't know, and those who know aren't saying."

At best, Muslim statements about their political goals are couched in mystical and eschatological innuendo or else in cryptic allusions to "a separate nation for ourselves, right here in America" or to "some good earth, right here in America, where we can go off to ourselves." Muhammad announced to some ten thousand listeners in Washington, D. C.:

You can't blame the government for not giving you anything when you are not asking for anything. . . . It is certainly evident by now that you were never intended to be a full citizen. . . . Your role was that of a slave and today, even . . . that intent underlies your role in the body politic.

. . . .

Our oppressors are determined to keep our eyes in the sky while they control the land under our feet, . . . smite our cheeks and rob our pockets.

. . . .

To integrate with evil is to be destroyed with evil. What we want—indeed, justice for us is to be set apart. We want, and must insist upon an area in this land that we can call our own, somewhere [where] we can hold our heads [up] with pride and dignity without the continued harassments and indignities of our oppressors.

. . . .

. . . let us carry in our hearts the doctrine of separation from our oppressors; let us demand a home we can call our own, support for ourselves until we are able to become self-sufficient.[61]

Usually the quantity of land mentioned is "two or three states," but the figure has sometimes been raised. In an address at the Muslim Convention of 1960, Muhammad suggested:

The best thing the white man can do is give us justice and stop giving us hell. I'm asking for justice. If they won't give us justice, then let us separate ourselves from them and live in four or five states in America, or leave the country altogether.[62]

Malcolm X thinks "nine or ten states would be enough." The Muslims have never indicated what states would be acceptable to them or just how they propose to acquire them, but the Southwest has featured prominently in speculation.

The Muslims often mention the alternative of leaving the country. In his column in the *Los Angeles Herald-Dispatch,* for example, Muhammad said: "All we are asking for is a separate state or territory. . . . It doesn't have to be in America."[63] But this alternative is never emphasized, and Muhammad repeatedly calls attention to the Black Nation's inherent right to land in America. This claim is grounded on two propositions: (1) the white man stole the country from the Indians, who are non-white peoples and brothers to the so-called Negroes, and (2) the Negroes worked for three hundred years as absolute slaves and an additional one hundred years as "free slaves," thereby earning a share in the country. Yet what share have they received?

> We are kicked around . . . until they say: "Move out n——r," even though they killed our people, the Indians, in order to possess the country for themselves.[64]

> We have not been given anything but hell in return for 400 years of hard labor, sweat and blood, without justice. We are not wanted in their society and are hunted like rabbits all over the country. . . .

> After 100 years of so-called freedom . . . the slavemasters have not offered you [a home] even in the worst part of this country, though our labor and our poor fathers' labor before us helped make America what it is.[65]

Malcolm X, speaking to a group of white listeners, has set forth a dramatic demand—not only for territory but also for a subsidy from the United States government. Millions of black men, he reminded his audience, "worked 300 years without a pay day. We feel that we've got something due us, and I don't mean this phony integration stuff." The United States, he declared, must "compensate us for the labor stolen from us." And he explained how:

The United States can subsidize Israel to start a state—Israel hasn't fought for this country. The United States can subsidize India and Latin America—and *they* tell the Americans to "go home!" We even subsidize Poland and Yugoslavia *and those are Communist countries!*

Why can't the Black Man in America have a piece of land with technical help and money to get his own nation established? What's so fantastic about that? We fought, died and helped to build this country, and since we can't be citizens here, then help us to build a nation of our own. We don't have to go to Africa. We can do it right here.[66]

There are indications that Muhammad does not really consider the physical separation of the races in this country a viable issue. He has offered no concrete proposal for effecting such a separation or for a partition of the country. The Muslims' real-estate holdings are scattered across the country, from Boston to Los Angeles, and they are preparing to spend at least $20 million to erect an Islamic Center in Chicago.

These facts, however, are capable of another and more sinister interpretation. The Muslims are convinced that "the white race . . . will never agree to divide America with us, though our blood is spilled on this soil and on foreign soil for the freedom of white Americans and their European friends."[67] But the white man's rule is at an end, and a "Superior Power" will now "create a 'New World,' a New People, a New Order, and a New Government."[68] What measures will this New Government take? If the Muslims will not leave America, and if the white man will not share the land with them, one drastic alternative remains:

The wicked must be punished for their wickedness poured out upon us. . . . This country is large enough to separate the two (black and white), and they both [could] live here, but that would not be successful. The best solution is for everyone to go to his own country. . . . The native home of the white race is in Europe.[69]

5 Reaching for the Masses

Unlike Athena, the Black Muslim Movement did not spring full-blown into maturity. It evolved over a generation and only gradually became a well-known symbol of protest—at least in the black ghettos of America's principal industrial cities. How shall we account for its growth and its attractiveness to the Negro masses as a social movement, quite apart from its identity as a religion?

Organizations such as the NAACP and the National Urban League, for all their virtues, have not caught the imagination and adherence of the Negro masses. Their memberships tend to comprise middle- and upper-class Negroes and whites, in each case the *least* disprivileged of their race. It is true that the lower-class Negro stands to benefit most from their services, for he is most deprived of the values they attempt to make available. But their philosophies are not directed toward him, and he has not taken them to his heart.

The Black Muslims, by contrast, are undeniably a mass movement. From their present base of more than 100,000 members, they are reaching for the support of the entire Negro lower class—and, ultimately, of all other black Americans. This ambition is of crucial importance, for it controls every public statement and activity of the Muslims, every gesture by which their myths and doctrines are expressed in action.

I. THE NATURE OF A MASS MOVEMENT

The Importance of Mass Membership

A mass movement usually begins with the degeneration of some familiar corporate structure—a church, in the sense of a religious denomination, or a major social or political unity—which has formerly maintained the social equilibrium. So long as this dominating structure is strong and vigorous in its social concern, mass movements do not develop. There is no need of them. But as these corporate ties dissolve—as the masses are dislocated from their "hereditary milieu"—many individuals become highly receptive to the new corporate unity implicit in a mass movement.[1]

Such people are the strength of a mass movement. Neither money nor prestige nor heritage approaches in importance the physical fact of a *participating* membership. The effectiveness of what a mass leader has to say depends upon how many people believe him and trust him for deliverance. Those who do believe him will be in the movement, and they are the most impressive arguments for the potential converts.

The principal rewards of a mass movement are always in the future, and the future takes on security in terms of the number of persons who are willing to identify themselves with it. The few are induced to follow the many, not because the collective mind of the many is presumed to be wiser, but because there is a certain loneliness in social isolation that is somewhat relieved by identification with a cause. Fifty million Frenchmen may very well be wrong, but they make reassuring company. Moreover, for the oppressed, the remotest hope is more acceptable than the present reality, and the strength of hope is intensified geometrically as those who share the hope increase in number.

A mass movement, therefore, does not begin with logic or a program, or even a defined goal. It begins with people who participate in a common hope for a better tomorrow. The task of the leader of a mass movement is to make that hope inclusive and vivid for all who find their present circumstances painful or unacceptable.

The True Believer[2]

It is a popular misconception that mass movements are formed by the most destitute elements of the society. This is almost never true. The destitute do not revolt. The mass movement may become a symbol of hope which draws the destitute to membership, but the movement draws its initial followers from the ranks of the merely discontented, those who have not yet lost all hope for better things. They see in the leader and his doctrine a chance to fulfill the desires and longings they have not quite relinquished, even in the face of the most discouraging adversity. In short, it is not present suffering but future expectation that impels the dissatisfied and the deprived to unite in protest.

The fanatical members of a mass movement, the "true believers," may vary greatly among themselves, but they have certain unmistakable traits in common. Their most pronounced characteristic is a desire for a personal rebirth—an escape to a new identity, in which they will be freed of their present restrictions and oppressions. A mass movement promises them a new "face." The old, unappreciated self is abandoned; in its place is a new self, neatly designed to inspire pride, confidence and hope.

Except for the opportunist and the adventurer, the mass movement offers no appeal to the individual interested in personal advancement on his own merit. Those who have learned to accept themselves or who have gained approval and acceptance in the society at large are not moved to exchange their individuality for a corporate identity. They do not wish to be lost in the mass. Only those who have lost all hope of gaining acceptance for themselves as they are—but who still hunger for acceptance—will seek to compel that acceptance by adopting a powerful corporate identity. The true believer, despised or ignored as John Smith, will be respected as, say, a Black Muslim; and he will count the submergence of his individual personality a trivial price to pay.

The true believer is ordinarily a misfit in the society he rejects. He may be a *temporary* misfit who has not yet found his niche—perhaps a returned veteran, an unemployed college graduate, a juvenile or a recent immigrant. Such people tend to exhibit a nervous restlessness and dissatisfaction. They envy the apparently unhampered progress of other men, and they are haunted by a fear that their best years will be wasted before they can realize their personal goals. These temporary misfits are receptive to the promises of the mass movement, but they are not totally committed to its doctrines, for they have not completely repudiated themselves. Any change in their personal fortunes will reconcile them to the larger society.

The *permanent* misfit's allegiance is without reservation, for he can find salvation only in escape from his repudiated self. Such a man may be an artist, composer, preacher, scientist or writer who has failed decisively to achieve a meaningful success. He may be an ex-criminal or a guilt-ridden individual striving to lose his past vileness by participating in a holy crusade. Perhaps the most tragic of the permanent misfits is the corporate minority, bent on assimilation but blocked by visibility—that "irreparable defect in body" which precludes acceptance. In such a minority:

. . . the individual stands alone, pitted against prejudice and discrimination. He is also burdened with the sense of guilt, however vague, of a renegade. . . . Within a minority bent on assimilation, the least and most successful (economically and culturally) are likely to be more frustrated than those in between. The man who fails sees himself as an outsider; and, in the case of a member of a minority group who wants to blend with the majority, failure intensifies the feeling of not belonging. . . . Thus it is to be expected that the least and most successful of a minority bent on assimilation should be the most responsive to the appeal of a proselytizing mass movement. . . . The least and most successful among the Negroes are the most race conscious.[3]

The true believer has no purpose and no goal except in relation to the movement with which he has identified himself. His acceptance and assimilation into the group is so complete that his personal identity *is* the corporate image. His confidence is the confidence born of the strength and unity of the movement, which can perform miracles of accomplishment beyond the reach of any individual. Most important, he is no longer alone. He is now accepted and wanted, rather than rejected and despised. And as long as the movement lives, the true believer cannot really die, for his life is in the corporate identity. To be expelled from it, or to have it destroyed by an external force, would be a death almost as real as physical death itself.

Leadership in the Mass Movement

The leader of a mass movement, like his true believers, is a product of the circumstances which make the movement possible. Ordinarily he is neither elected nor appointed, though he may have already held a post at some level within the movement. More often than not, the leader is simply "acclaimed" or "recognized," with formal investiture coming later if at all.

It has been said that the successful leader is a man who determines where his followers want to go and leads them there. Such a description applies *a fortiori* to the leader of a mass movement. Whatever his morals or his motives, he must have an almost uncanny sensitivity—an ability to empathize with and reflect the unspoken (and often unrecognized) yearnings of the people he undertakes to lead. He must, in his own behavior, reassure them by displaying a complete absence of fear and a constant concern for their welfare. He must demonstrate an unshakable conviction in the ultimate success of his cause, in which he alone is aware of some unique and essential truth.

The leader's most important asset is his ability to surround himself with a small coterie of worshipers who draw their inspiration from him, are categorically willing to accept his will as their own and are themselves capable leaders and organizers. No other single factor will more clearly determine his failure or success. But the leader can never rely wholly on his lieutenants; he must be indomitable himself. He must have "a joy in defiance . . . faith in his destiny and luck; a capacity for passionate hatred; contempt for the present . . . [and] a disregard of consistency and fairness."[4] He must also be able to estimate and manipulate the human craving for the sense of security inherent in a communion of cause and kind. Assemblages, parades, rituals, ceremonies, uniforms—all the badges of belonging—are part of his repertoire of leadership and control.

Originality is *not* important: the leader of a mass movement appropriates from every source whatever ideas or techniques he finds useful and presents them as originating with his own people. Nor must he be a thinker in his own right. Many times in history, the leaders of mass movements have been brilliant men, but their appeal was not rooted in the quality of their ideas. "What counts is the arrogant gesture, the complete disregard of the opinion of others, the singlehanded defiance of the world."[5]

The mass movement tends to be associated with the person of the leader as though it were his creation. In reality, the leader does not create the movement; he capitalizes upon conditions which are the product of social interactions too diverse and too momentous to be the work of one man. In a very real sense, mass movements are set up and "waiting to happen" before the leader arrives on the scene.

There is a period of waiting in the wings—often a very long period— for all the great leaders whose entrance on the scene seems to us a most crucial point in the course of a mass movement. Accidents and the activities of other men have to set the stage for them before they can enter and start their performance. "The commanding man in a momentous day seems only to be the last accident in a series."[6]

But a coalescence of the peculiarly volatile elements of social change does not automatically produce a mass movement. The right man must be there. The elements must come together in the presence of the unique personality which can successfully catalyze or ignite them.

The Instruments of Unification

The characteristic feature of a mass movement is its unique capacity for united action without consideration for the individual sacrifices of its members. The personal self is lost in the corporate whole and is expendable in the interests of the whole. Personal privacy, personal judgment and often personal possessions, freedom and life itself are laid upon the corporate altar. The mass movement exists as an instrument for united action and self-sacrifice, not for the advancement of individuals. Whenever there is a relaxation of collectivity, or when individual self-interest appears, the distinguishing character and the effectiveness of the movement are lost.

Absolute self-sacrifice is the lifeblood of the movement; contempt for death is the sure sign of faith. The true believer places all his trust in the destiny of the movement, its doctrines and its leader. He forsakes all values not sanctioned by the movement and not among its stated objectives. He lives not for the present but for the future; and not for his own future, but for the glorious triumph of his cause. He has renounced all self-interest, and even his most pragmatic affairs—earning a living, raising a family—assume the character of a holy crusade.

What seems to count more than possession of instruments of power is faith in the future . . . extravagant hope, even when not backed by actual power, is likely to generate a most reckless daring. For the hopeful can draw strength from the most ridiculous sources of power —a slogan, a word, a button. No faith is potent unless it . . . has a millennial component.[7]

A mass movement, then, is unified first by faith, carried to the extreme of self-sacrifice. It is unified also by its doctrines, for the mass movement claims to possess the absolute truth—an esoteric knowledge of the past, a pellucid understanding of the present, a perfect awareness of the future. This "truth" is a formidable source of the movement's power, and the true believer "knows" the "truth" through faith. He knows it with his heart rather than with his mind.

The doctrines of a mass movement derive their power not from their meaning but from their certitude. The leader's utterances may be replete with the grossest nonsense, and rational critics may search them in vain for some clue to his power. But they miss the point. Reason and truth are not important; the masses are roused to action by what they *accept* as true. A proposition that can be tested can be proved false, but not a prophecy or a revelation. A doctrine that is understood loses its power to compel its hearers: he who accepts a mystery can only obey, but he who understands it draws the power into himself. The true believer, however, wants only to accept. Understanding is personal, and he has renounced self, so he feels no need to understand. He has no doubts; he truly believes.

Self-mastery is another potent instrument of unification for the mass movement. On the one hand, as the members overcome in themselves the decadent habits and corrupt appetites of the rejected society, their own last shreds of identification with that society are symbolically overcome. On the other hand, certain moral commitments claimed by the general society but imperfectly observed by it take on an exaggerated importance within the movement. As the members successfully (indeed, fanatically) honor these commitments, they assert their moral superiority over all those from whom they have set themselves apart. The true believer is thus, in one sense, inevitably ambivalent: he seeks the approval of the general society by accomplishing what it has failed to accomplish, yet he scorns that society as worthless and its opinions as insignificant.

The mass movement also establishes its own exclusive code of behavior and institutes its own taboos. In the Black Muslim Movement, for example, every Muslim is committed to defend and protect every other "brother," even, if necessary, at the forfeiture of his life. Timidity or any hint of reluctance in this regard is absolutely taboo, and the rare lapses are punished summarily by ostracism or rejection by the group. Moreover, there can be no deviation from the "party line" as defined by the Messenger and enunciated by his ministers. Even "independent interpretations" are absolutely taboo. The ministers speak with the voice of Muhammad; the laity speak with the voice of the ministers; and on subjects on which the Messenger has not spoken, no one else in the Movement will venture to speak. In every facet of behavior and belief, the true believer must relentlessly master his own errant impulses and mold himself to the movement's unique image. But in doing so, he lowers still further the stubborn barriers of personal will that stand between his old, rejected self and his new corporate identity.

Finally, the mass movement is drawn together and held together by hatred, "the most accessible and comprehensive of all unifying agents." Eric Hoffer describes the effect of hatred upon the true believer:

It pulls and whirls the individual away from his own self, makes him oblivious of his weal and future, frees him of jealousies and self-seeking. He becomes an anonymous particle quivering with a craving to fuse and coalesce with his like into one flaming mass. . . . Common hatred unites the most heterogeneous elements.[8]

Hatred requires an object, a devil.

Mass movements can rise and spread without belief in a God, but never without belief in a devil. Usually the strength of a mass movement is proportionate to the vividness and tangibility of its devil.[9]

The genius of the leader of a mass movement is displayed in his timing and his choice of who the devil is to be. The devil must be an individual or group which is a socially legitimate hate-object, but he must also be omnipresent. Every difficulty must be ascribed to his evil nature, and every accomplishment must be vaunted as a triumph over him.

Hatred of the devil is the driving force of a mass movement. It is, without doubt, the most immediate instrument of unification. And, to complete the circle, it is the final product of every mass movement.

. . . we have never, since the world began, heard of a merciful nation. Nor . . . of a merciful church or a merciful revolutionary party. The hatred and cruelty which have their source in selfishness are ineffectual things compared with the venom and ruthlessness born of selflessness . . . we usually blame this shameful perversion on a cynical, power-hungry leadership. Actually, it is the unification set in motion by these enthusiasms, rather than the manipulations of a scheming leadership, that transmutes noble impulses into a reality of hatred and violence. The deindividualization which is a prerequisite for thorough integration and selfless dedication is also, to a considerable extent, a process of dehumanization.[10]

II. THE BLACK MUSLIMS AS A MASS MOVEMENT

Reaching for the Masses

Under Fard, the Muslims never had more than 8,000 members, although the conditions for rapid growth were almost ideal. Today the Muslims are flourishing: more than 100,000 members, with more being assimilated every day. The difference lies in this: Fard never had a movement. He only had a cult.

Muhammad's strategy has been to put the cult on parade—on the streets, in the press, in the temples, *wherever there are people*. And he has done this with impressive success. For local action, he has had an able corps of ministers in the field; but there were not many at first, and their fight was uphill. The press gave him his first major assist, for it made him "controversial": as a columnist in one of the most important Negro papers in the country, he became a conversation piece for hundreds of thousands of Negroes across America. Thousands of letters were sent to Muhammad and to the *Pittsburgh Courier,* denouncing and defending both the Messenger and the newspaper which provided space for his message.

People went to the temples to see the man whose columns they read. For the most part they were simply curious, but Muhammad and his ministers are masters at capturing the curious. In the temples Muhammad preached a somewhat different message—not completely different, but different in emphasis. His writings in the newspapers were generally filled with vague and cryptic biblical interpretations. But in the privacy of the temples, the white man was unmasked; his mistreatment of the so-called Negro was rehearsed in bizarre detail and with militant outrage.

Moreover, Muhammad appealed to the newcomers not as individuals but as a crowd. All persons entering a temple were (and still are) searched for weapons as a precaution against the assassination of a minister. This requirement intrigued the curious and excited their sense of personal importance. Even to be thought capable of assassinating an important leader was gratifying to some who, in the structure of things, had no real identity whatsoever. At the same time, they were awed and flattered at being admitted, while all white men were rigidly excluded. The initiative had passed to the Muslims: it was now the newcomers who were tentatively accepted, but on trial.

Inside the temples, they were fascinated by the black-suited young males with the red ties and the military bearing. They were impressed by Muhammad's bold denunciation of the white man, and they were enlightened by hearing for the first time the "truth" about themselves, the Black Nation of Islam. For the most receptive among them, the potential true believers, a new vision dawned. They joined—a few at first and then more and more—and the character of the association began to change. The cult had quietly died. The Movement had begun.

The Negro press helped to supply the initial impetus that brought Muhammad and the Muslims to the attention of his potential followers. The white press has made him famous, and notoriety has sharply enhanced his attraction for the masses. In the summer of 1959, Mike Wallace presented a television documentary featuring the Muslim leader,[11] and articles soon followed in *Time, U.S. News and World Report, Reader's Digest* and other elements of the national press. Muhammad's total following was then less than 30,000. A month after he had been "discovered" by the mass media, his following had doubled, and it has continued to spiral ever since. Ironically, many of these magazines and newspapers sought to "expose" Muhammad as "a purveyor of cold black hatred,"[12] or otherwise as a social anomaly with no real future. They underestimated his appeal to an important segment of the dissatisfied black masses, who, being born with a cause, needed only a leader. A New England journalist correctly assesses Muhammad's timeliness as a leader for the disprivileged:

Muhammad cannot be laughed at as Father Divine has been. Muhammad's movement, with its promises of swiftly approaching social and economic superiority for the Negro race, has captured the imagination of a segment of the suppressed and inarticulate Negro masses as few things have since Marcus Garvey. . . .[13]

Muhammad's first and most crucial task is to keep the Movement a *movement* rather than permit it to become an institution. This does not mean that the Muslims must forsake structure and direction; on the contrary, they have one of the most effective organizational structures to be seen outside the military. But to lure the masses, they must seem to be going somewhere, not settling down. They must reflect and mobilize the masses' own dissatisfaction and urgency, building these into the corporate identity. A successful mass movement is always arriving, but never quite arrives.

Muhammad is not unaware of the frustrations and the free-floating hostilities which are the corollaries of America's caste system, and he will continue to use these as capital in his program to recruit 5 million Negroes by the end of 1964. This is, to be sure, an ambitious undertaking; but it is well to remember that only Billy Graham has attracted and converted more people in recent years than has Elijah Muhammad, Messenger of Allah.

Lures for the True Believer

To clinch the conversion of those true believers who approach the Movement in simple curiosity, Muhammad offers the lure of personal rebirth. The true believer who becomes a Muslim casts off at last his old self and takes on a new identity. He changes his name, his religion, his homeland, his "natural" language, his moral and cultural values, his very purpose in living. He is no longer a Negro, so long despised by the white man that he has come almost to despise himself. Now he is a Black Man—divine, ruler of the universe, different only in degree from Allah Himself. He is no longer discontent and baffled, harried by social obloquy and a gnawing sense of personal inadequacy. Now he is a Muslim, bearing in himself the power of the Black Nation and its glorious destiny. His new life is not an easy one: it demands unquestioning faith, unrelenting self-mastery, unremitting hatred. He may have to sacrifice his family and friends, his trade or profession, if they do not serve his new-found cause. But he is not alone, and he now knows *why* his life matters. He has seen the truth, and the truth has set him free.

When he has seen the light and has decided to join the Movement, the potential convert is made to pass through a number of barriers before he is admitted. First he is given a copy of the following letter, which he himself must copy by hand:

Address
City and State
Date

Mr. W. F. Muhammad
4847 So. Woodlawn Avenue
Chicago 15, Illinois

Dear Savior Allah, Our Deliverer:

I have been attending the teachings of Islam by one of your Ministers, two or three times. I believe in It, and I bear witness that there is no God but Thee, and that Muhammad is Thy Servant and Apostle. I desire to reclaim my Own. Please give me my Original name. My slave name is as follows:

Name
Address
City and State

The applicant's letter is sent to Chicago, where it is scrutinized. If it contains any errors, it is returned and must be recopied correctly. If the letter is perfect, the applicant receives a questionnaire concerning his marital status and dependents. When this and other forms have been completed and approved, the convert enters his new life as a member of the Black Nation of Islam.

To commemorate his rebirth, the convert drops his last name and is known simply by his first name and the letter X. To facilitate identification among Muslims having the same first name and belonging to the same temple, numbers are prefixed to the X. Thus the first man named John to join the temple is named John X; the second becomes John 2X; and so on. Some temples have gone as high as X to the "17th power"! At a later date, Muhammad may grant the convert a new—that is, an "original"—surname, such as Shabazz.

The symbol X has a double meaning: implying "ex," it signifies that the Muslim is no longer what he was; and as "X," it signifies an unknown quality or quantity. It at once repudiates the white man's name and announces the rebirth of Black Man, endowed with a set of qualities the white man does not know. "In short," Malcolm X explains, " 'X' is for mystery. The mystery confronting the Negro as to who he was before the white man made him a slave and put a European label on him. That mystery is now resolved. But 'X' is also for the mystery confronting the white man as to what the Negro has become." That mystery will be resolved only when the teachings of Elijah Muhammad have been received by enough Negroes to counter "three hundred years of systematic brainwashing by the white man." When the Lost Nation of Islam in the West has learned its true identity, has gained a realistic appreciation of its past accomplishments and has seen the "truth about the white man," then the white man will see the Negro in a new light—"and he will have no reason to rejoice."

Most Muslims also retain their "slave" surnames for use in such pragmatic affairs as signing checks. On these occasions, however, the surname is always preceded by an X to indicate that the Muslim repudiates it. On other occasions, Muslims may use the surname Shabazz. For example, when Malcolm X toured Egypt and several other Moslem countries in Africa and Asia in the summer of 1959, he traveled as Malik Shabazz "so that my brothers in the East would recognize me as one of them." If he had used his "European" name (Malcolm Little), he explained, he would have been rejected as an imposter or ridiculed for re-taining that symbol of the white man's ownership.

This change of name is, of course, only the most outward token of rebirth. Perhaps the deepest change promised—and delivered—is the release of energies that had been dammed or buried in the old personality. This release may account in part for the regeneration of criminals, alcoholics and narcotic addicts which is a hallmark of the Movement. At the other extreme, it is often apparent in a change from gentle bewilderment to dogmatic and barely leashed hostility. "When I was in the Pacific," said a Muslim veteran of World War II, "I prayed to God every day that He would not let me die in the jungle, fighting some Japanese who had never done anything to me. I was a Christian then. Now I pray to Allah to let me live to help my people find out who their real enemies are, right here in America."

Recruitment

In pursuit of his goal to make Muslims out of Negro Chris-tians and the unchurched, Muhammad has an ambitious program of recruitment. His ministers go into jails and penitentiaries, pool halls and bars, barbershops and drugstores to talk about Islam. They invade the college campuses, the settlement houses and the YMCAs. Young Muslim brothers pass out literature in front of the Negro Christian churches on Sunday morning, inviting the Christians to attend lectures at the Muslim temples in the after-noon. They speak from street corners and in parks, and they distribute literature wherever large crowds of Negroes are gath-ered. Invariably, the proselytizers are young, personable, urbane and well-dressed men of confidence and conviction.

It is a Muslim boast that although the Negro intellectual will be hardest to reach ("he has been brainwashed more thor-oughly than any of the rest of us"), he will ultimately have no choice other than to embrace Islam. He can never be more than marginally acceptable to the white man, so "he will have nobody to lead and no one to honor him when the common people have all become Muslims." Muhammad himself has a sort of calculated patience with the Negro upper classes. He regards them as doubly cursed: "they have stayed in the white man's schools too long, learning nothing of themselves," and they are fervid in their "hopes that the white man is going to change and treat them like men instead of boys." Malcolm X is more philosophical: "The American Black Man has worked hard to accomplish something and to be somebody. The whole system was against him, but some made it to a point where the white man will show some isolated individuals a little respect; not much, but more than he shows the rest of us. That man isn't going to join us until the white man is more respectful of us than of him." [14]

In their proselytizing, the Muslims carefully select their approach and their language—and often their speaker—to match the particular audience in mind. For example, Muhammad's newspaper column, formerly in the *Pittsburgh Courier* and now in the *Los Angeles Herald-Dispatch,* is aimed at a lower-class readership. It is filled with biblical eschatology, numerology and "mystery," all to the embarrassment and shame of the educated classes. However, the pitch here is being made not to the educated classes but to the masses, who are successfully attracted by such techniques. Inside the brotherhood these exotic elements are deemphasized, and more practical concerns are introduced.

When the Muslim is called upon to confront a highly critical audience, the whole panoply of the occult is usually discarded, except when it is needed to protect the speaker or the Movement against too close examination. In the privacy of his home, Mr. Muhammad is not only "rational," but gracious and friendly as well. He does not greet his guests with *"As-salaam-alaikum"* unless they happen to be Muslims. There are no guards anywhere about the house, and none of the physical trappings of the Movement is in evidence. Conversation is at a level consistent with his appraisal of the visitor. To be sure, Muhammad has an uncamouflaged hostility against the white man, but this hostility does not dominate his private conversation. The Messenger's concern is more likely to center around the Black Man's economic plight. On the other hand, he may become totally incomprehensible about any matter he does not wish to discuss, usually calling upon "Allah" in answer to any questions which might put him at a disadvantage or prematurely disclose his plans.

The same is true of Malcolm X, who has been characterized as "whip-smart"[15] and is certainly able to think on his feet under adverse conditions. Despite his conversational adroitness, or perhaps because of it, Malcolm will take refuge behind any convenient obfuscation rather than to allow himself to be trapped into saying more than he thinks expedient. If he does not invoke Allah, he will refer the insistent prober to Mr. Muhammad—who will probably invoke Allah.

The Muslims boast of a considerable amount of professional talent, especially in the area of musical entertainment. Minister Louis X of Boston is perhaps not a typical example, but he does illustrate the emphasis upon the performing arts which are useful in attracting young Negroes into the Muslim fold. The rather handsome and personable minister plays the violin well and is accomplished on several other instruments. As a calypso singer, he was commanding five to six hundred dollars a week in some of the better night clubs before he renounced Christianity and became a Muslim. Since then he has performed only under the aegis of Islam. He has written and directed two stage productions, *Orgena* and *The Trial,* both propaganda pieces designed to show the cupidity of the white man and the depths to which the Negro has fallen in trying to be like him. In *The Trial,* as we have seen, the white man finally pays for his crimes against humanity, and the Black Nation is restored to its former moral and cultural excellence. Louis has also written and recorded several popular Muslim songs, the best known of which are *White Man's Heaven Is Black Man's Hell!* and *Look At My Chains!*

Dramatic productions, songs and other such entertainment are effective recruiting devices. "People who can put on a drama like that—and who wrote it themselves are not just 'everyday' folks," a Boston taxi driver remarked. But Muhammad does not make entertainment ability the chief attraction of his Movement. Indeed, he is careful to emphasize that the Negro has already done too much singing and dancing, when he should have been giving his attention to more serious matters like factories and supermarkets. Apart from the public meetings and publications, a good deal of recruiting is done in jails and prisons, among men and women whose resentment against society increases with each day of imprisonment. Here their smoldering hatred against the white man builds up to the point of explosion. But Muhammad's ministers are trained to prevent any such release; they are adept at channeling aggression and hostility into a kind of leakproof reservoir for future use. No act of violence or retaliation against the white man is permitted. Instead, Muslims who join the sect while in prison invariably improve in behavior and outlook. Every Muslim *must* respect constituted authority—no matter what the authority may be. This is one of the cardinal rules of membership in the sect.

The black prisoner is reminded that he is in an institution administered by whites, guarded by whites, built by whites. Even the chaplains are white, "to continue to force upon you the poisonous doctrine that you are blessed by being persecuted." The judge who tried him, the jury who heard his case, the officers who arrested him—all were white. Can he, then, be justly imprisoned?

If in fact you *did* steal, from whom did you steal? Only the white man has anything, and if you stole from him, you got but a fraction of what he owes you. Did you kill? If you killed a white man, they murder us at will. They decorate their trees with the bodies of our people. Or they kill us by "law," but they cannot enforce the same "law" to protect us or let us vote.[16]

If prisoners have committed crimes against other black men, they are told they committed these "unnatural acts" out of frustration and the inability to "see who the real devil is." "You may have killed your black brother with your hand, but in your heart you have tried to kill your true tormentor."

When the prisoner is discharged, he is "not wanted by the Christian churches who teach love and forgiveness," but a ready-made fellowship awaits him at the Muslim temple. The new brother is welcomed and immediately made to feel a part of the group. A job is found for him, usually in one of the Muslim enterprises, and in a short time he is indistinguishable from any other Muslim. The routine of work, coupled with the obligations of the temple, leave him little time for regression or for any contacts with the criminal element.

Occasionally, a man or woman will join the Muslims "to keep out of trouble" or to find help in trying to overcome addiction to dope or alcohol. One woman in Milwaukee said that she joined "because I was tired of hating myself every time I looked in the mirror."

Muhammad's reclamation program promises a kind of moral and social perfectionism, which is available to all who adopt Islam. In his public addresses, he chides the Negro community for its juvenile delinquency, which is "caused by parental immorality" and "rips apart the seams of the Christian society." In Islam, echoes Malcolm X, "we don't have any delinquency, either juvenile or adult, and if Mr. Muhammad is given a chance he will clean up the slums and the ghettos—something all the leaders and the social workers and the policemen put together have not been able to do."

The Muslims visualize the reclamation of thousands of Negroes who, through ignorance, despair and defeat, have found themselves in the gutter or in jail. They have had some impressive successes in rehabilitating certain categories of social outcasts, including narcotic addicts and alcoholics. Muhammad operates on the premise that "knowledge of self" and of the "truth about the white man"—when tied in with a constructive program, such as building the "Black Nation"—is sufficient to reclaim the most incorrigible. "By nature," the Muslims are taught, "you are divine." Their social tragedies are caused by the white devil's "tricknology," but truth and hard work will soon make them free.

Visit to a Temple

The real recruitment is done in the temples, for there the import of Muhammad's message may be heard at best advantage. The temple is typically located in the area of densest concentration in the black ghetto. In this way, the bars, pool halls and chicken shacks—all crowded with potential converts—are readily accessible to the proselytizing Muslim brothers. Conversely, the temple is in a neighborhood familiar and convenient to most of those to whom its basic appeal is directed. On Wednesday nights the clean-shaven, dark-suited Muslims may be seen posted near the liquor stores or canvassing the bars and cafes, "fishing for the dead"—that is, inviting the most lost of the Lost Nation to repair to the nearby temple to learn the truth about themselves and their future.

On Sunday mornings the crusading brothers may station themselves outside the Christian churches—High-Church or apostolic, cathedral or store-front, it doesn't matter to the self-confident Muslims, for the message they have is ultimately intended for the entire Black Nation. They march silently up and down in front of the churches, passing out handbills inviting the Christians to come to the Muslim temple that afternoon "to hear the truth." The "pickets" are polite and friendly, quietly dressed and soft-spoken. But most impressive of all is their self-assurance, their utter confidence in their "program for the Black Man which does not require you to love those who do not love you."

The temple itself may be a vacant store or a lodge hall, if the Muslims have but newly organized or if the Movement has not yet caught on in that vicinity. Where the size of the congregation warrants, the Muslims have typically bought abandoned Jewish temples or Christian churches as the whites have fled from the changing neighborhood. Occasionally the nascent Muslim organizations meet in Negro churches or even in funeral chapels.

Arriving at the temple, the new visitor may discover that it has a number rather than a name. A large sign across the front of the building or a signboard on the temple lawn may proclaim it to be, say, MUHAMMAD'S TEMPLE OF ISLAM NO. 5. However, because law enforcement and other agencies have shown increasing interest in the Movement in recent times, the wily Muslim leader has now stopped numbering his temples in order to keep the strength of the Movement secret.

The lawn bulletin, as in Christian churches, announces the speaker for the day. Nationally popular speakers other than Muhammad include Malcolm X of New York, Louis X of Boston and Wallace Muhammad, the Messenger's son, who leads the Philadelphia temple. Whenever a program of unusual importance is held at a local temple, it is supported by busloads of Muslims from all nearby cities and from national headquarters in Chicago. At a rally held by the Atlanta Temple in September 1960, Muslim caravans came from as far away as Boston and Los Angeles. This kind of mobility promotes a rather widespread cohesiveness within the brotherhood; most of the ministers eventually become known to all other ministers and to congregations scattered across the country.

The Negro visitor is welcomed at the entrance to the temple by a committee of the dark-suited brethren. The white visitor is politely but firmly turned away, with an explanation that "this is a meeting for the victims of the white man and not for the white man himself." It may be further explained that what will be said in the temple "may sound offensive" to white people and that white visitors who become offended may find themselves in danger; consequently "it will be better for all concerned if only black people attend."

Negroes are readily admitted and are shown into the temple with elaborate courtesy and ceremony. In an anteroom just off the sanctuary, a Muslim sister waits to record the visitors' names and addresses, which are then added to the temple's mailing list. Following this registration, the visitor is asked to submit to "a little ceremony we always go through." The "little ceremony" is, in fact, an elaborate and systematic search for concealed weapons. All pocket knives, nail files and any other instruments capable of inflicting serious injury are taken from the visitor and checked in a plastic bag, along with lip rouge, chewing gum, cigarettes and all other "articles of defilement." The visitor is asked to open his wallet and remove his money. Both the wallet and the money are then examined, but the owner is permitted to retain these.

Two Muslims are assigned to go over each new arrival, and they do it with a thoroughness that would delight the heart of a police sergeant. Pockets must be turned inside out; coat lapels, collars and trouser cuffs are all given attention. The trouser legs must be raised to show that nothing is concealed in the socks. While the visitor's arms are held aloft, a Muslim brother places his outspread hands on either side of the neck and in one continuous sweep carefully trails them down the sides of the body to the ankles. The armpits and the inside of a man's legs are given close attention. Women are given similar treatment in a room set aside for that purpose.

The Muslims are remarkably adept in the business of the "ceremony." The whole thing takes only about a minute and is done with as little inconvenience and embarrassment to the be-wildered newcomer as possible. On special occasions, such as when the Messenger or Malcolm X is speaking, a double line of perhaps fifty to sixty Muslim brothers is assigned to this detail, thus enabling several thousand people to be "cleared" and seated within an hour or two preceding the meeting. At the big meetings the paramilitary FOI is in charge, and Muslims as well as non-Muslims are searched.

Once the visitor has been cleared, he is escorted into the sanctuary by one of the Muslims. The entrance to this room is typically guarded on the inside by two members of the FOI, who stand, one on each side of the doorway, facing the front of the room. If there is a double entrance (as in most churches), guards are posted at each. The entrances near the chancel at the front of the room are similarly guarded. There may also be two guards flanking the speaker, one on each side; or there may be a guard opposite the front row of seats on each side of the room. The escort will lead the visitor to the front of the room, making certain that all seats on the front row are filled first, and so on with the succeeding rows. Men are seated to the right, women to the left. There is no mixed seating whatsoever.

Before the minister enters to deliver the main lecture for the day, one of the brothers may instruct the audience in a Muslim prayer or in the understanding of certain Arabic phrases. The prayer posture may be taught—palms upward, face to the East—and its meaning explained.

There is a flurry of excitement when the minister enters. He walks rapidly to the lectern and bows slightly, with his palms up and slightly extended. Then he smiles at his congregation and greets them in Arabic: *"As-salaam alaikum!"* ("Peace be unto you!") The greeting is returned in unison: *"Wa-alaikum salaam!"* ("And unto you be peace!") This exchange is usually made three times, after which the minister launches immediately into his address, which is the heart of the service and usually lasts two or three hours. Unlike the traditional Christian sermon, it is not confined to a single topic each week. Instead, the minister at-tempts every week to present the entire gamut of Muhammad's teachings. He speaks almost without pause and is interrupted

only by the changing of the guard—a ceremony in which, at intervals, the guards at the rear of the hall march forward, exchange
phrases in Arabic with the guards down front and then exchange
stations with them.

Throughout the lecture, the audience is attentive and earnest.
It is eager and seems enraptured by its exclusive possession of the
truth; yet it is always restrained. There are no "happy" people in
the congregation, and the foot-thumping, head-wagging-amen
stereotype of the store-front Negro churchgoer is conspicuously
absent. There is no singing and no "shouting." Emotional displays are limited to frequent ejaculations of "That's right!" when
the minister scores a point upon which there is wide agreement.
Often, the minister asks a rhetorical question for emotional effect.
He may wonder, for example, "Now what do you think would
happen if you tried to do some of the things the Constitution says
you have a right to do?" At this there is an uneasy rumble of
snickering, interspersed with the cynical response: "Now *that's* a
good question, Brother Minister! That's a *good* question!"

While the minister lectures, money receptacles are in continuous circulation, and the challenge to "support your own" is
insistently urged by young ushers moving among the audience.
The receptacles are not inconspicuous: they are plastic waste-
baskets or large brown paper bags. Such collections are a recent
innovation. The Muslim brothers formerly took no public offer-
ings and announced proudly: "Islam takes care of its own." Now
they explain that, since Muhammad has become well-known and
"his aims and integrity are established," the public can be permitted to contribute toward his work, "especially the proposed
building of an Islamic Center in Chicago."

The minister nearly always begins his lecture by writing
several Arabic phrases on a blackboard, explaining that Arabic
is the original language of the Black Man and that he must begin
to relearn the language of which the white man has deprived him.
The first phrase is the Muslim greeting: *As-salaam alaikum*. The
proper response is then written and explained: *Wa-alaikum
salaam*. "It is proper," the minister explains, "to begin the study
of Islam and the worship of Allah in the presence of peace. Islam

is the religion of peace, and Muslims should be at peace with each other and, insofar as is possible, with all others."

Peace having been disposed of, the minister launches into a long discussion of the primacy of the Black Man and his remarkable accomplishments. To this end, he cites pertinent passages from the Islamic Quran, the Old Testament and other literature, as well as the writings of Muhammed himself. The hearers are reminded that their earlier knowledge of themselves and their past has been derived from the spurious teachings of the white man, who has "prostituted truth and defiled history to serve his own ends." Black Men must no longer accept the white man's teachings at face value. They must search out the facts and make intelligent judgments for themselves. The ministers will help them, for "the Messenger knows the truth about the white man" and he has taught his ministers well.

Often the minister reads passages from well-known historical, sociological or anthropological works and finds in them inconspicuous references to the Black Man's true history in the world. Black Men in Asia and Africa were enjoying advanced civilizations when the white man was eating his meat raw in the caves of Europe. Yet the whites, through their control of informational media (including the black preachers), have succeeded in making the so-called Negroes accept themselves as inferior.

Black Men sat on the thrones of Egypt and Ethiopia, fought beside the Romans in conquering the savages of Britain, discovered America long before Columbus and then piloted the ship on which Columbus sailed. Black Men ruled Spain and Southern Europe, reigned as popes in the Eternal City of Rome and built great civilizations on the west coast of Africa. They produced many Moslem scholars of whom the white Christians profess to be ignorant, though the white civilization has stolen much knowledge from them. But the whites have taught the so-called Negro nothing of all this, and he has a mental block against searching out the information for himself. The so-called Negro doesn't want to know about his own history; he wants to know about the white man's history. He has been taught that his own history will only deposit him in the jungle, whereas the white man's history begins with Socrates dying nobly to illustrate a moral principle.

Occasionally the minister chides the audience for its skepticism: "I know you don't believe me because I happen to be a Black Man. Well, you can look it up in a book I'm going to tell you about that was written by a white man." He then reads off references, which his hearers are challenged to check for themselves. A single documented statement, however, may become the basis of a wide range of generalized *non sequiturs*. The fact that a North Carolina slaveholder had an Arabic-speaking Moslem slave of unusual mathematical ability may be offered as evidence that *all* slaves brought to America were Moslem, Arabic-speaking and learned.

Similarly, historical facts may be indiscriminately mingled with myths and countermyths. The information that Aesop was a Negro and that the great University of Sankore in Timbuktu sent its professors to lecture in the universities of Cairo, Granada and Morocco at a time when Europe was just emerging from the Dark Ages—allegations easily documented from standard sources [17]—may be interspersed among claims that "all history is written in advance by twenty-four Black Scientists" under a twenty-fifth Black Man who serves as "Judge," or that the tribe of Shabazz (to which all Black Men belong) are the "Original Men" who "came with the earth sixty-six trillion years ago."

The minister next turns his attention to the evil and divisive influences of the white man and to the white man's equally repulsive religion. The white man has come but lately to the table of civilization. "When the black princes of Asia and Africa were wearing silks and plotting the stars, the white man was crawling around on his all-fours in the caves of Europe. The reason why the white man keeps dogs in the house today, and sleeps with them and rides them about in cars is that he slept with the dogs in the caves of Europe and he has never broken the habit." [18]

The audience is urged to give the Christian religion "back to the white man," for it is a religion of slavery and death. Negroes must also "give the white man back the names he has labeled you with," for these are badges of slavery. "If a Chinaman tells you his name is 'Whitfield,' you know there's something wrong somewhere. Well, there's also something wrong about a Black Man named 'Jones'." [19] Wherever the white man's name is attached to the so-called Negro, it is a symbol of possession. "Every time you sign your name you tell the world you're still the white man's chattel. If your body happens to be partly free, you're still his chattel in mind."

At this point, the minister may point to a painting which, in most temples, hangs on the wall behind the lectern. On the right half of the canvas are shown the symbols of Islam—the star and crescent—and the legend "Freedom-Justice-Equality." On the left are depicted the American flag, the Christian cross and a Negro hanging by his neck from a tree. These three, the minister explains, are the symbols of Christianity and what it has offered the Black Man. But now the Black Man has a choice: Islam, or continued abuse in subservience to the white Christians.

The men are reminded that they have been helpless even when their homes have been invaded. Resistance, even to protect their families, has meant death. Further, their economic conditions are so contrived that they must send their womenfolk out to work in the homes and offices of Christian white men. This is no accident: the white man controls the economy, and he knows the Black Man is at his mercy. He deliberatly "castrates" the Black Man by paying his wife higher wages, so that the male is no longer head of his family. The wife then comes to despise her husband and to admire the white man, who is economically independent. And the white man not only employs the Black Man's women but proceeds "forthwith to send them home to their black husbands with blue-eyed babies." "These same robbers," says Muhammad, "disgrace and corrupt them with all kinds of diseases besides spotting up [their] children like the animal family."[20]

We stand by with folded arms, cowards to the core, and allow the human brute . . . to take our women . . . the most priceless gift of a nation. . . . We cannot produce a pure, chaste nation with a "free-for-all" woman. If we [cannot] protect her from the human beast's advances, we should kill ourselves and our women.[21]

Christianity is dealt with summarily. It is considered a religion of ignominy and disgrace for the Black Man, but of great convenience and practicality for the white man. For the white man neither believes its teachings nor makes any attempt to practice them. The white man wants the so-called Negro to accept

Christianity and live according to its teachings; but he then laughs at the so-called Negro for being a fool.

"Love thy neighbor;" I have yet to meet one white man that loved his neighbor. . . . "Thou shalt not kill;" I have yet to meet such a Christian. . . . Where is a good Christian among this race?[22]

. . . you fear and love [the white Christians] though you are even disgraced, beaten and killed by them, from your ministers of their slavery religion . . . down to the lowly, ignorant man in the mud. You have made yourselves the most foolish people on earth by loving and following after the ways of Slavemasters, whom Allah has revealed to me to be none other than real devils, and that their so-called Christianity is not His religion, nor the religion of Jesus or any other prophet of Allah (God).[23]

The audience is encouraged to disavow a religion which worships "a dead Jesus and his dead disciples," for such behavior distracts them from the business of trying to live in *this* world. "The white man has 'given you Jesus' while he has robbed you blind." Heaven is right here, and we must try to share in it now, rather than after death. Jesus has not "gone anywhere."

No one after death has ever gone any place but where they were carried. There is no heaven or hell other than on earth for you and me, and Jesus was no exception. His body is still . . . in Palestine and will remain there.[24]

With this transition, the minister next gives his attention to the Messenger's economic program. The hearers are chided for thrift-lessness, conspicuous consumption and living beyond their means. Such self-indulgence will not build the Black Nation. The white man still owns the so-called Negro, because the white man owns the factories, the land, the houses and everything else needed for survival. When he decides to kill a Negro, he does not shoot him —except for amusement. "All he needs to do is to deny the Negro a job, and he will soon be just as dead." The Negro, in an attempt to protect himself against economic reprisal, adapts a posture of servility. "The so-called Negro's principles are always in pawn to the Slavemaster. The white man can make him bark and roll over any day in the week!" He is no more than a "free slave," for he dares not assert his manhood, no matter what indignities are heaped upon him or what atrocities are directed his way.

"Mr. Muhammad has an economic program," the minister continues, "which, if followed, will soon free the Black Man and make him equal to the other nations of the world." But the Black Man must be prepared to work:

Many of us, the so-called Negroes, today are so lazy that we are willing to suffer anything rather than go to work. It is true that God has come to sit us in heaven, but not a heaven wherein we won't have to work.[25]

Integration comes under heavy attack. It is anathema to the Movement, and the minister is trained to denounce it with especial vehemence. He may read from Muhammad's *The Supreme Wisdom,* in which the Messenger condemns integration as a kind of social opiate.

The Slavemaster's children are doing everything in their power to prevent the so-called Negroes from accepting their own God and salvation, by putting on a great show of false love and friendship.

This is being done through "integration," as it is called; that is, so-called Negroes and whites mixing together such as in schools, churches, and even intermarriage. . . . The poor slaves really think they are entering a condition of heaven with their former slaveholders, but it will prove to be their doom.

Today . . . we are living in a time of great separation between the blacks and white. . . . The so-called Negroes must now return to their own; nothing else will solve the problem.[26]

The integration controversy is presented as a private quarrel between Northern and Southern whites:

The Northern whites don't really care about the Negroes, but they don't like it because the crackers in the South disgrace the country and embarrass the nation. They can't keep out of the Black Man's bed, and they have to keep lynching Negroes to try to keep it covered up. Now today, this makes for bad international relations. But the Southern cracker isn't going to clean himself up and stay on his side of town just to please the Yankees or to put the country in a better light. He can't. He was born a dog, and he'll be a dog. But he'll get up on Sunday morning and look pious in his pew![27]

The minister denounces integration as a stratagem of the white man to insure his survival in a world he has managed badly.

The white man's time is up, and he knows it. He has no friends anywhere. He now hopes that by integrating with the rising Black Man, he can avoid paying for the long list of crimes he has perpetrated against humanity. So he has undertaken to "sweetheart" with the only people who are stupid enough to listen, the dupes he has trained to love him.

If the so-called American Negro were not so much in love with his deceivers, he would be preparing to be master now, rather than continuing to be satisfied as a free slave. For the white man's doom is sure.

The minister then speaks again of Islam, the religion of "peace, justice and equality." It is the *only* religion, he asserts, in which the Black Man in America—or anywhere else in the world—can find communion in brotherhood. Islam is hateful to the white man because it "equalizes" him, and "the white man would rather be dead than to be equal." But there are as many professing believers in Islam alone as there are white men in the entire world, and all non-white men everywhere are *by nature* Muslims, whether they profess it or not. The white race is thus hopelessly outnumbered by the Muslim brotherhood, which stretches across the world.

The *Holy Quran* of Islam is the "book which makes a distinction between the God of the righteous and the God of evil." This is the book which the Slavemaster has willfully kept from the blacks in America, for it contains all knowledge: "the Guidance of Light and Truth and of Wisdom and Judgment."

This book the *Holy Quran Sharrieff*, pulls the cover off the covered and shows the nation for the first time that which deceived 90 percent of the people of the earth without knowledge of the deceiver.[28]

At present, the *Holy Quran* must be taught by the leaders, but all Muslims should learn Arabic (which is taught at some temples) so that they may read it for themselves in the original. Meanwhile, only those translations approved by Muhammad should be used.[29]

Near the end of the meeting and at the conclusion of the minister's lecture, the congregation is asked whether it agrees with what has been said. Any who do not agree are asked to state the points of disagreement, so that the minister may try to provide "the clarification necessary to unity." If the minister cannot provide a satisfactory answer, he promises to relay the question to the Messenger himself for resolution. No questions or problems are deemed beyond the capacities of the Messenger, for "it is because of his wisdom and insight that he has been chosen leader of the Black Nation."

When all questions raised from the floor by "those not yet returned to Islam" have been spoken to, the minister invites those who believe what they have heard and who have the courage of their convictions to come forward and declare for Islam. There are rarely more than fifteen or twenty in any one meeting; but in a three-hour lecture before 8,500 persons in Los Angeles' Olympic Auditorium, "Mr. Elijah Muhammad . . . persuaded more than 143 Christians to renounce Christianity and embrace Islam."[30]

Those who elect to join are warmly welcomed by the Muslim brotherhood and are assigned to classes of instruction. Those who are impressed, but are not yet willing to separate themselves from the Christian tradition, are urged to continue attending the public meetings, in the expectation that they will eventually overcome this hesitation. The merely curious and those suspected of being "stooges for the FBI" are not encouraged to return.

Schools and the Center

A powerful and long-range recruiting device of the Movement is its parochial schools, with their massive emphasis on education about the Black Man—his resplendent past, his divine nature, his triumphant future. Many lower-class Negroes find this approach, for all its exaggerations, a welcome change from the white-oriented teaching in nearly all public schools. The desire to have their children "learn something about themselves" is surprisingly strong, particularly now that the new African states have gained their independence. These parents are also impressed with the schools as irrefutable evidence of the Muslims' determination to free themselves from all white influence and to prepare their youth for roles as reclaimers of the Black Man's heritage. Finally, the schools have important status-value as "private schools" for the low-income families, who could never hope to afford the luxury of ordinary private schools.

There are now two active parochial schools (known as Universities of Islam) in Chicago and Detroit, and plans have been made to have a school attached to each temple. The University of Islam in Chicago includes grades one to twelve and is accredited by the agencies which rate the city's public schools. It is housed in a modern building and has an enrollment of about three hundred students. The University of Islam in Detroit has about one hundred students. In both the Chicago and the Detroit schools, the "Future Leaders of Islam" attend classes fifty weeks a year. Both are staffed with Christian as well as Muslim personnel. Efforts are now under way to establish schools at other large temples, but securing teachers has proved to be a severe problem.

In both schools Arabic is taught from the third grade on, for a mastery of his language is held to be the Black Man's key to a knowledge of his past and to acceptability in the universal brotherhood of Islam. Much is made of the fact that Muhammad's young son, Akbar, a graduate of the University of Islam in Chicago, acted as interpreter for his father's party much of the time during their recent tour of Islamic countries in Africa and Asia.

The Detroit school dates back to the early years of the Movement, and it has been a constant thorn in the side of the Detroit police and school officials. In 1934, Muhammad was found guilty of contributing to the delinquency of a minor and given six months probation when he refused to withdraw his children from the University of Islam and enroll them in the city's public schools. At about the same time, when the city attempted to interfere with the operation of the school, the Muslims began "a severe riot" in which the Muslims "tried to storm the police headquarters. Fearful of race riots, the judges of the recorder's office released with suspended sentences almost all of the rioters."[31] But the trouble continued:

Several . . . cult members were in and out of court on . . . charges, most resulting from their insistence on sending their children to cult schools. "Universities of Islam" were operated in various places around Detroit for more than a decade as the Board of Education sought to close them. . . . The school system finally decided to "join" the Muslims instead of fighting them. . . . Cult leaders, working through their attorney . . . got together with the State Departmen of Public Instruction representatives to work out an approved private school for the cult. The court cases were dropped on the assumption the school had been approved. . . .[32]

The school was closed again in August 1959, after "a State Police sergeant, an agent of the State Department of Public Instruction, two Buildings and Safety Engineering Department inspectors, a Health Department investigator, and a Detroit Fire Department inspector poked through the musty, crumbling former theatre building. . . ."[33] A few weeks later, the school was again in operation.

The Muslims place a high premium upon special education for wives and mothers, and their Muslim Girls' training and General Civilization Class is an effective means of drawing Negro women into the Movement. The MGT, as it is generally known, concentrates primarily on the art of homemaking. It meets on week nights at the local temples, and the women are "taught how to sew, cook, keep house, rear their children, care for their husbands, and how to behave at home and abroad." High moral behavior is an absolute requirement, for "a Muslim can rise no higher than his women." The MGT also has a Junior Division for girls aged fifteen to nineteen.

Perhaps the most ambitious undertaking Muhammad has announced for the immediate future is the building of an Islamic Center in Chicago. The center is to include "a mosque in which to pray . . . an educational institution in which to enlighten our youth, a library in which to deepen their knowledge and understanding, a hospital in which to cure the sick and strengthen the healthy."[34] The initial cost of the center is put at $20 million, and funds are solicited from all who attend the various meetings of the Muslims, on the promise that the facilities of the center will not be restricted to Muslims.

The Muslims have already acquired a five-acre tract on Chicago's far South Side for which they paid a reputed $150,000. When residents in the area became convinced that the Muslims really intend to build the center, they sought to have the tract condemned for a public park. The Muslims countered by hiring Chicago's famous civil rights attorney, Robert Ming, to represent them; and an angry Muhammad lashed out at the Negroes trying to block his program in terms reminscent of Garvey:

The short-sighted so-called Negroes seem to rather have a playground to sit, eat and sleep on [and] to be criticized by the civilized people of earth as the laziest and most foolish people of all. . . . I warn you my people who are trying to oppose me and my followers—to the joy of our enemies, (the devils) by our Allah, all of your efforts shall fail . . . if we are forced by the city to give it up or sell, by the help of our God, Allah—we will most certainly retaliate; this we are assured of.[35]

Mr. Muhammad Speaks

The Black Muslims have spared no effort to contact the Negro masses through every available medium of mass communication. Wherever Muhammad speaks, his audiences are numbered in the thousands; and since 1959 his rallies have been increasingly frequent. Baltimore, Pittsburgh, New York, Boston, Philadelphia, Los Angeles, Chicago, Atlanta, Washington and other cities across the country have turned out impressive crowds to hear the Messenger. Nowhere have fewer than four thousand persons gathered to hear his call for "a separate place for the Black Nation." Crowds of eight to ten thousand are the rule.

For several years, Muhammad's column in the *Pittsburgh Courier* attracted wide attention among Negroes and stirred a lively debate between those who supported his views and those who were indignant that he was granted space in the paper. During his tenure as a *Courier* columnist, no other single writer drew as many letters to the editor; and the newspaper, which had been steadily losing readers, suddenly found its circulation increasing. This was partially due to the fact that the Muslims took to the street corners and the housing projects to hawk the papers—each brother being assigned a quota. In 1959, however, the controlling interest in the paper was bought by S. B. Fuller, a Chicago manufacturer, and Muhammad's column was dropped.

Subsequently the column began to appear in the weekly *Los Angeles Herald-Dispatch,* which has become in effect the official Muslim organ. Since its alliance with the Muslims, the *Dispatch,* which is only eight years old, has begun to publish a regional edition in Chicago, and local offices have been opened in other cities where there are large numbers of Muslims. The paper is published by Sanford Alexander of Los Angeles. Raymond Sharrieff, son-in-law of Muhammad and Supreme Captain of the FOI, is in charge of its Chicago offices. The paper is sold at all Muslim enterprises across the country, and individual Muslims are given quotas to sell in the black ghettos. Its present circulation is approximately 40,000 a week.

Malcolm X refers to the *Dispatch* as "the most outspoken newspaper in America . . . 100 per cent pro-black." The paper denounces "the so-called Negro leaders," ridicules the Negro's commitment to non-violence and passive resistance, and supports the Black Muslims unequivocally. It says candidly:

. . . Mr. Muhammad's program . . . and the racial policy of the *Herald-Dispatch* is one and the same. . . . Mr. Muhammad maintains and the *Herald-Dispatch* concurs, that the salvation for the so-called American Negro is unity of purpose . . . one goal, spiritually, economically, and politically, such as embracing Islam, . . . building business enterprises among the black race, supporting the Negro businessman, learning self-respect. And above all else, [we must] stop begging our oppressor for the crumbs from his table. Prepare for the day when his beastlike action against the non-white population . . . will be stopped with force.[36]

The feature news of each issue of the *Dispatch* is predominantly concerned with Muslim affairs, and the addresses of Muhammad, Malcolm X and others prominent in the Movement are given extensive coverage. Guest columns by various Muslim ministers are featured regularly, as are stories about the activities of local temples. Muhammad's "Economic Blueprint" is printed in most issues. The back page is ordinarily devoted entirely to a graphic projection of the proposed Islamic Center, plus a listing of the Muslim temples and their addresses. Considerable space is devoted to advertising from Muslim temples, enterprises and individuals.

News of interest to the general Negro community is also published in the *Dispatch,* but relatively little space is given to social events—an important feature in most Negro newspapers. Some straight news pertaining to Christian churches is carried, as is news about such organizations as the NAACP. Foreign news is usually limited to items concerning the Afro-Asian community.

In February 1960, the *Dispatch* presented Elijah Muhammad an award on the occasion of its eighth anniversary celebration. In anticipation of the event, the *Dispatch* said editorially:

Mr. Muhammad has succeeded in organizing approximately one half million so-called Negroes. . . . He is uplifting fallen humanity. He is not concerned with other races, he teaches the so-called Negro to be pro-black. This is not teaching hate . . . because of his teachings, his program of positive action, the *Herald-Dispatch* will give him the highest Achievement Award ever given to an individual by this publication. . . .[37]

Both Christianity and Judaism come under frequent attack from the *Dispatch*. While it categorically denies religious bias, it publishes material such as this—from an editorial entitled "The Evils of Christianity":

The Christian, the white man with a gun and a Bible in one hand and a bottle of gin in the other . . . enslaved [the Black Man] . . . [and is guilty of] economic oppression, lynchings, bombing of [Negro] churches, segregation, disenfranchisement. . . . Christianity in Germany used fiendish gas ovens to "scientifically" rid the world of millions of Jews; the U. S. under Christianity performed the most heinous crime ever committed on the planet Earth—the dropping of the atomic bombs on the Japanese. . . .[38]

The "Christian Belgians" are charged with slaughtering the Congolese; the "Christian French," with bombing the Algerians and Tunisians, "supported by the Christian United States and Britain." In a particularly bitter editorial, the *Dispatch* challenged its readers as follows:

We ask Negroes: where was Ralph Bunche, the stooge of the Western Powers when the Belgians murdered 10,000 Africans on January 4, 5, and 6, 1959? We ask the Negroes where was the United Nations when the South Africans were shooting down Africans like flies? . . . Where was Ralph Bunche when the British, using rockets were killing the Africans in Kenya? . . . Russia saved Egypt in 1956. . . . Russia ordered Israel out of the Sinai Desert . . . it was Russia again who ordered the Belgians out of the Congo. We are thankful for Russia.[39]

This praise of Russia, incidentally, is the *Dispatch*'s only significant departure from the Muslim line. Muhammad holds no brief for *any* white nation, including the Soviet Union. He apparently permits this pro-Russian slant only because it has the virtue of discomfiting the local "Slavemasters."

Judaism, "from which Christianity spread"—the *Dispatch* does not mention Islam's similar origin—is condemned for "her brutal treatment of the Palestine Arabs who had befriended the Jews in an hour of need." The Jews are referred to as "educated and highly cultured," and it is emphasized that their "crimes were conducted with the aid and sanction of the Christian countries." All Negroes are called upon to "renounce Christianity in all its facets, [for] Christianity . . . is not for the Black Man."[40]

The Muslims also have an ever-increasing number of special publications designed to attract the attention of the black masses to Muhammad's work and teachings.

The Supreme Wisdom: Solution to the So-Called Negroes' Problem is the hornbook of the Movement. In its fifty-six pages, Muhammad addresses himself to such diverse topics as "The Bible and its Teachings," "Christianity," "What Our Enemy Is Doing," "No 'Integration,'" "Kinky Hair," "The Hog and Its Eaters," "Heaven on Earth" and "Other Notable Aspects of Islam." An early edition lists ten formal requirements of practice, or "Principles of Belief," including the following: "Keep up prayer; speak the truth regardless of circumstances; keep clean internally and externally at all times; set at liberty the captured believer; fear no one but Allah, and kill no one whom Allah has not ordered you to kill." *The Supreme Wisdom* is perhaps the Muslims' earliest venture in publishing and has been through several editions, but on the whole it is poorly written and poorly organized. Not many outside the fold have seen it.

In 1959 and 1960, the Muslims launched a number of publications in keeping with their new resolve to add a million converts to Muhammad's following by the end of 1961. One such publication was *The Messenger,* a magazine edited by the ubiquitous Malcolm X and devoted to a pictorial presentation of "typical Muslim activities." Several pages are devoted to the Muslim schools and show the eager young faces of the Muslim children in their classes. Other sections show Muslim women (busy with the tasks of homemaking), the Muslims' various commercial enter-prises and a display of newspapers headlining news about Mus-lims. There is a feature story on "a typical Muslim family"—that of Supreme Captain Raymond Sharrieff. Subsequent issues were planned but were never published.

One issue of *The Islamic News,* a tabloid-sized paper, ap-peared in July 1959. Its eight pages were mainly devoted to an "Exclusive Verbatim Transcript of [Muhammad's] Historic Wash-ington Speech." The issue is obviously the work of a professional journalist, and the speech as presented is certainly not a "verbatim transcript." This address is particularly important, however, be-cause in it Muhammad considered himself to be tweaking the nose of the government, which, on his previous visit to Washington during the "lean years" of the Movement, had humiliated him and put him in jail.

Another tabloid-sized Muslim paper, *Mr. Muhammad Speaks,* bills itself as "a militant monthly dedicated to Justice for the Black Man." This paper was launched in May 1960 and went on sale at fifteen cents. It is devoted to the general news of Muslim interest, including features of special interest to women. This is probably the best publication the Muslims have, and the hand of a professional journalist is apparent in its layout and composition. It is published at 113 Lenox Avenue, in "The Heart of Harlem." The photography tends to be unusually effective, and the paper sells readily wherever it appears on the streets in Negro neighborhoods. Venders are often stationed outside NAACP meetings, churches and other places where large groups of Negroes congregate.

In July 1960, a pocket-sized magazine called *Salaam* ap-peared. It is essentially a picture magazine, and its first issue featured Muhammad's trip to Mecca, the University of Islam in Detroit and the 1960 Muslim Convention in Chicago. *Salaam* is published in Philadelphia by L. Masco Young.

Yet another pocket-sized Muslim magazine is *Muhammad Speaks to the Blackman*. It is a shallow publication, playing upon racial feeling in such a way as to be nauseous even to some pro-Muslims. Dan Burley, a well-known Chicago newspaperman, is listed as editor. Other Muslim publications appear sporadically as the need for them is indicated.

In addition to these publications and such attention as they receive in the non-Muslim Negro press, the Muslims lose no opportunity to offer themselves to public attention through television and radio. The chief spokesman for interpreting the Movement through these media is the ubiquitous Malcolm X, whose adroitness and cunning, displayed during many of his numerous radio interviews, led a Boston critic to name him "the Harlem Asp." Also known as "the Big X," Malcolm has tilted with such TV notables as Mike Wallace and has been interviewed on radio or television by such top-flight journalists as Nat Hentoff, Louis Lomax and Chuck Stone. As a guest on the two-and-a-half-hour-long Jerry Williams show on radio station WMEX in Boston, Malcolm turned what was intended to be a half-hour interview into a two-and-a-half-hour marathon.

The Muslims also have a regular and extensive series of weekly radio lectures. In December 1960, a listing of "Muhammad's Nationwide Radio Schedule" in *Mr. Muhammad Speaks* covered seven stations, each reaching cities within a hundred-mile-or-more radius of a major metropolitan area. (The stations were KAPZ, St. Louis; WEAW-FM, Chicago-Milwaukee-Indianapolis; WERD, Atlanta; WHAT, Philadelphia; WJLB, Detroit-Toledo; WNTA and WNTA-FM, New York City; and WSID, Baltimore-Washington, D. C.) The list keeps growing, but the Muslim leadership is looking far beyond this limited expedient. The next major enterprise the Movement hopes to undertake in its constant reaching for the masses is its own radio station—"The Voice of Islam," broadcasting from "the wilderness of North America."

6 Tensions:
Outside the Movement

The Black Muslims are psychologically indrawn: they feel responsible only to each other and derive most of their satisfaction from their own mutual approval. Yet they are also aware of the world around them—and smugly aware that the world is aware of them.

To a great extent, the Muslims define their Movement by negative contrast to their most important audiences: Negroes, Jews, the orthodox Moslems in America and the hated whites. They assert their own strength and purity by castigating the weakness and depravity they claim to see among these strangers. The Movement, they imply, is in no way ignorant, corrupted or impotent. It is not at all like the world from which they have drawn themselves apart.

But more is involved in the traffic between the Movement and its surrounding world than a mere exercise in self-glorification. The Muslim statements are often complex, foreshadowing ultimate goals and hopes even while they make explicit the dogma of the moment. And in the response of the Negro, Jewish, Moslem and white communities to the Black Muslim challenge, it is possible to read some hints, at least, of the onrushing future.

I. THE NEGRO COMMUNITY

Individual Negro Leadership

The sudden prominence of the Black Muslim Movement and its rapidly increasing appeal to the Negro masses have become a source of major concern for the recognized Negro leadership. Some of this concern may be attributed to professional jealousy, for each Muslim was once potentially a member of a different

Negro organization. But beneath this surface jealousy lie far more serious apprehensions—a recognition of the Muslims as a dangerous threat to the areas of harmony that have been won through years of painstaking interracial negotiation and experimentation.

Negro leadership in America—politicians, intellectuals and businessmen—has been uniformly dedicated to the principle of cooperation with the white man in any attempt to relieve the Negro's condition. Muhammad's harangues on "the truth about the white man" are therefore considered dangerous and destructive, regardless of their truth or falsity. One leader who has spent a lifetime in patient negotiation with the white community declared that Muhammad's allegations are "intemperate enough to be insulting and true enough to be embarrassing."

The strategy of Negro leadership has characteristically been to avoid embarrassing the white man, even at the cost of some delay in attaining a desired end. This has not been accidental: the American Negro has clung tenaciously to his belief in the American Creed and the Christian ideal, and he has wanted to believe in the white man's essential integrity. Indeed, he has been much more willing to see the mote in his own eye than to argue about the beam in the eye of the white man. John Steinbeck sensed this when he wrote:

I am constantly amazed at the qualities we expect in Negroes. No race has ever offered another such high regard. We expect Negroes to be wiser than we are, more tolerant than we are, braver, more dignified than we, more self-controlled and self-disciplined. . . . We expect them to obey rules of conduct we flout, to be more courteous, more gallant, more proud, more steadfast. In a word, while maintaining that Negroes are inferior to us, by our unquestioning faith in them we prove our conviction that they are superior in many fields, even fields we are presumed to be trained and conditioned in and they are not.[1]

Negro leadership has never seriously considered whether the Negro might solve his problems without help. It holds that the Negro is an integral part of the American society, that his problem is America's problem—the problem of all the people, created by all the people—and that it is to the interest of all the people to participate in its solution. Besides, in the complex set of relationships that constitutes a modern society, it is unrealistic to think of any one group solving an intergroup problem alone—except by annihilating the offending group or by a complete physical separation from them. Few Negro leaders have envisaged either extreme.

The Black Muslims do not repudiate either possibility. On the contrary, they already are demanding physical separation; and while they are cautious in discussing the *means* by which the white man may be annihilated, they proclaim openly that his time is up. Listen to Minister Malcolm X as he addresses a white audience at Boston University:

A child stays within the mother until the time of birth. When the time of birth arrives, the child must be separated or it will destroy the mother and itself. The mother can't carry the child after its time—the child wants to be free. It cries for a world of its own. If the mother will not give it up naturally, the doctors must forcibly take it from her, which sometimes causes her death. If she can set it free naturally, easily, so much the better; if not, it must be taken. Twenty million so-called Negroes in America number a nation within a nation, crying for freedom. We must be free. We must be born. We must be separated or cause the destruction of both.[2]

This precept—that separation is the only final solution to the race problem in this country and throughout the world—is appalling to most Negroes. A white newspaper has caught the responsible mood of the Negro community with unusual clarity:

In the long struggle over racial discrimination in the United States, the American Negro has almost always behaved with fortitude and restraint.

He has pressed the battle for his rights through orderly and legal means. He has borne insult and injury without resorting to violence. He has faced the hate-mongers without adopting hatred as his creed.

His passive resistance campaign against discrimination on busses in Montgomery, Alabama, showed a moral strength and self-discipline that has few parallels in our history.[3]

When Negro leadership attempted to ignore Muhammad and his Muslims, Malcolm X complained:

Mr. Muhammad has done more to make the Black Man in America think than all the Negro teachers and leaders together. . . . If he were not responsible for doing this, he would not be the object of so much comment and so much concern. For a long time, they tried to cover him up—to put him under the rug. They figured he would just evaporate or go away. No matter what he did, nothing was said about it in the white press or any other press. It looked like it was an agreed method to just not say anything about him.[4]

But the Movement could not be realistically ignored. Muhammad was drawing thousands of Negroes wherever he spoke, and it was inevitable that Negro leadership would have to take official recognition of him.

The politicians were among the first to yield. In Harlem, at a two-day "Unity Feast" held in July 1958, Muhammad was greeted by Manhattan Borough President Hulan Jack, who referred to him as "our distinguished visitor from Chicago" and welcomed him on behalf of Manhattan's 2 million residents. City Councilman Earl Brown told the 8,000 Muslims and other nationalists present: "I have been inspired by being with you. . . . As I gaze upon you I recognize fully our power as a people." Judge Carson DeWitt Baker and State Senator James Watson were also present. U. S. Congressman Adam Clayton Powell wired his regrets at being unable to attend and offered his sentiments for the success of the meeting. The celebration was also attended by J. A. Rogers, historian and columnist for the *Pittsburgh Courier;* Col. Walters of the Universal Negro Improvement Association; Noel Austin, Director of the Manhattan Elks Civil Liberties League; and other notables of political, labor and fraternal organizations.[5]

Muslim relations with Negro politicians are more consistently cordial than their relations with any other group of Negro leaders, even though Muslims have yet to demonstrate their voting strength. In August 1960, for example, Martin Luther King, Jackie Robinson, Adam Clayton Powell, Thurgood Marshall, Hulan Jack, Roy Wilkins and other Negro leaders were invited to attend a Harlem rally and "debate key issues" before the public. Seven thousand Negroes came to hear them, but only Hulan Jack put in an appearance. Mr. Jack expressed great appreciation and admiration for Elijah Muhammad as "a spiritual leader whose purpose is to bring about better understanding and cooperation." Malcolm X, who hosted the meeting, called upon all Negro leaders to set aside "petty differences" and to "reason together and keep open minds." Some leaders had failed to appear, he explained, because they were afraid "of irking their white bosses [or] embarrassing their white liberal friends."

An earlier Leadership Conference, held in Harlem in January 1960, was attended by an impressive array of New York politicians—this time including Adam Powell. Malcolm X commended these leaders for "at last catching up with the progressive thinking of the enlightened Negro masses." He also warned them that, while the Muslims have thus far refrained from active political participation, they should not be discounted when political decisions are made that affect the Negro community.

Of the American Negroes connected with politics at any level, only United Nations Under Secretary Ralph Bunche has come under direct fire from the Black Muslims. They have excoriated him as "the George Washington of Israel," presumably because they suspect him of favoring Israel in his negotiation of the Israeli-Arab dispute. This negotiation was, however, hailed as a diplomatic achievement; it brought Dr. Bunche a Nobel Prize in spite of the denunciation of the Black Nation of Islam.[6]

Negro intellectuals have systematically ignored Muhammad. Like most Negroes outside the lower class, they have not felt impelled to attend his meetings; their knowledge of the Muslims has come, for the most part, through occasional conversations with persons who have read about the Movement. In a nationwide sampling of intellectual opinion, a surprising percentage of "informed" Negro intellectuals was found to know practically nothing about the Movement,[7] even though it has been constantly reported in the Negro press for several years, featured in almost all of the national news magazines and covered repeatedly in the white press for at least two years! Even in the cities where Muslim activities regularly outdraw Christian and fraternal affairs and receive national coverage, the intellectuals seem unaware of the Muslims' existence.

Some of this "ignorance" is, of course, a kind of psychological insulation. It is a refusal to acknowledge the existence of *any* phenomenon that might be interpreted—by the white community, at least—as casting doubt on the Negro's social and intellectual

maturity. At first the intellectuals considered it a badge of status
to "know nothing of these people." They "rarely read the Negro
press," and none of their friends were aware of any Muslim
activity. After a spate of articles on the Black Muslim in *Time,
The New York Times, The Christian Science Monitor, Reader's
Digest* and other middle-class media, the intellectuals at last admitted having "heard something about the Movement" but tended
to dismiss it as "just another Harlem-type cult of ignorant Negroes." An article by Nat Hentoff in *The Reporter* magazine, in
August 1960, brought polite inquiries from the Negro elite. (It
is interesting that some Negro intellectuals first heard of the
Muslims through white contacts.) The "Muslim question" is
gradually—and belatedly—becoming a frequent topic of conversation among the intelligentsia.

The Muslims are ambivalent toward the intellectuals, who
they say, "have been in the white man's schools longer and have
been more thoroughly brainwashed." Those few who join the
sect are acclaimed as the true race leaders, who have sacrificed
status to service, and great pride is taken in their "professional"
or "college" training. But intellectuals are more acceptable than
other Negroes to the white community in situations approaching
equality, and nearly all of them spurn Muslim-type protest organizations. Such intellectuals are scored for permitting the white man
to "make fools and Uncle Toms out of our educated and professional class of people with a false show of social equality."[8]
The Muslims also charge the intellectuals with "giving their education back to the teachers" rather than teaching in the Negro
schools and colleges, where they are more sorely needed.

The Muslims do not expect to make many converts among
the Negro intellectuals, for these are held to be the "satisfied
Black Men" who are least concerned with the problems confronting the majority of Negroes. To the intellectuals, on the other
hand, the Black Muslim Movement looms as a threat—not to
themselves, but to their hopes and aspirations for the Negro in
America.

Negro big-businessmen, like Negro politicians, are very much
aware of the Muslims—and especially of their economic potential.
They do not like Muhammad's religious and racial extremism,

but they welcome his continued stress upon economic self-sufficiency and upon racial solidarity in protecting and strengthening Negro financial interests. Those who do business with the Muslims have found them reliable and businesslike. The Muslims do not buy beyond their means, but they tend to buy merchandise of good quality, usually for cash.

Negro businesses were well represented at the 1960 Muslim Convention in Chicago. Banks, insurance companies, retail stores and service enterprises accepted Muhammad's invitation to display their wares and advertise their services at special "bazaars" in the giant Chicago Coliseum, where the convention was held. However, one executive of a Negro insurance company, not represented at the convention, has said privately:

In my opinion the "Muslim" movement or cult has not had, and will not have in the future, any appreciable appeal to American Negroes in either the Low- Middle- or Upper- social Class. . . . It is my further opinion that this movement is rendering a definite disservice to the effort being made in the realm of human relations to make democracy in its fullest sense a reality in this country, and should be resisted to the utmost by the intelligent leadership of our group, as well as the authorities vested with the responsibility of guaranteeing the security of our country against such dangerous and radical movements.

Whether he speaks for a significant number of Negro businessmen, only the future will tell.

The Negro Press

The important elements of the Negro press have not supported Muhammad, nor have they in any way endorsed the Muslim teachings. They have, however, given impetus to the Movement by providing the medium through which it became known to the Negro community as a whole. In this, the press has had little choice: it exists to keep the public informed, and the Muslims were and are news.

The Muslim leadership is fully aware of the importance of the press to its interests. In the *Messenger* magazine, a Muslim publication, Editor Malcolm X devoted two full pages to an article expressing his support of the Negro press:

The daily [white] press can make even the "Negro" public eat your flesh with its powerful . . . propaganda. . . . The Negro press may have its shortcomings, but when the die is cast and your "downtown" friends ready you for the dogs, there must be a NEGRO PRESS to present your case to the "Negro" public. The Negro press is our only medium for voicing the true plight of our oppressed people to the world.[9]

He gave specific endorsement to four Negro newspapers: the *Pittsburgh Courier,* the *Los Angeles Herald-Dispatch,* the *New Jersey Herald News* and the *New York Amsterdam News.* Readers were encouraged to examine each of the Negro papers and "then support the one you find to be the most fearless, uncompromising, and outspoken in behalf of our downtrodden people."

The *Pittsburgh Courier,* with a circulation of 300,000, is the largest Negro newspaper in the country. It has a nationwide coverage, implemented through several regional editions (such as the *New York Courier*), and it was the first paper to give any significant coverage to the Black Muslim Movement. For about three years, from 1956 until the summer of 1959, it served in some ways as a spokesman for the Movement. It carried Muhammad's column, as well as news about Muslim activities, and in 1957 it presented Muhammad with the "Courier Achievement Award."

The *Courier's* editors and columnists also came frequently to the Muslims' defense. For example, George S. Schuyler, New York editor of the *Courier* and one of the most widely read Negro journalists in the world, wrote in his column, "Views and Reviews":

The recent uproar over Mr. Muhammad's movement . . . seems to me to be quite superficial. . . . There is no point in inveighing against Mr. Muhammad's followers as anti-white when the whole climate surrounding them is anti-black. . . . Mr. Muhammad may be a rogue and a charlatan, but when anybody can get tens of thousands of Negroes to practice economic solidarity, respect their women, alter their atrocious diet, give up liquor, stop crime, juvenile delinquency and adultery, he is doing more for the Negro's welfare than any current Negro leader I know.[10]

In October 1959, the *Courier* took *Time* magazine to task for "flippancy" in its treatment of the facts in an exposé of Muhammad. The *Courier* said editorially:

Time magazine . . . is relentless in its frenetic search for *le bon mot*. It seems frequently more interested in the good word than in the good reputation. If it can get its writers to turn a good, or bad, phrase, so long as it "clicks," *Time's* editors do not seem to be concerned. They have the same penchant for "facts" unadorned or unexplained.[11]

The *Courier* was complaining about *Time's* unamplified reference to Elijah Muhammad's arrest on a charge of contributing to the delinquency of a minor in 1934 and to *Time's* assertion that the Muslim leader was jailed for draft-dodging in 1941. The *Courier* editorial pointed out that the charge of "contributing to the delinquency of a minor" was brought against Muhammad for refusing to withdraw his children from the sect's parochial school and send them to public schools. With reference to Muhammad's alleged draft-dodging, the *Courier* pointed out that Muhammad was forty-five years old in 1941 and, therefore, ineligible for the draft. It did not offer the further clarification that Muhammad was jailed for exhorting his *followers* not to register for the draft.

In 1959, when ownership of the *Courier* passed to more conservative hands, Muhammad's column was discontinued, and coverage of Muslim affairs was sharply curtailed. The Messenger's column soon began to appear in another Negro paper, the *Los Angeles Herald-Dispatch,* which quickly became the de facto official organ of the Black Muslim Movement.

The *New York Amsterdam News* is the only other newspaper of significant circulation giving important coverage to the Muslims. The *News* displays little if any overt bias, toward the Movement or against it. It gives considerable attention to Muslim affairs, particularly in New York City, where there is a large Muslim contingent; but its policy is clearly one of impartial reporting. The *News* treats the Muslims as an important and potentially powerful group in the Harlem community, but not as unusual or bizarre. (Harlem abounds in exotic cults, sects and nationalistic organizations, and the *News* displays a certain sophistication regarding all such movements.)

Characteristically, the *News* invited an African Moslem, Isa S. Wali, to write a series of articles interpreting orthodox Islam for its readers. Against this background, it invited its readers to judge for themselves whether the Black Muslims are a bona fide Islamic sect. The paper observed:

Due to the rapid growth of the followers of Elijah Muhammad in Harlem, one of the most frequently asked questions in Harlem today is "What is Islam?"

Mr. Muhammad's followers call themselves Moslems and their religion Islam. There are those who dispute their claims and charge that they are not true Moslems and that their religion is not true Islam.

Without attempting to take any sides in the controversy, the *Amsterdam News* herewith publishes this interpretation of Islam as it was interpreted by a Moslem of Africa at the second annual conference of the American Society of African Culture.

The hope is that our readers, having been told just what Islam is, will be able themselves to determine who is not practicing it.[12]

One of the few papers which has ever been harshly critical of the Muslims is *The New Crusader,* a tabloid published in Chicago. In the autumn of 1959, when Balm L. Leavell, Jr., was editor, the *Crusader* published a series of articles "exposing" Muhammad. The paper has a limited circulation, however, even in Chicago, where it must compete with the long-established *Chicago Daily Defender*. Outside Chicago, the *Crusader* is virtually unknown.

The *Crusader* devoted several issues to its exposé[13] and claimed that, on one occasion, the Muslims bought 10,000 copies of the paper in bundles as they hit the newsstands and burned them in the streets "to curtail circulation of any unfavorable stories about their leader." The keystone of the exposé was an article quoting Talib Ahmad Dawud, a rival Moslem leader, who denied that Muhammad was a bona fide Moslem or that he would be permitted to make the pilgrimage to Mecca—a prediction that turned out to be mistaken.

It is worth noting that even this paper did not criticize Muhammad's racial attitudes, preferring to question his religion instead. Indeed, the *Crusader's* racial views appear to parallel closely those of Muhammad and the *Herald-Dispatch*. In an editorial which appeared in the same issue with an installment of the "exposé," the *Crusader* said:

. . . Negroes have labored so long under the illusion that there is a
WHITE SUPREMACY, that . . . IT'S TIME we got some IDEA
ABOUT BLACK ALSO BEING SUPREME! . . . History bears out
the contention that the NEGRO IS OF SUPERIOR BACKGROUND.
. . . No, we don't go along with Rev. King on hollering down BLACK
SUPREMACY . . . our leaders, INCLUDING DR. KING, persist
in teaching that old time religion in which THE WHITE MAN IS
ALWAYS SUPREME. . . . Most Negroes today are hungry for
AGGRESSIVE LEADERSHIP. . . . They WANT ACTION NOW,
VIOLENT ACTION if the situation calls for it. That's why ELIJAH
MUHAMMAD is TROUBLING THE WHITE FOLKS TODAY.
. . . WE NEED BLACK SUPREMACY to get Negroes OFF THEIR
KNEES in churches that preach a WHITE HEAVEN, a WHITE
GOD, and a WHITE UNIVERSE.[14]

At one time it was obvious to anyone who read the *Crusader*
that it was anti-Muslim, even though its principal circulation is
among the classes from which the Muslim membership is drawn.
The coincidence was striking. But times change, and the *Crusader*
is no longer anti-Muslim. By a not quite so striking coincidence,
the *Crusader*'s new editor is also the editor of one of Muhammad's newest pocket-sized magazines, *Muhammad Speaks to the
Blackman.*

Institutional Negro Leadership

The National Association for the Advancement of Colored
People is the organization upon which most American Negroes
have, in recent years, pinned their hopes for a solution to the
problem of racial subordination. In earlier generations they had
relied respectively upon the church, the major political parties
and the moral consciousness of the "better class" white people.
Failed each time they trusted, they now rely only upon themselves
and their individual well-wishers, expressing their moral and civic
convictions through the NAACP.

The NAACP, in turn, has displayed an unparalleled confidence in the adequacy of the law, the competence of its own
lawyers, the sense of moral responsibility in our judiciary and the
integrity of those sworn to enforce the courts' decisions. The
NAACP's legal arm has won some encouraging legal decisions,
which—when the white community has not openly flouted them—

have helped to make the Negro's lot as an American citizen increasingly tolerable.

But to many Negro Americans, the way of the NAACP is too slow, too expensive and too uncertain. The fact that the NAACP has accomplished more concrete results than has religion, politics or the appeal to moral responsibility seems inconsequential in today's jet age. Negroes cannot understand why they must spend time and money again and again to have the courts secure for them privileges that all other Americans—and many resident aliens—take for granted. This is especially true of those furthest down the social scale, those who lack the sophistication necessary to rationalize their status but no longer accept it as necessary or inevitable.

The Black Muslims are just such a group. They do not trust the NAACP, partly because they do not understand either the organization or the complex of politico-social relations that make it necessary. Yet even those Muslims who claim to understand the NAACP vigorously reject it. They reject it because white people, and Negroes who want the white man's acceptance, are identified with it. The Muslims claim that, in some way, *any* group the white man is identified with inhibits or qualifies the Negro's sense of freedom and equality.

At first, the leadership of the Black Muslims was not antagonistic toward the NAACP. It had courted the notion that, as soon as Negroes understood the Movement, they would all embrace it —leaders and laymen alike. The total orientation of the Black Muslim is away from the white man; and this is not merely a creedal expression but an attitude that informs his whole way of life. It is inconceivable to the Muslim that, after "learning the truth," any sensible Negro would prefer to retain his white associations. The Muslim leadership fully expected—and still does expect, though more patiently—that Negro leadership would join freely in the "United Front of Black Men." Moreover, the Movement abhors all intraracial strife and will sedulously avoid it, except when it feels compelled to maintain face.

In an interview in April 1959, Muhammad praised the NAACP as doing a good job "within its limitations." The "limitations" were, of course, its interracial board and its dependence upon white philanthropy. Muhammad's preference is *not* to destroy interracial contacts willy-nilly wherever they exist, even those of a practical nature. What he wants is a "Black Council" *above* such contacts, a council that will coordinate a grand strategy looking forward to eventual independence from all contact with the white man. Presumably, as the leader of a disciplined body of young Muslims in every major Negro community in the country, Mr. Muhammad would head such a council. This idea is, needless to say, rather less than acceptable to the NAACP.

At first, the NAACP, like most other Negro organizations, paid no official attention to the Muslims. The NAACP itself was under fire from conservatives for "pushing too fast," and it may well have been relieved by the sudden arrival of a group which is bent on pushing very much faster. During a television interview in July 1959, Roy Wilkins, Executive Secretary of the NAACP, was asked what he thought of the Muslims. He replied only that "for years the NAACP has been opposed to white extremists preaching hatred of Negro people, and we are equally opposed to Negro extremists preaching against white people simply for the sake of whiteness." The following month, however, after some excitement in the white press about "the Muslim menace," Negroes and whites alike demanded an official statement from the NAACP. Most hoped that the statement would be a strong indictment, and Mr. Wilkins complied:

The NAACP opposes and regards as dangerous any group, white or black, political or religious, that preaches hatred among men. Hatred destroys men—the haters and the hated.

The so-called Moslems who teach black supremacy and hatred of all white people have gained a following only because America has been so slow in granting equal opportunities and has permitted the abuse and persecution of Negro citizens. At this very moment the Congress is shadowboxing with a milk-and-water civil rights bill. All this furnishes ammunition for the use of opportunistic leaders.

The clearest rejection of the "hate-white" doctrine of these so-called Moslems is to be found in the new states of Africa where leaders recognize the need for cooperation with white nations and with their economies.

Prime Minister Nkrumah of Ghana cannot build the Volta Dam with hot-air hatred from American Negro cultists.[15]

The most comprehensive statement on the Muslims issued
by an NAACP official was made by Derrick Bell, Executive Secretary of the Pittsburgh Branch, in a radio address over station
KDKA. Mr. Bell addressed himself principally to certain "sincere
individuals" who had advised that the NAACP "must denounce
the Muslims in no uncertain terms" and suggested "full page ads
in the local newspapers" for the purpose. Many concerned persons had offered money to finance such an advertisement. Others
called for a condemnation of the *Pittsburgh Courier* for publishing
Muhammad's column. In answer, Mr. Bell said in part:

I question the wisdom of either of these proposals . . . not because
either the NAACP or I agree with the . . . Muslims. On the contrary
we could not disagree more. We are convinced that . . . racial superiority is just as wrong when preached by black men as by white
men. Those who have . . . watched the NAACP's struggle for freedom . . . will not likely confuse the NAACP with the Muslims merely
because there are Negroes in both groups. . . . [Further] to urge
the *Courier* to discontinue a column which thousands of its readers
find of interest [is not the remedy]. The Muslims would simply find
another medium to disseminate the same material.[16]

Thurgood Marshall, chief legal counsel for the NAACP,
was less diplomatic and considerably more direct. In an address
at Princeton University, Marshall denounced the Muslims as "run
by a bunch of thugs organized from prisons and jails, and financed,
I am sure, by Nasser or some Arab group." He called the Muslims "vicious" and a real threat to the FBI, the NAACP and all
state law-enforcement agencies.[17]

The Muslims then fought back. Malcolm X referred to
Marshall as a "twentieth century Uncle Tom" and declared that
Muhammad was "too busy to worry about the envious yapping
of every jealous dog that is paid to bark at him." The *Los Angeles
Herald-Dispatch* devoted its editorial columns to a discussion of
"The Ugly American"—that is, "the American Negro who has
made a career of being a good Uncle Tom." Yet the *Dispatch*
offered Marshall an excuse by blaming "Zionism" for the statement he had made at Princeton:

Marshall is a competent attorney who has consciously or unconsciously accepted Zionism as his philosophy. While speaking at
Princeton University to a group of white Americans, he denounced the

followers of the Islamic faith as "a bunch of thugs financed by Nasser or some Arab group." This is Zionist ideology at its ugliest. . . . The Zionists are the most subtle, successful, and insidious [hate group] . . . and have injected their poison into the ugly American, the Uncle Tom.[18]

The Jews, said the *Dispatch,* have infiltrated the NAACP, whose primary function is to promote the interests of the Jews in the guise of helping the Negro.

In the early thirty's, a large percentage of European Jews were engaged in trade, living in the rear of stores, markets and generally making their living from the Negro in the Negro community. Thus they had an excellent opportunity to study the habits and weaknesses of the Negro. The depression of the 30's, through the activities of the Communist Party, allowed the Jews to further intrench themselves into the community, to infect his thinking to the extent that by 1940 the Negro was almost entirely dependent upon the Jews and had accepted the thinking and ideology of the Jewish people. In the late 30's and by the early 50's the Jews had finally gained control of the NAACP.[19]

The NAACP has permitted itself to be sidetracked by the Jews into a struggle for integration. But integration is a stratagem of the Jews "to divert the Negro from basic economic problems by keeping him chasing butterflies," while the Jew works feverishly to establish himself economically at the Negro's expense. Each time the Black Man tries to establish his own leadership, he is blocked by the Jews, who fear an ultimate economic loss if the Negro takes over his own destiny.

Our main task then in 1960 is to rid ourselves of this phony Jewish leadership, to work and cooperate with all groups but as equals and not to permit ourselves to be dominated by any of them.[20]

As if to prove their willingness to forget past differences with the NAACP, the Muslims opened 1960 with a significant gesture. Wallace D. Muhammad, 26-year-old son of Elijah and minister of the Philadelphia Temple, helped to launch an NAACP fund drive on behalf of Mrs. Daisy Bates, NAACP regional executive, and her husband, who had lost their newspaper and their personal fortune because of their activities in the integration crisis. Young Muhammad contributed fifty dollars with the assurance that:

We Muslims have always admired Mrs. Daisy Bates for her strong courage in the face of great odds in the Little Rock, Arkansas situation. And since our organization, under the leadership of Mr. Elijah Muhammad is striving for the same goal as the NAACP in their fight for our people's rights in this country, we feel that Mrs. Bates is more than deserving of this small contribution. . . .[21]

This overture was a significant reversal of the behavior charged to Muslims in New York less than two months earlier. At a reception given in Harlem for President and Mrs. Séku Touré of the Republic of Guinea, L. Joseph Overton, president of the New York branch NAACP, was so roundly booed that he was unable to perform his scheduled function as master of ceremonies. Overton is popular with Harlem's black nationalists; his NAACP is not. The Muslims had not sponsored the reception, but they were present in force, and they were accused by their critics of starting the demonstration against the NAACP, which then became "spontaneous."

Malcolm X categorically denied this accusation. He warned that the Negro masses are unsympathetic to any Negro leader "handpicked by the white man," but he denounced this act of discourtesy as "a terrible thing." James Lawson, president of the United African Nationalist Movement, who had directed the reception, supported Malcolm's position. He insisted that the booing had not been organized. Rather, he said, it was "spontaneous and unanimous," for "the name 'NAACP' is tantamount to waving a red flag in front of a bull." The common people, Lawson said, remember the NAACP as "the enemy of Marcus Garvey and Booker T. Washington, and they did not want the mention of that group on any program honoring the African Chief of State."

Whatever the Muslims' share of responsibility for the demonstration, Mr. Overton—whom the Harlem Muslims call "one of the few NAACP leaders who knows anything at all about what the common people are thinking"—seems to have remained unperturbed. *The New York Times* later reported:

Despite his unpleasant experience at the reception for President Touré, Mr. Overton was moved in a recent interview to praise the Temple of Islam [i.e., the Black Muslims]. Since his work for the NAACP is in Harlem, this may be an indication of the movement's strength.

"I daresay there is no group with higher moral standards," Mr. Overton commented. "Many vices have been dominated; mutual love has been cultivated."

Mr. Overton expressed confidence that his type of "grassroots leadership" would lead to a measure of understanding with Malcolm X and his followers.[22]

In return, Malcolm X has said that "Overton is out there in the street with the rest of us. He's got some idea of what the Black Man wants—what he's thinking. It's not so with the others. Every time I've seen Roy Wilkins he's been at the Waldorf, or in the vicinity of the Waldorf. I have never seen him with black people unless they were looking for white people!"

In short, those NAACP leaders who live closest to the experiences of the Muslim class seem to have a more sympathetic understanding of the Movement. They do not condone the Muslims' extremist policies, nor do they share the Muslims' extreme antipathy for and distrust of the white man. But they can appreciate the individual Muslim's sense of futility—his awareness that he is hemmed in by immense forces which are brutally indifferent to his sense of dignity and personal worth.

The Muslims look upon the National Urban League, like the NAACP, as "controlled by white men, for its existence is dependent upon white philanthropy." Like the NAACP, it is no more than a way station: "It is not the answer."

Because of the nature of its program, the Urban League has not been brought into direct conflict with the Movement. Some league officials, however, have expressed concern about the negative publicity they feel the Muslims have brought upon the whole Negro community. Executive Secretary Lester B. Granger concedes that the Muslims have momentarily caught the public attention, but he insists that they are only a temporary symptom of the present crisis in race relations. "These racist, hate movements," he believes, appear at intervals of crisis, spend themselves and fade into oblivion, while the truly significant improvements in the Negro's status are being made through patient cooperation of Negroes and whites, working together in the common interest.

The Urban League has issued no official statement regarding

the Muslims. Asked about this apparent lack of official concern, Mr. Granger explained:

It is true that there has been expressed a great deal of interest in this variant among Negro protest expressions. However, my own feeling is that the discussion has been out of all proportion to the significance of the movement whether one gauges that significance in the relationship to the number it involves or the historical record of similar movements that have regularly occurred over a period of more than 40 years.

In short, I do not believe that any good purpose is served by having an organization such as mine make an official expression of opinion in view of the many truly significant developments with which we are concerned.[23]

Not all of the Urban League's executives in the local offices across the country share Mr. Granger's detached aloofness. In Ohio, for example, Andrew G. Freeman, executive director of the Columbus Urban League, felt constrained to sound a public note of warning:

The basic faiths with which we are familiar meet the needs of all men. Our philosophy of government is based on the belief in the brotherhood of man under God. Any teaching contrary to this principle is extremely dangerous and should be viewed with concern.[24]

Edwin C. Berry, director of the Chicago Urban League, was more emphatic, perhaps because his work brings him into more personal contact with the average Negro. In an informal statement that has been widely quoted in the national press, Berry said: "A guy like this Muslim leader makes more sense than I do to the man on the street who's getting his teeth kicked out. I have a sinking feeling that Elijah Muhammad is very significant."[25]

The Black Muslims are emphatically opposed to passive resistance as it has been expressed by the followers of Martin Luther King, Jr., and in the wave of "sit-ins" conducted by college students across the country. They oppose King because he emphasizes the Christian principle of loving the oppressor rather than retaliating against him. This is precisely the "slave philosophy" the Muslims have sought to escape in their repudiation of Christianity. Hence, King represents to the Muslims a capitulation to the cunning Christian strategy of the white man. "How long do you think we'd last," asked a Muslim leader, "if the white man thought we'd all bow our heads and present our necks to the axe? About long enough for him to get the axe!"

The Muslims score King for having "turned many potential freedom-fighting Negroes into contented, docile slaves," [26] and his "fitness to lead American Negroes" is questioned. His decision to leave Montgomery to become associate minister at his father's church in Atlanta brought a bitter denunciation from the *Los Angeles Herald-Dispatch:*

In February, this same Reverend Martin Luther King, the Darling of the South, Honey Boy of the North, is now moving his headquarters from the increasingly hostile atmosphere of Alabama to the more lucrative haven of Atlanta. Is this a retreat from the bloody racial struggle soon to erupt in Alabama? Has his philosophy developed from "turn the other cheek" to "turn and run away"?

If all of us are going to die and go to heaven as the Negro Christian ministers have been preaching, why must Reverend King flee the "portals of death" in Alabama, conveniently seeking safer refuge among the wealthier Negroes of Atlanta? . . .

Reverend Martin Luther King could clear his conscience simply by taking a firm stand on the side of TRUTH. Tell the Negroes in America the TRUTH—that they will never get anything up in the sky after they die, nor will they ever get anything here on earth either until they are ready and willing to shed blood or die fighting for it.[27]

Dr. King did not reply to this attack; but in an earlier address before the National Bar Association, meeting in Milwaukee, he had cited the Muslims as "one of the hate groups arising in our midst which would preach a doctrine of black supremacy," a new kind of bigotry as bad as the old one of white supremacy.

The Muslims ridicule the charge that teaching the Negro to defend his person and his dignity has anything to do with black supremacy. The Black Man is by nature peaceful and respectful, but it is also the nature of a man to fight to protect himself. The so-called Negro, however, has been so psychologically paralyzed by the black preachers and their religion that he is no longer a man.

No one can react to persecution like this but the Negro, and he does it under the counseling of the Negro preacher. . . . Were it not for the Negro pastor, our people would be just like the Hungarians, we'd be fighters. . . . The Negro is a fighting man all right. He fought in Korea; he fought in Germany; he fought in the jungles of Iwo Jima. But that same Negro will come back here, and the white man will hang his mother on a tree, and he will take the Bible and say, "Forgive them Lord, for they know not what they do." This Negro preacher makes them that way. . . . Where there is a slave like that, why you have a slave-making religion.[28]

Nothing short of "an eye for an eye" will have a lasting impression upon the white man, for he "has never stolen an acre of land or chained a single black to be his slave without force." Hence Malcolm urges the Black Man to "be peaceful and loving. Agree with everyone, but if anyone comes to take advantage of you, do the same thing the white man does; *lay down your life!* and the Black Man will be respected all over the planet Earth."[29]

Passivity, say the Muslims, robs the Negro of his only weapon. This is especially true in America, where the white men are morally indifferent and the Negroes are a numerical minority. One Muslim brother explained: "When the Ghanaians got ready for the British to go, they told the British to 'get out!' and the British got out. The same was true of the Belgians—and when they were a little slow, why the Congolese helped them to go. But the Ghanaians and the Congolese were at home and in the majority. When the South Africans get ready for the white man to go, why they can just all sit down, and the white man has to go or starve. It's not so here. When the white man here gets tired of your 'sitting down' or 'sitting in,' you *know* what he's going to do."

Martin Luther King was challenged by Malcolm X to "come to Harlem and prove that 'peaceful suffering' is the solution to the atrocities suffered daily by Negroes throughout America."[30] Dr. King did not respond. The Muslims then announced that they would hold a rally in Atlanta to demonstrate that Southern Negroes were "tired of suffering, peacefully or otherwise."

The sit-ins are denounced, not for passivity, but for aggressively "going into these stores where we are neither wanted nor invited." Instead of pointlessly jeopardizing their lives, Negroes are urged to "ignore the whites and develop [their] own business as [the whites] have." Separatism, the Muslims point out, hits the white man where it hurts. The whites have begun a nationwide campaign against Muhammad as a "hate teacher" because he excludes whites from his temples "on the same basis that Negroes are excluded from white churches." This is proof that if Negroes want the white man's respect, they need only turn the white man's policy against him.

The sit-ins are described as being led by CORE (Committee on Racial Equality), "an organization with headquarters in New York on Park Row. . . . Its policies have been . . . supported by the usual phony Negro leadership, such as Jackie Robinson, Roy Wilkins and Martin Luther King." [31] These leaders are accused of putting the lives of Negro children on the line "while they sip cocktails in the lounges of Fifth Avenue." The Muslim leaders, in contrast, do not "send our women and children into the lair of the beast. We go ourselves, but not just to sit beside him or to eat in his presence."

For the most part, Dr. King and other leaders associated with the nonviolent approach to America's racial problem have either ignored the Muslims or deplored their publicly-expressed "invitation to annihilation" (as one Southern professor termed it). Those who guide the passive resistance movements feel they have nothing important to gain from answering the Muslims' charges and that they stand almost no chance of enlisting the Muslims' support. No constructive communication can take place between the two groups until one or the other is ready to modify substantially its point of view. This accommodation seems hardly likely to occur.

The Negro Christian Churches

At first the Negro churches were inclined to accept the Black Muslims as another Christian denomination, and in at least one instance a Muslim minister is said to have belonged to a local Pastor's Alliance. The report is not incredible, for the Muslim ministers tend to be young and personable, and not much attention is paid to the *nature* of a church in the average American community. Further, the range of religious beliefs and affiliations among Negroes in the large cities tends to be quite wide; in the pastors' organizations, the behavior and presentability of the minister is often the chief criterion of acceptability. What a man preaches in his own church is not usually open to question, and few of his colleagues would inquire into it. A Muslim minister, therefore, would be accepted without question so long as no specific complaint was raised. And this leniency is not unusual; it is true of nearly all community organizations. It is a matter of record, for example, that a Troy (N.Y.) Muslim was a prominent Mason and NAACP president, as well as a scoutmaster and a member of the Advisory Council of the Juvenile Court.[32]

During the period of the Movement's recent growth, (that is, from about 1955), Muslim ministers frequently addressed Christian congregations. Although such occurrences are considerably less frequent now, they are by no means rare. One interesting recent development in invitations to the Muslim minister is a shift away from the lower-class pulpits, which once welcomed him, and toward various organizations (such as men's groups) in the upper-class churches, whose curiosity has been aroused.

Before the summer of 1959, Christian churches rarely denied the Black Muslims the use of their churches for meetings and special services. The traditional spirit of helpfulness was extended to the Muslims quite as readily as to any other religious group. After the Muslims were discovered by the national press, this practice was sharply curtailed, and it became increasingly difficult for the Muslims to obtain any accommodations in Christian churches in most cities. The following incident, reported in the *Indianapolis Times,* is a case in point:

A rally by an extremist Negro cult was cancelled yesterday when a Methodist Church locked the group out of the church sanctuary. About 50 followers of Elijah Muhammad, self-styled "messenger of Allah," milled around outside the Gorham Methodist Church, 11th and Missouri, after the church's board of trustees decided at the last minute to deny them use of the sanctuary.

The meeting was switched to Greater Zion Baptist Church, 701 N. Tremont, but then was cancelled because of the large number of police and newspaper reporters present. . . .

The Reverend G. N. Hardin, pastor of the Methodist Negro Church [*sic*], said his group decided to bar the cultists, because "the Moslems are not Christian as we see it. We do not know that what is printed [about the Moslems] is true, but it doesn't appear they are a Christian group."[33]

The Muslims chide the Negro ministers for bowing to the white man in denying the Muslims use of their sanctuaries. Why should Negro Christians, who themselves are not permitted to worship in the white churches, let the white man tell them whom they may have as guests in their own sanctuaries? Yet even when the Muslims were welcomed, they subjected their hosts to a constant and embarrassing criticism. For example:

Speaking for more than 2,000 Moslems and non-Moslems last Tuesday, Elijah Muhammad told his enthusiastic audience, "I will gladly go to prison, sacrifice my very life itself, for the freedom and rights of the 17,000,000 Negroes in America."

The spacious King Solomon's Baptist Church, 6124 14th Street [Detroit], was packed to capacity with an overflow crowd of Negro Christians and Moslems, many of whom had taken off from their jobs to see and hear the noted spiritual leader. . . .

[Said Muhammad:] "Since the Negro Church has failed to do that which we are doing, the Negro Church should be glad to join in and work with us."

He called on the Negro pastors to accept Islam and unite with the Moslems. "Let us use the Moslem Crescent, which is the sign of LIFE . . . instead of the white man's cross, which is the sign of slavery, suffering and death. Tell the white man that since he has not given the Negro Christians justice in his Christian religion, you are now going back to the Islamic religion of your foreparents . . . a religion of TRUTH, in which we get freedom, justice and equality. . . . A religion that gives us dignity, unity, and makes us FEARLESS. . . ."[34]

On another occasion, in Los Angeles, three Negro ministers were described as having "hot-footed it out of a meeting" at which Malcolm X blamed the Negro clergy for "the Negro's deplorable economic condition" and charged them with helping the white man to keep the Negro Christian in poverty:

He said $90,000,000 is spent annually in Los Angeles in upkeeping Negro preachers and churches, while [only] $60,000,000 is spent for houses and furniture combined. . . . Malcolm X then pleaded with the Negro preachers to return to their churches and put their members' money to work "for the members" . . . building factories and supermarkets instead of [more] churches.[35]

Some churches have found themselves picketed, in effect, by pairs of quiet young Muslims who pass out literature near their doors on Sunday morning. Police in Springfield, Massachusetts, patrolled the areas around three Negro churches after the pastors complained of such activities,[36] and there have been similar complaints from other parts of the country.

The ministers themselves, like Christianity and the churches, have been the target of direct and vicious attacks. Muslim leaders urge the Negro laity to "pay no more attention to [these] black friends of the white Slavemasters [for] they have not been able to help you in all these years."[37]

The ignorant, greedy Negro preachers . . . are the willing tools of the very ones who are responsible for our people's miserable plight. . . . [The white man] has trained these ignorant, greedy Negro preachers to parrot his religious lies to us, a pacifying religion that was skilfully designed to brainwash us and keep us in "our place."[38]

On the whole, the Christian ministers have responded with restraint. They have typically deplored the Movement's extremism and its flagrant attacks on Christianity. Yet, because of widespread segregation and other signs of racial bias within the church and throughout the Christian world, many ministers feel vulnerable. They cannot in good conscience flatly reject the Black Muslim position as a whole. Most have taken a position similar to that of The Reverend William M. James, Minister of the Metropolitan Community Methodist Church in Harlem, who repudiated black racism as unjustifiable and unavailing but pointed out that it is rooted in the persecution and the denial of common opportunities to American Negroes. "Social disease breeds diseased leadership," he asserted and urged those interested in eliminating Muslim-type movements to help the Negro break out of his "ghetto encirclement."[39]

The Muslims have also exhibited some ambivalence—or at least a willingness to work with Negroes who refuse to give up their Christian faith. Even while denouncing the value of Christianity, Muhammad pleads for the cooperation of Christians and Muslims in their areas of mutual concern.

Let us lay aside, for the moment, our differences of faith and remember that we are members of the same [Black] Nation regardless of religious beliefs. Let us think of the condition of the world and of our future as a people. We can no more depend on the future of the white race, for they have no future. The time is far spent, and their sun is set.[40]

But this expediency is temporary. Muhammad's long-range goal is to win all Negro Christians to Islam. Some Christians are receptive, and the Movement keeps growing, but nearly all defections thus far have been individual. There have been almost no mass defections as far as is known.

Perhaps the only known case of a wholesale transfer of religious loyalties was that of a Baptist church in Richmond, which, after two addresses by a Muslim minister, voted to become a Muslim temple. Thereupon the minister dropped his "slave name" and became David X. It may be significant that this church was won to Muhammad during a period of extreme racial unrest, when Virginians had closed their schools rather than admit Negroes and had set up segregated schools for white children in the Christian churches.

The Negro Man in the Street

In his current struggle for social dignity and a larger share in the common values of the community, the American Negro is generally ambivalent about means. Should he merely support his leaders, or should he take direct action on his own initiative? Increasingly he does both, for the man in the street, whether white-collar or in overalls, is generally impatient with the progress his leaders are making. Mrs. Rosa Parker, the gentle and unassuming seamstress who created the "Montgomery situation" by asserting her right to sit where she chose on a public bus, is a vivid illustration of this attitude. Mrs. Parker believed in and supported the Negro leadership in Montgomery; but her soul was as tired as her feet, and she could not wait any longer for deliverance at their hands.

In Memphis, sometime before the public busses were desegregated, a Negro laborer boarded a bus in an outlying Negro section during the evening rush hour. Two Negro women who had boarded earlier were seated midway in the bus. As the bus approached the downtown area and more whites began to come aboard, the Negro women were required two or three times to give up their seats and move farther back. Finally the Negro laborer could stand it no longer. Taking an old linoleum knife from the bag of tools he was carrying, he rushed up to where the women were now sitting. "Ladies," he said, with tears streaming from his face, "don't y'all move back no doggone more! If you do, I'm going to have to hurt you. And if anybody on here tries to *make* y'all move *just one more time,* then my life ain't worth a quarter. We done moved back enough, and ain't none of us gon' move no further!"[41]

When the local Negro leadership in Memphis could not wrest a guarantee from management that Negro women would be extended the same courtesies in the downtown department stores as were white patrons, the women began canceling their accounts on their own accord. Thereafter, those who could afford to do so did their shopping in periodic trips to cities as far away as St. Louis and Chicago. "If I can't be 'Mrs.' and have the use of a dinky dressing room on Main Street in Memphis," said one indignant Negro matron, "I can be 'Madame' in a State Street salon in Chicago."

The college sit-ins are yet another illustration of the Negro's ambivalence toward his established leadership—and, perhaps, of the leadership's misjudgment of the prevailing mood in the Negro community. The college students had long been among the most ardent supporters of the relatively conservative protest organizations, such as the NAACP. Yet the sit-ins took the NAACP by surprise, as they did the rest of the established Negro leadership.

The man in the street is waiting and pushing and hoping; but he is also looking around for alternatives. The disease of racial discrimination has been with us longer than is reasonable to expect in an enlightened society; and in an atomic age, the traditional remedies make haste too slowly. The Negro wants to be first class *now.* Anyone who fails to understand this has seriously misjudged the temper of the times.

Among the Negroes of the middle class, Muhammad's call for a united front is not wholly devoid of appeal. There has been a common notion that the Negroes' vulnerability has stemmed, at least in part, from their own apparent inability to stand together and make a common cause in the fight against discrimination. The superstition that "Negroes cannot stick together, especially in a crisis," has long been accepted as a fact. The "Great Walk" at Montgomery and the more recent sit-ins in various communities have done much to disprove this superstition and to make the average Negro more receptive to proposals for group protest. Most middle-class Negroes, however, are determined to keep within the broad limits of the "democratic" and "American" tradition. They are drawn to the idea of a *united* front but repelled by the idea of a *black* front. Similarly, the Negro middle class shares the increasing race-consciousness of the entire Negro community; but it interprets this as a unity-in-determination to resist oppression, rather than as an aggressive "front."

Muhammad's Movement is one of rigid discipline, aimed at controlling the total behavior of the individual. This factor alone is sufficiently repulsive to dissuade the majority of the middle class from any "committed" participation, for while the middle class is highly conformist, it is oriented toward the prevailing values and taboos of the general society. The middle-class Negro also refuses to identify with the Muslims, by and large, because he associates them with potential violence or because "the government is after them." (Some non-Muslims report that a visit to one of the temples has been followed by a visit from the FBI.) But above all, the middle-class Negro is loath to add a new philosophy of racial subordination to that already imposed by the white majority. While acknowledging his latent hostility to the white man, he is not willing to give over his entire life to a fanatic hatred. He is in search of freedom, not vengeance.

Nevertheless, some small businessmen and tradesmen have been forced to the reluctant conclusion that they must support a movement like Muhammad's or perish. Faced with the choice, they have joined the Movement. Muhammad has, ironically, predicted that this would happen. He has insisted that the white man will not do business with Negroes and that integration can only weaken the Negro businessman's support in the black community. Only race pride, he has said, and a determination to "support your own kind" can save the Negro businessman from extinction.

But even among those who have joined or who favor the Movement, sympathy is generally focused not on the doctrine of racial hostility but on the issues of economic policy, race pride and moral uplift. Such expressions as the following are not infrequent among the middle class (and they have their corollaries among the more economically and socially depressed Negroes in the slums and on the street corners):

One Chicago businessman said, "When Mr. Muhammad urges Negroes to build up solid economic holdings in the community, I agree with him 100 per cent. But I can't go along with some of his other ideas."

A Philadelphia lawyer's comment was, "He's merely trying to give the Negro the education and understanding strictly from an economic point of view, that the Jew has been getting and using for centuries. It would be a tough job, but organizing the Negro's financial intelligence into one solid buying power would be a good thing. We don't stick together and pool our capital as other groups do."

In Los Angeles, a real estate broker's comment was, "I don't know too much about the other things they want, but if they can get colored people to support colored business 100 per cent, I wouldn't be able to count all the money I'd make selling houses."

A Hartford, Conn., man said ". . . if . . . [Negroes] want better schools, good jobs and homes they should follow the leadership of Elijah Muhammad. We need to turn to Elijah Muhammad, for he is telling the Negro to unite because unity is the key to their freedom."[42]

Finally, the chance to identify with an organization that boldly attacks social and religious conventions is for some middle-class Negroes an irresistible challenge. This is especially true of a handful of young "rebels" who resent the contemporary emphasis on conformity in general and who particularly resent the idea of conforming to a social status that implies docility and an admission of inferiority. The few college students who have joined the Movement are of this class, as are many of the Muslim veterans of the armed services, who nurse their resentment of the "reward" they received for defending the nation against its enemies.

The lower-class man in the street has more immediate motivations for his attitude toward the Movement. In the crowded slums of the big cities, it is difficult to find anyone who has not heard of Muhammad and his Black Muslims. Even among those who have not joined the Movement, there is a strong admiration for the Muslim leadership and often an openly expressed identification with most of what they stand for. Typical is the statement by a Detroit youth that Mister Muhammad and Minister Malcolm are "telling the truth if they get killed for it," while the other Negro leaders "keep on messing around with The Man (i.e., the white man), when they know he ain't going to ever act right." In the pool halls, the barber shops, the taverns and cafes and on the street corners, Muhammad is an inevitable topic of conversation; and more often than not, his defenders are in the majority.

To many who have despaired of ever seeing American democracy become "color-blind," Muhammad represents the only available alternative. The emotions of the disprivileged lie close to the surface; and the church, which managed for so long to sublimate the Negro's resentments, finds its task increasingly difficult. Even the store-front "shouting" missions have lost much of their attraction for the Negro whose frustrations are choking him. The Muslims are saying bluntly many of the words he wants to hear. And the Muslims symbolize *action*.

Like their counterparts in the middle class, the Negroes furthest down are impatient with the techniques of "education and negotiation." They cannot see why people as well-educated as the white man is alleged to be "can't tell the difference between right and wrong." It seems to them obviously wrong that people who are not white should be treated differently from those who are, especially in a country where all are supposed to be equal under the laws of the land. They reject the Negro leadership's involved explanations about "white moderates" and "men of good will." They do not understand how "a handful of Ku Klux congressmen from Georgia and Mississippi can make the North, the East, the West, the Mid-West and all the rest of the country" conform to what is obviously an unjust position. They are inclined to doubt the alleged "good will" of *any* white man, and they tend to be ready to accept Muhammad's allegation that the white man's "tricknology" has brainwashed the Negro leaders and bought them out with "iced tea and worthless promises."

The followers of Marcus Garvey are represented in the Muslim temples in substantial numbers, as are the Moorish Scientists. But there are also thousands of Muslims who have had no previous contact with black nationalism. What they have had is an unfortunate contact with the enduring corrosion of prejudice and discrimination—and they are looking for a way out.

Some potential converts in the lower class reject the Movement because of its spartan requirements. Women tend to object to the Muslim ban on cosmetics and to various other restrictions pertaining to dress. The requirement of strict sexual morality and the categorical prohibition of alcohol and tobacco alienate many young men for whom the Muslims' religious and racial teachings are not a formidable barrier. Those who join the Movement tend to have been so impressed with the futility of established techniques for improving their lot that they are willing to make the required adjustments in personal behavior in exchange for a new emotional outlook.

And those who do not become members may have guilt feelings because they are *not* in the Movement! In Chicago, for example, a young deliveryman was asked if he were a Muslim. "No sir," he replied, "but God knows I ought to be. I guess I just ain't got guts enough." Respectable Negro leadership knows that Muhammad's solution to the race problem is not viable, but the lower-class man in the street is far from certain. For him it is a question of "guts," his *own* guts. He seems to take for granted that the Muslims' courage is superior to his own.

Yet this is not the whole story. Sometimes it is easier to call oneself a coward than it is to call oneself a fool. Even in the lower class, the man in the street is loath to give up his belief that the American Creed will one day be realized, but his continuing faith has exposed him only to fresh disappointments and ridicule. In his most bitter moments, he may accuse himself of lacking the courage to give up a dream that will never come true. He has not yet capitulated. But his faith is sorely tested; and if racial oppression is allowed to persist in America, only the Muslims stand to gain.

II. THE JEWISH COMMUNITY

The Black Muslims deny that they have a special antipathy for Jews, and the Muslim leaders have been unable to discover a significant reservoir of hatred for Jews *as Jews* among the rank and file. There is latent admiration for the Jewish "psychology" and for the Jew's alleged business acumen, and there is great sympathy for the Jews as a minority group who "were roasted like peanuts by the white man in Europe." On the other hand, some Muslims openly detest Jews as renegade Black Men and as leeches on the so-called Negro community.

Among the Muslim leaders and influential laymen, there appears to be some ambivalence about classifying the Jews as white. There is a feeling in some quarters that the Jews, as Semites, are "not quite white" and should be grouped with the Arabs as members of the Black Nation. "How can we be accused of being anti-Semitic," one Muslim minister asked, "when our Arab brothers are Semitic?" For those who accept this implication, the Jews are traitors: Black Men who reject their true identity, scorn their black brothers and pass themselves off as white.

This attitude, however, is quite rare. The Muslim laity tends simply to dismiss the Jews as white, without making further distinction. "The Jew is a white man. He is accepted as a white man, and that is how he wants it. He can go places we can't go." Jews may live in ghettos, but their ghettos are in white neighborhoods, "except when they are complete parasites upon the Black community." Even when a Jew lives above his own store in a black ghetto, he is not really part of the black community, for he fraternizes with black men only so far as is necessary to promote his business. The Jew clings to his white identity even though he is persecuted by other white men. "The Anglo-Saxons look down on the Jew. The Jew hates the Anglo-Saxon but considers himself better than a Black Man."

But there are differences among white men, and generally you find them in certain kinds of activities. For example, "the Anglo-Saxons are diplomats and statesmen; the Italians are criminals and racketeers; the stupid Irishmen are cops; the Germans

are good scientists; the Jews are the brains of the white race."
They are the thinkers and the writers, and they are shrewd enough
to manipulate the rest of the whites—to say nothing of the so-
called Negroes. "Every Jew is a born psychologist," and he uses
his "psychology" to accomplish his ends. The so-called Negro
begs for what he wants, or relies on the white man's "Christian
spirit." The white man tries to buy his way with money. "The
Jew wastes neither his love nor his money: he 'psyches' his way
to the top. One Jew is smarter than a roomful of 'white men.' He
can spend a quarter and make a million dollars; or he can rob you
blind while he's telling you a funny joke."

The Jews are believed to have a stranglehold on public
opinion through their control of mass communication. They are
said to own the radio and television stations, along with many
magazines and newspapers. They hire gentiles to "front" for
them so as not to antagonize the public; but on crucial issues,
such as the Suez Canal, they control the thinking of the people.
And they use this power to forward the Zionist cause. Malcolm X
declares:

We make no distinction between Jews and non-Jews so long as they
are all white. To do so would be to imply that we like some whites
better than others. This would be discrimination, and we do not
believe in discrimination. However, the Jews, with the help of Christians in America and Europe, drove our Muslim brothers (i.e., the
Arabs) out of their homeland, where they had been settled for centuries, and took over the land for themselves. This every Muslim
resents.

In America, the Jews sap the very life-blood of the so-called Negroes
to maintain the state of Israel, its armies and its continued aggression
against our brothers in the East. This every Black Man resents.

The European and American Christians helped to establish Israel
in order to get rid of the Jews so that they could take over their
businesses as they did the American Japanese during the war. The
scheme failed, and the joke is on the white man. The American Jews
aren't going anywhere. Israel is just an international poor house
which is maintained by money sucked from the poor suckers in
America.[43]

Muslims are especially resentful of Jews who live in the

Negro community. "The Jew comes in and brings his family. He opens a business and hires his wife, his mother-in-law, all his brothers-in-law, and then he sends to the old country to get his father and mother, sisters and brothers—even his uncles—and he hires all of them. Meanwhile, the so-called Negroes are footing the bill, but there isn't a black face behind a single counter in the store." Soon the Jew will open another business—a laundromat, perhaps. He will then shift some of his relatives there. Still later he will open a liquor store, "because by now he's got enough money to buy off the crooks downtown." Soon he follows his Negro customer home and buys the flat he lives in. By that time, the Jew is providing the Negro with his food, his clothes, his services, his home and the whiskey he has to have to keep from hating himself. "But the Jew doesn't live above the business any more. He's moved on out to the suburbs and is living in the best house black money can buy."

To the Negro in the black ghetto, the Jew is as highly "visible" as are the handful of Negroes who escape the ghetto and penetrate the white communities. Consequently, the negative image of the Jewish merchant is likely to be extremely exaggerated. The Jew's presence among the Negroes—and his racial and social separation from them—make him a readily available scapegoat, an easy target for the pent-up frustrations engendered by the "place" the Negroes have been assigned by the larger society.

The Jew not only dominates the Black Man economically, the Muslims aver; he manipulates the Negro organizations as well. The NAACP, for example, is the Jews' "tiger," and from time to time they unleash it on the prejudiced Christians. But for all practical purposes, the NAACP is a "paper tiger," since every law enforcement agency in the country is in the hands of the white man. The Jew knows this, but he keeps the so-called Negroes agitated about such nonsense as sitting beside a white man on a bus, thus keeping them too busy to think about building supermarkets and department stores. Meanwhile, the white man is so busy trying to segregate the Negroes in the back of the bus that *he* has no time for business. The Jew then steps in and provides the food, clothes and services for both contestants. He may even provide the bus! And he is certain to provide the Negro with enough money to keep the fight going.

If the Jew wants the so-called Negroes to attack a white man, he circulates the rumor that the white man is prejudiced— a fact that every Negro with any sense knows to begin with. If the Jew wants to get rid of a troublesome *Negro* leader, the Jew does not attack him directly. Instead, he invites a *second* Negro to dinner, lets the Negro shake hands with his wife and assures the Negro that everybody is equal. "Hearing that kind of talk and being treated like that by a white man, the second Negro gets so 'hopped up' he will not only go out and organize a campaign against the Negro the Jew doesn't like, but he will kill his own mother if she gets in his way before that 'fix' he got from being invited out by the white folks wears off!" Meanwhile, the Jew sits back and enjoys the show, while remaining a "friend" to everybody.

These, then, are the prevailing attitudes the Black Muslims have adopted toward the Jews. Some of the beliefs are stereotypes held in common with the white community; some are endemic in the general Negro community; some are uniquely Muslim. But none of the beliefs are more virulent than those held about the white man in general. The Jews have not been singled out as a special target of a concentrated attack. Such an emphasis might easily occur, however, as the Black Muslims cement their identification with Afro-Asian Islam.

The Jews, for their part, have paid little official attention to the Muslim movement, but they do have an intelligent awareness of its existence. So long as the Muslims remain a local sect without the official recognition of international Islam, the American Jew sees no reason to be concerned. Negro sects and cults abound, and while they are often given to much sound and fury, they have seldom been a real threat to any other minority. On the other hand, the American Jews are not unaware of the pressures of international Islam on the national state of Israel, nor of the attempts of some segments of international Islam to enlist anti-Jewish support wherever it may be found.

At least one United States Senator has seen enough evidence of anti-Semitism in the Black Muslim movement to warrant bringing the organization to the attention of Congress. Senator Kenneth B. Keating of New York, a Presbyterian, deplored this "anti-Jewish propaganda":

A very disturbing development has been the emergence of a new hate group in the United States which call themselves "Moslems." [Their] leader preaches a cult of racism for Negroes and extreme anti-Semitism.[44]

Surprisingly, Mr. Keating saw the Muslims as reflecting "a new trend in Moscow," rather than domestic competitions or the machinations of international Islam. He emphasized that "the name adopted by the fanatical organization" insulted the members of the Moslem faith; and he was careful to point out that orthodox Moslems have "absolutely no relationship to this group," whereas "it obviously serves the Communist interests to promote dissensions among Negroes in this country and to incite hatred against Americans of Jewish faith."

III. THE AMERICAN ISLAMIC COMMUNITY

The Black Muslims are almost unanimously rejected by the orthodox Moslem groups in America. Race is probably not a major factor in this rejection: there is a marked clannishness among American Moslems of European descent, but some of the earliest Moslem converts in America were Negro followers of Soufi Abdul-Hamid, an American Negro who embraced Islam during his travels in Asia,[45] and Negro Moslems remain scattered about the country in small numbers. The rejection is based, rather, on Muhammad's extreme racial views, his emphatic militancy and his unhistoric teachings about the Black Nation. American Moslems do not wish to be identified with such doctrines.

The Black Muslims, in return, assert that whatever the white man touches, he taints. Just as the so-called Negroes, in their attempts to appropriate the white man's culture, have been corrupted by its disvalues, so the American Moslems have suffered the corrosive influences of white, Western Christianity. In their yearning to gain the white man's approval, they sometimes behave suspiciously like the blue-eyed devils themselves. "No Muslim will reject another Muslim," Malcolm X argues, "except where the devils have made him forget who he is." The American Moslems who join the white man in denouncing the Black Muslims are little better than the so-called Negroes who have been "Tom-ing" for generations. When they finally see the Movement through their own *Muslim* eyes, rather than through the distorted lenses of the white Christians, they will rally to Muhammad and recognize him as the true Messenger of Allah Himself.

The Federation of Islamic Associations is the official Moslem organization in the United States and Canada. However,

. . . the Negro society in Chicago led by Elijah Muhammad is not affiliated and it is not recognized as truly Moslem. Although he conducts the largest Arabic school in the United States, and claims to use the Qur'an as the basis for his teachings, the Federation officers . . . have remained suspicious of him.[46]

Some Moslem leaders, such as Jamil Diab of Chicago, have issued statements dissociating themselves and their followers from the Black Muslims. Diab denounced the Muslims as "a cult totally lacking in the requisites which constitute any Moslem Group." He asserted that they have "penetrated into the Afro-American society . . . [where] they propagate their views in the name of Islam. They start controversies everywhere . . . [and carry on] propaganda in an aggressive manner." Because of them, "an insidious stigma" has become attached to *all* Islamic societies in America.

Muhammad smiles mysteriously when Shaikh Diab's criticisms are laid before him, for it is rumored that the Shaikh (who is a Palestinian Arab) was once a close adviser to the Messenger and that he taught Arabic for several years at the University of Islam in Chicago. Muhammad and Diab are said to have split over questions of ritual. The Shaikh apparently sought to form the Muslims into an orthodox Moslem organization, but practically none of the rank and file followed his lead.

Another challenger to Muhammad's religious authenticity and to his leadership of Americans in the Islamic movement is Talib Ahmad Dawud, bearded leader of the Muslim Brotherhood, USA. Dawud, who was converted by Gulam Yaslum, an Ahmadiyya missionary from India, has described Muhammad as "plain Elijah Poole of Sandersville, Georgia," and "no Muslim." In an abortive bid for the Black Muslim leadership, Dawud lent his name to a series of articles in a Chicago newspaper aimed at exposing Muhammad and discrediting him with his followers. Mr. Dawud, who had just returned from his pilgrimage to Mecca, based his arguments against Muhammad's authenticity primarily upon an assertion that the Hajj Committee, which rules on the acceptability of Moslem pilgrims, would not admit the self-styled Messenger to the Holy City. Muhammad was, in fact, received in Mecca a few weeks later, and Dawud was badly trounced.

Actually, it never seemed likely that the Imam would make any serious inroads on the Black Muslim membership. His own brotherhood has only a few hundred members, many of whom are popular entertainers or musicians—Dawud's wife is jazz singer Dakota Staton—and they seem to have none of the fanatical devotion to their leader that the Muslims show for Muhammad. Nor does Dawud enjoy unqualified recognition as a leader in the American Moslem community.

Most of the authentic Moslem groups in this country have stood back from the fray, and their aloofness has strengthened rather than weakened the strategy of the Black Muslim leaders. Left to his own devices, Muhammad is able to exert a kind of papal absolutism in the direction and development of his Movement. At the same time, he has been able to cultivate the good will and respect of a significant corps of informal representatives of Afro-Asian Islam. His temples are often visited by Moslem students studying in America, some of whom address his followers or participate in the temple affairs.

In Harlem, an organization called Asian-African Drums serves as an important liaison between the Black Muslims and various Moslem nationals from Asia and Africa, particularly Arab nationals. The Muslims do no proselytizing at the Drums meetings, which are kept on the level of friendly contact. The Drums organization is headed by Abdul Basit Naeem, a Pakistani Moslem, who has served as Muhammad's chief apologist and interpreter to the world of orthodox Islam. To Mr. Naeem, Muhammad is "the humblest of all important black men alive . . . extremely gentle, very courteous and kind . . . [and] the core of Mr. Elijah Muhammad's teachings is, of course, the faith of Islam. . . .

The book of Mr. Elijah Muhammad is the book of ALL Muslims,
known as the Holy Qur'an." Further, "his work and teachings are
not entirely unknown to other Moslems . . . including the beloved
president of the United Arab Republic, Gamal Abdel Nasser."[47]

Mr. Naeem, an ardent supporter of the Movement, is a
Pakistani journalist and lecturer with twelve years' residence in
the United States. He is a graduate of a Midwestern university
and the publisher of a Moslem magazine called *The Moslem
World and the U.S.A.*

Not all the contacts with extranational Moslems in America
have been through Black Muslim-sponsored organizations. The
Black Muslims have participated in various Moslem affairs held
on the campuses of some American universities, such as the
celebration of Pakistan Independence Day at the University of
Southern California in 1958,[48] and they have been represented
at conferences concerned with the interests of various Moslem
states. At one such conference, held in Hollywood in 1958 and
sponsored by Dr. Mohammad T. Mehdi of the Arab Information
Center in San Francisco, Malcolm X boldly demanded attention
for the Black Muslims as a potential power in the sphere of international politics. "The Arabs, as a colored people," he said,
"should and must make more effort to reach the millions of colored people in America who are related to the Arabs by blood.
These millions of colored peoples would be completely in sympathy with the Arab cause!"[49]

IV. THE WHITE COMMUNITY

One might expect—from the Muslims' diatribes against the
white man and from their commitment to retaliation—that there
would be constant open conflict between the Muslims and the
white community. But few open battles have been joined thus
far. The Black Muslims do not pretend to love the white man,
but they avoid overt antagonism. They shun the white community
entirely, except for requisites of work or business, and they do
not seek the white man's social acceptance. Muslim women particularly are forbidden contact with either sex of the white race,
on the theory that "no white man has honorable intentions toward

any black woman" and that white women are "immoral by nature." The white women are said to corrupt the minds of the black women, who then try to imitate them by "displaying their bodies, neglecting their children and abandoning their men."

In his communication with the white man, the Muslim tends to be both polite and direct, a technique which helps to avoid tension and misunderstanding. Speaking to a white group, Malcolm X declared:

I don't want you to think I'm being disrespectful to you as white people. I am being frank, and I think a frank statement will give you a better insight into the mind of the Black Man than statements you get from people who call themselves "Negroes," and who usually tell you what they want you to hear . . . [in the interest of creating] a better possibility of getting some of the crumbs you may let fall from your table. Well, I am not looking for crumbs, so I am not trying to disillusion you. . . . Diplomacy fools people. Diplomacy misleads people. It is better to be frank. . . .[50]

The white community is constantly assured that the Muslims are not anti-white simply "because they tell you what they think, nor anti-American because they say that America made our fathers slaves and refuses to give us civil rights." Malcolm assures the white man that "you can go anywhere among us and receive more courtesy and real respect than you can among the so-called Negro leaders who lick your hand for crumbs." But the white man must wake up, for "the Negro you used to know is dead."

According to Malcolm X, much of the white man's ignorance of the Black Man's true nature results from his habit of picking Negro leaders who, "since their jobs depend upon his pleasure, only report to him what will make him happy. But these leaders don't have things under control. And they can't control this generation with anything less than freedom and justice." The white man's educational system also contributes to his unrealistic view of things.

The educational system . . . is designed to make you think you are God. . . . There is no one else like you and everyone else is below you. . . . You can't blame the American [man in the street] for looking down on the Black Man when every day he is brainwashed by the movies, the television, radio and the newspapers. . . . He is taught in school that he is the best, and that anyone not as white as you cannot be on your level.[51]

The white man is urged to treat the Negro with respect and to provide an opportunity for him to learn "something about himself." Only then can there be any hope of peace between the races. When the Negro learns the truth about himself, he will not seek integration with the white man; he will be proud to associate with his own kind. When this happens, the white man will no longer have to worry about the Negro becoming his "brother-in-law," and each race will respect the other for wanting to maintain racial purity. As things are now, the Negro has not been educated: he has been trained.

He is like a dog—a watchdog. You don't give him credit for intelligence, you give him credit for being well-trained. You sic him on the Japanese and tell him to bite them, and he will run out and bite the Japanese. You tell him to bite, and he will bite the Germans, the Koreans. He will bite anyone you say bite. Now you don't give him any credit for having done a good job. You give yourself credit for having trained him so well. Now when he comes back from biting the Germans and the Japanese, you can hang his mother on a tree and have his wife before his eyes and he will stand there whimpering with his knees knocking and his tail between his legs. Why? Because he's waiting for you to say "sic 'em!" That's what he's been trained to do.[52]

The white men in America are like diners at a banquet table. The Negro is there, too, but the white men pass the dishes back and forth in front of him without ever letting him be served. The Negro is not a diner; he is simply at the table looking on. The white men think he should be satisfied with being present: "To be in the presence of so many fine people who are enjoying themselves at such a sumptuous feast—you'd think he would be grateful." But the Negro has got knots in his stomach because he is hungry; and since he helped to kill the game, he thinks it's his right to eat. Now.

In the same way, the white man tries to pacify the Negro by telling him that he is a citizen. But the Negro is waking up to that. He has learned that he is a full-fledged citizen in wartime and at taxtime, but at no other time.

They tell us that we are all citizens, that we were born in this country. Well, a cat can have kittens in an oven but that doesn't make them biscuits! The Black Man in America can never be called an American until he is enjoying what America is offering to everybody else. . . . Twenty million black people here in America today are called "second-class" citizens. We don't accept that. You are either a citizen or you are not a citizen. No country has citizenship by degrees.[53]

In the summer of 1960, Muhammad broke precedent and allowed whites to attend some of his public rallies. Until then, no whites had been admitted to any group addressed by the Messenger; and whites are still barred from the temples themselves. The sudden change in policy was partly inspired by criticism which likened the "crepe-black" Muslim organization to the "lily-white" white citizens councils. But it was equally inspired by Muhammad's certainty of mass support from the Negroes of Chicago and Harlem, and his desire to demonstrate his strength to any whites who cared to come.

In Harlem, where one of the "open" rallies was held, Malcolm X announced that "because of the grave race crisis that faces the Western world [and] to which white America is trying to blind itself, these white people need someone to tell them what time it is." In the audience of seven thousand people was a sprinkling of whites, scattered throughout the hall. Some of these whites joined in the Muslim prayers, facing east with their palms upraised, and some even applauded parts of Muhammad's address. Most, however, simply sat and took notes or stared in unbelief.

While the white man in the street has not commented, the Movement has often excited his attention. On learning of its existence (but almost never with any detailed knowledge), some individuals and groups have regarded it with a degree of approval. A white woman in Boston applauded Malcolm X's extended interview on radio station WMEX and opined that "this Movement will do more for the Negro and the whole country than anything the Negroes have tried so far." A well-known Texas millionaire, perhaps not unsympathetic to Muhammad's advocacy of racial separation, is alleged to have shown his approval of the Movement by an outright gift of several thousand dollars. But most white people who learn of the Movement tend to consider it a preternaturally extreme and dangerous social aberration. They are anxious to be reassured that it "has reached its peak" and that "most Negroes do not really feel like that."

The Movement has caught the attention of researchers in colleges and universities across the country. Professors and graduate students in such widely separated schools as Harvard, Radcliffe, Union Theological Seminary and the Universities of Chicago, Missouri and Michigan are now studying the Black Muslims. Law enforcement agencies and their libraries in many cities across the country are amassing data on the Movement.

The tendency in the white-controlled mass media until very recent times was to ignore the Movement, but its importance in the current racial crisis has warmed the microphones and loosened the typewriter keys. Apparently these media now feel that the people have a right to know about the Muslims, who are undoubtedly the fastest-growing movement in the country and potentially one of the most dangerous. Since 1959, extensive coverage has been given the Muslims in *Time, The New York Times, The Christian Science Monitor, Reader's Digest, The Reporter, U. S. News and World Report, Chicago's American, Providence Bulletin, The Denver Post, Chicago Sun-Times, Springfield* (Massachusetts) *Daily News, Columbus* (Ohio) *Dispatch, New York Post, The Detroit Free Press, The Boston Herald, The Minneapolis Tribune, The Boston Globe* and many other newspapers and periodicals.

What do they say, the writers in these "white" media, which mold opinion for millions of Americans? What is their image of the Black Muslims? Most of the news stories are essentially descriptive; almost all turn hopefully to the established Negro leadership for interpretation of the Movement. However, some eidtorial comment has appeared.

Time refers to Elijah Muhammad as a "scowling, incendiary speaker . . . pouring out his scorn upon all 'white devils,' 'satisfied black men,' the 'poison' Bible, Christianity's 'slavemaster doctrine,' and America's 'white for white' justice." *Time* considers Muhammad to be a "purveyor of . . . cold black hatred . . . calmly feeding the rankling frustration of urban Negroes." The Muslim leader is held to be "well beyond the run-of-the-street crackpot Negro nationalist groups . . . [and] of rising concern to respectable Negro civic leaders, to the [NAACP], to police departments in half a dozen cities, and to the FBI."[54]

The Christian Science Monitor is more positive in its views. While finding that "Mr. Muhammad's counsel is not entirely free of animosity," it suggests that out of Muhammad's guidance "appears to have come an environment which . . . has made possible a degree of middle-class respectability for many Negroes whose lives before had been crude at best." Yet the *Monitor* recognizes the Black Muslims as "one of the most controversial and curious organizations of Negroes"[55] and generously estimates that the Movement has gathered "some 200,000 of the 20,000,000 non-whites into its fold in the last three years."[56]

"It was inevitable," says *The Denver Post* "that some Negroes would prove unable to keep their heads as the struggle [over racial discrimination] continued." And it warns that "the excesses of a Negro hate group can poison the whole integration movement in the United States and jeopardize the progress that has already been made."[57] *The Providence Bulletin* observes that "thousands of Negroes are turning their backs on Christianity and embracing a highly nationalistic religion that takes Islam for its spiritual basis." The *Bulletin* believes that "the Movement has weight" and that "Muhammad cannot be laughed at as Father Divine has been. . . . The Black Muslim Movement is a force to take seriously, . . . [for] the Messenger isn't just a-whistling 'Dixie.' "[58]

In Boston, the *Herald* deplores Muhammad's "black supremacy" doctrines and declares them to be "as disgraceful and inflammatory as those of the Ku Klux Klan." It points out that "on a Harlem street corner where a member of the Temple harangues a group it is wise for a white man to pass by quickly"— a circumstance which is, "of course, deplored by the best Negro civic leaders."[59] *The Detroit Free Press* asks "Is the [Muslim] cult dangerous?" and then assures its readers that "Detroit police keep an eye on it. State Police routinely pick up lists of students attending the University of Islam. The FBI watches."[60]

On September 3, 1959, Bill Stout of CBS-TV in Los Angeles reported that "the Negro group called Moslems, a religious sect dedicated to black supremacy and the destruction of the white race," had mushroomed from 300 members to "more than 3,000" in Los Angeles in six months. He quoted "a Los Angeles leader of the Moslem group [as saying] at a recent meeting, 'No torture of the whites—just annihilation.' " The TV newscaster called the Los Angeles temple "the biggest in the country," and he marveled that there had been "no public notice of the Moslem sect in this area." What Mr. Stout probably did not know is that in Los Angeles, as in many other cities, there is (or was) a tacit agreement between law enforcement officials and the major news media to bar publicity about the Movement. Without the aid of the press, it was hoped, the movement would soon wither.

That hope persists, and *The Reporter* magazine finds it "difficult to see how a militant movement like the Temples of Islam can attract a wide following." It quotes with apparent finality the sentiments of a Negro integration leader who told that magazine "I don't think they'll get much stronger," but who then immediately asserted that "We [Negroes] have a right to our crackpots as you do to yours." *The Reporter* predicts that "Malcolm X may yet be an executive in the Urban League, but Elijah Muhammad is more likely to end as Marcus Garvey did—with little left but pictures of himself addressing huge crowds years before."[61] However, Pulitzer Prizewinner Harry Ashmore, writing in *The Boston Globe,* tempers his similar optimism. The Muslims, he feels, "are not themselves going anywhere. But as long as they are around and talking it is a reasonable assumption that the great mass of American Negro people are not going to be content to stand still."[62]

7 Tensions: Inside the Movement

For the time being, the Black Muslims are presenting a monolithic face to the outside world. They are on the upswing, rapidly gaining membership and power and their resultant excitement and self-confidence breed a natural sense of unity. They feel beset by a powerful enemy—a supposed threat which impels them to minimize internal conflicts and pull together. And they are genuinely unified in their dedication to Elijah Muhammad, the Messenger, whose force of personality overrides any divisive tensions.

Yet some tensions are already perceptible within the Movement, and these seem likely to increase with time. There are problems both of definition and of control. As the Movement solidifies, it will have to make more and more explicit its relationship to both the white American and the international Islamic worlds. For the moment, the Muslim leaders are purposefully vague on these points. When they must declare themselves, the present quiet disagreements within the leadership will most likely become sharp and bitter factionalism. And as the Movement grows in size and influence, it will become more and more a tempting prize for those who covet power. Rivalries within the leadership already exist, as well as a latent reliance on force. These rivalries may erupt quickly when Muhammad dies.

The future of the Movement—and of the world on which it has an impact—will be greatly affected by these internal tensions. They are, of course, extremely difficult to pin down precisely; they are the Movement's best-guarded secrets. But a certain amount of information is available, and from this a broad outline of the internal tensions can be fairly accurately sketched.

179

I. THE CONCENTRATION OF POWER

The Long Road from Sandersville

"And after these things I saw another angel come down from heaven, having great power; and the earth was lightened with his glory. And he cried mightily with a strong voice, saying, Babylon the great is fallen, is fallen, and is become the habitation of devils, and the hold of every foul spirit. . . ."

The Supreme Wisdom, sacred text of the Black Muslim Movement, teaches that this angel having great power (mentioned in the eighteenth chapter of Revelation) was "no other than Master W. F. Fard Muhammad, the Great Mahdi." The Mahdi came for the express purpose of enlightening the so-called Negroes and pronouncing judgment on the white devils, who had enslaved the Black Nation and still hold them in "mental slavery." The Great Mahdi "announced the immediate doom of America," for "America committed suicide when she brought the so-called Negroes into slavery." He urged all Black Men to resume their true religion, Islam, and their true identity. Each Black Man who took this momentous step he blessed with a holy name of Allah's —on written application and for a ten-dollar fee. This name was the applicant's "true name," concealed from him by the Slave-masters and restored through Fard's divine knowledge. The restoration of this true name at once identified the Muslim with the Black Nation and provided him with an Afro-Asian history. "The name," the Muslims say, "is everything."

Among those blessed by the Mahdi during his sojourn in the Wilderness of North America was the son of a Georgia preacher for whom the devil-ridden city of Detroit had proved to be less than the Promised Land. This convert's "slave name" had been Elijah Poole; the Great Mahdi rechristened him Elijah Karriem and later, to show his increasing favor, Elijah Muhammad.

Poole (who has also been known as Gulam Bogans, Muhammad Rassouli, Elijah Muck Muhd and various other aliases) was born in Sandersville, Georgia, a rural hamlet[1] midway between Macon and Augusta, on October 7, 1897. He is one of thirteen

children born to Wali and Marie Poole. His father was a Baptist
preacher—a fact which is doubtless reflected in Elijah's charismatic gifts—and both parents had been slaves of a white family
of the same surname. Elijah completed the fourth grade. At sixteen he left home. Ten years later, in 1923, he and his wife
Clara (Evans), with their two children, moved to Detroit. Poole
had heard rhapsodic praise of the city from Negroes of his own
home town who had moved there after the end of World War I,
but the rhapsodies turned out to have been exaggerated. He
worked in factories, holding several different jobs, until the
Depression set in late in 1929. A year or so later he came under
the spell of Fard, who, he recalls gratefully, took him "out of
the gutter in the streets of Detroit and in three and a half years
taught [him] the knowledge of Islam."

From the start, Muhammad's relationship with Fard seems
to have been a close one. One old-timer remembers Muhammad
as "doing errands for the Prophet" (as Fard himself was then
known) and helping him "put out some kind of paper." In 1932,
Muhammad established the Southside Mosque—later called Temple No. 2—in Chicago and apparently ran it for some time. The
following year, when Fard was trying to elude the police, he
sought refuge with Muhammad in Chicago. A Detroit Muslim
had been convicted in 1932 of a sacrificial killing of one of his
"brothers."[2] Thereupon, says Muhammad:

He [Fard] was persecuted, sent to jail in 1932, and ordered out of
Detroit, Michigan, May 26, 1933. He came to Chicago in the same
year, [was] arrested almost immediately and placed behind prison
bars. He submitted himself with all humility to his persecutors. Each
time he was arrested he sent for me that I may see and learn the
price of truth for us (the so-called Negroes).[3]

Muhammad's willingness to conceal Fard and brave the law for
his sake must have cemented their mutual trust and respect.
Muhammad soon became Fard's chief minister and gradually took
over the leadership of the Detroit temple. Before long, he was
charged by Fard with full administrative responsibility for the
Movement and was being groomed as Fard's successor.

Not all of the Black Nation in Detroit took kindly to Muhammad's favored position with the Mahdi. Some of his antag-

onists rejected his second rechristening (from Elijah Karriem to Elijah Muhammad). When Fard disappeared in June 1934, with Muhammad as his logical successor, they immediately spread rumors that Muhammad had induced Fard to offer himself as a human sacrifice. Fard was still considered a prophet, not an incarnation of Allah and it was a common belief among his followers that a Muslim who immolated himself could become "Savior of the world." The rumors were never substantiated, of course, and they do not square with anything that is known about the relationship between the two men. Still, it is interesting to note that Fard is honored by Muslims everywhere as the "Savior" and is celebrated as such every year on his birthday, February 26.

Whatever its merits, this unsparing hostility to Muhammad split the Movement into factions. After Fard's disappearance, Muhammad withdrew to Chicago and designated Temple No. 2 as the new headquarters of the Movement. His faction became known as the "Temple People" and their meeting places as "Muhammad's Temples of Islam." Fard was deified and was thenceforth referred to as Allah; Muhammad took upon himself the mantle of Prophet and presented himself as the sole Messenger of Allah. Human sacrifice was never again mentioned as a Muslim doctrine. But the most important change was an expansion of the horizon of ambition: Muhammad was determined to bring into the light of the divine knowledge every Black Man in America.

As his chief minister—a post roughly analogous to the one he had held under Fard—Muhammad appointed a Haitian, Theodore Rozier, who had never known Fard. The dissident factions repudiated Rozier on the ground that he "never saw the Savior" and that his "second-hand revelation" was not sufficient qualification for the role. Their real objection, however, seems to have been to Muhammad's audacity, for he was already beginning to identify himself as the only channel through which Fard's "truth" could be brought to the sleeping Black Nation. In any case, Rozier was not a successful proselytizer; he could not capture the imagination of the people. Muhammad gradually won back most of the dissidents—his own brother, Wilfred X, is now minister of the Detroit temple—but the Movement made only small inroads on the Negro community. Not until the late 1940s, when "the Big X" became the right hand of the Messenger, did the Movement begin to catch fire.

Muhammad's association with Fard, "the Supreme Being among all Black Men," invests him with a status and power that have never been successfully challenged. The Muslim lay brother often expresses the wish, gravely and wistfully, that he might have seen Allah (that is, Fard), much as the devout Christian wishes he might have known Jesus when he was on earth. But Muhammad proclaims in *The Supreme Wisdom:* "I know Allah, and I am with him." And in Chicago he informed some ten thousand followers and curiosity seekers:

I am not trembling. I am the man, I am the Messenger. . . . I came directly from God. I am guided by God. I am in communication with God, and I know God. If God is not with me . . . protecting me, how can I come and say things no other man has said and get away with it?[4]

The Messenger assures his listeners that the world will soon know who sent him, and he admonishes the Negro Christians that "God is here in person; so stop looking for a dead Jesus and pray to HIM . . . who is ALIVE and not a spook."[5]

Muhammad is known not only as "Messenger" and "Prophet" but also as "Spiritual Head of the Muslims in the West," "Divine Leader" and "The Reformer." His ministers most often refer to him as "The Honorable Elijah Muhammad" or as "The Messenger of Allah to the Lost-Found Nation of Islam in the Wilderness of North America." Occasionally the less formal reference "Brother Elijah Muhammad" is used.

Muhammad is a slight, brown, quickly energetic man of about sixty-three. He often works an eighteen-hour day, pausing for his one daily meal at six in the evening. In his private life he is calm and temperate—a sharp contrast to his writings and to the fanatical intensity he inspires in the tens of thousands who call him the Messenger. His face is rather lean and angular, although his receding hairline broadens his forehead in a suggestion of strength and intelligence. His lips are thin; his eyes quick and penetrating. He has no features that are pronouncedly within the Negro stereotype. One recent writer has described him as "a slight man with a zealot's intense solemnity . . . [and] a quick, intuitive intelligence."[6] He lives on Chicago's South Side and has an unusually large family, six sons and a daughter.

For the most part, Muhammad speaks, writes and directs the activities of his burgeoning movement from his Chicago headquarters, Muhammad's Temple of Islam No. 2. Administrative policy has been set chiefly through written directives and conferences in Chicago and enforced through a few lieutenants of demonstrated loyalty. But as the Movement has gathered momentum, the Messenger himself has had to travel more and more. The response his presence evokes in the black masses is phenomenal, especially in the light of his barely literate oral delivery. Wherever he has gone, his visits have been followed by spurts in the temple membership.

The announcement that the Messenger is to visit a particular temple is a signal for feverish activity on the part of the members. Cleanliness, always emphasized in the teachings at the temple, is given additional stress. In the Muslim homes, the best furnishings and utensils are brought from under wraps and put on display. The Muslim restaurants and other businesses are given new coats of paint, and pictures of the Messenger are prominently displayed. All this despite the fact that Muhammad rarely sees the results. He almost always remains in seclusion at his hotel or in the home of the host minister until it is time for his address, and he seldom misses the first flight available after his public appearance.

Several days before the Messenger is scheduled to arrive, members of the FOI security corps cover every inch of the route he is to travel from the airport to the temple. On the day of his arrival, Muslim guards are posted at strategic points along his route several hours in advance. Each guard is briefed as to precisely what he should do in the event of an emergency. The penalty for carelessness or error is severe.

The Messenger always travels with a personal security force, comprised of three or four members of the FOI from Temple No. 2. This guard is often headed by Supreme Captain Raymond Sharrieff in person. When Muhammad deplanes, he is always preceded and covered from behind by this personal guard. As soon as he is on the ground, the local security force takes over. The Messenger is immediately surrounded by a force of from twelve to twenty men, and other Muslims are scattered "inconspicuously" among the crowds at the airport. An additional force in several automobiles takes over as he leaves the airport, some preceding and others following the car in which the Messenger is riding. The FOI captain of the local temple, riding in one of the lead cars, exchanges signals with individual guards previously stationed along the way. Should the guard not return the proper signal, the entire force is put on "emergency alert" and an alternate route is chosen.

Muhammad's arrival at the temple or auditorium causes much excitement. The crowds usually begin arriving two or three hours in advance. By the time Muhammad arrives, those who can be accommodated in the hall have been searched and seated— men to the right, women to the left. The Muslim women march in as a separate group and occupy a section of the hall reserved for them. They are dressed in flowing white gowns and shawls, and wear no makeup. Scores of Muslim brothers are on security duty inside the building—at the doors and in the restrooms and hallways. The hall will have been thoroughly searched at least twice before the public is admitted, and roving patrols are constantly on the lookout for trouble. As many as a hundred men may be assigned the task of securing the inside of the building and searching each member of the audience.

Outside, Muslims are on constant patrol on foot or in cars, ranging several blocks around the area. In a meeting held in Atlanta in September 1960, the FOI even placed a patrol on the roof of the Magnolia Ballroom, where the Prophet was to speak. In Boston, a few months earlier, the FOI set up a counterwatch on what they took to be "agents" watching them from an office building across the street from the John Hancock Hall, where Muhammad was speaking.

When the Messenger finally arrives outside the hall, an Honor Guard escorts him along the sidewalk down a double row of Muslims and so into the building. (At a meeting held in the Uline Arena in Washington, D. C., in the summer of 1959, Muhammad marched from his car down an aisle of eight hundred

Black Muslims, standing shoulder to shoulder all the way from the street to the rostrum.) As he enters the hall and comes before his audience, there is a quiet stir, an excitement compounded of awe, pride and reverence. This decorous intensity of response is maintained throughout his speech, punctuated only by the usual affirmations: "That's right! That's right!" But the Messenger's charismatic presence seems to cause a vibrancy in the air—a vibrancy that lingers long after he has finished his speech and departed, quickly and quietly, from the hall.

In the informality of his home, Muhammad conveys the impression of an almost wistful gentility and kindness, and the visitor is immediately impressed by his deep feeling of responsibility for "his people." He is peculiarly sensitive to attacks by Negro leadership and is perplexed that "the educated ones who should know more than the rest of us cannot see the truth of what I am teaching." He attempts to avoid controversy with other Negro leaders, believing that eventually all will recognize that "the salvation of the so-called Negro in this country depends upon the unity of all Black Men" and that this unity can come only when Negroes are willing to "see the white man for what he is" and reject him.

Muhammad has a personal antipathy toward white domination that borders on the pathological, and it is almost exclusively in this reference that his passions are likely to escape restraint. Yet he denies teaching hatred.

They say that I am a preacher of racial hatred, but the fact is that the white people don't like the truth, especially if it speaks *against* them. . . . It is a terrible thing for such people . . . to charge me with teaching race hatred when their feet are on my people's neck and they tell us to our face that they hate the black people. . . . Remember now, they even teach you that you must not hate them for hating you.[7]

Muhammad enjoins his followers never to initiate violence but to retaliate if they are attacked. He ridicules the whites for demanding that Black Men turn the other cheek, when they themselves will kill even without provocation.

It is against the law of nature. The Christian government of America can't do it. The Pope of Rome can't do it. If you and I don't wake up to that knowledge and execute the law of an eye for an eye, we might as well be dead and forgotten.[8]

The white man's greatest fear, Muhammad believes, is that the Black Man will know the truth about him and will unite against him. As a result, the white community slanders the Muslims and treats them like criminals. The white men "claim the truth to be subversive and hate-teaching. . . . They tap our telephones, eavesdrop and follow us around . . . use tape-recording machines [and] the hypocrites and stool pigeons among us to keep up to date on what we say and do. They are even bold enough to ask [our own] relatives to help them do [us] evil!"[9] This accusation is only slightly if at all exaggerated. The FBI and local police *do* keep Muhammad and his Movement under close scrutiny, from outside and probably also from within.

Muhammad seems to live comfortably in this atmosphere of hostility and counter-hostility, but he is rarely without an awareness of danger. He observes characteristically:

I have it from the mouth of God that the enemy had better try to protect my life and see that I continue to live. Because if anything happens to me, I will be the last one that they murder. And if any of my followers are harmed, ten of the enemy's best ones will be killed.[10]

The Messenger has already tangled twice with the law—and lost. In 1934, when he refused to transfer his child from a University of Islam to a public school, he was found guilty of contributing to the delinquency of a minor and was placed on six months' probation. In 1942 he was arrested by federal authorities in Chicago and this time was obliged to serve time in prison. In a story headlined "12 Negro Chiefs Seized by FBI in Sedition Raid," the *Chicago Tribune* gave the following account:

Arrest of more than 80 Negroes, members and leaders of three organizations, on charges of sedition, conspiracy, and violation of the draft laws was announced by the Federal Bureau of Investigation here.

Twelve of those arrested are considered leaders in the groups. They were charged with . . . conspiracy to promote the success of the enemy, making false statements to those about to be inducted into the armed forces, [and] disrupting morale and causing mutiny.

. . . The three organizations are known as "The Peace Movement of Ethiopia," . . . "The Brotherhood of Liberty for Black People of America," and an organization known as "The Temple of Islam." . . . Elijah Poole, who calls himself Elijah Muhammad, was [among those] arrested. . . . Elijah is also known as Elijah Muck Muhd, and is known as "The Prophet."[11]

Arrested with Muhammad was Lenzie Karien, identified as one of the Ministers of Islam. Both Muhammad and Karien admitted sympathy for Japan, but Chicago FBI Chief Johnson said "no definite connection had been found by his men between Negro organizations and Japanese activity in this country."[12] Nonetheless, indictments were drawn on the ground that the three organizations were "alleged to have taught Negroes that their interests were in a Japanese victory, and that they were racially akin to the Japanese. . . . J. Albert Woll, U. S. District Attorney, . . . said the defendants made statements 'as vicious as any ever uncovered by a grand jury.' "[13] For these "vicious" statements, Muhammad went to federal prison at Milan, Michigan, until 1946. He apparently was able to direct the Movement even while in jail, for it gained strength during those years.

After his release, Muhammad repeated and elaborated on the sentiments that had brought him to jail. He taught that the white man is—and has been since his creation—the oppressor of all who are not white; and he asserted that all who are not white are, by the white man's own social definition, black. Consequently, he reasoned, it made little sense for Negroes in this country to fight against the Japanese, who are equally victims of the white man's hatred and color prejudice. World War II was not a battle in which the American Negro ought to have been forced to participate. The Black Man's war is "the Battle of Armageddon," which will be fought "in the wilderness of North America." It is, in Muhammad's words, "a battle for freedom, justice and equality —to success or to the death."

Muhammad is ostensibly not troubled about what direction the Movement will take when he returns to Allah, or about who will succeed him. "Allah will see that the work is carried on," he insists with conviction. Yet Muhammad, more than anyone else, must recall the schisms that rent the Movement after Fard disappeared in 1934, and it would be hazardous to take his apparent naivete at face value. He must sense, as many observers do, that the struggle for succession is already on and that the image of the united front that the Black Nation has labored so hard to build will once again be fractured when the Messenger's voice is heard no more. It will be interesting to see who, if anyone, will be able to pick up the pieces and fit them together again.

Malcolm X: First Plenipotentiary

No one man could carry alone Muhammad's immense burden of responsibility. In directing the complex affairs of the rapidly growing Black Nation—coordinating its program, managing its economic enterprises, founding new temples, and so on—he relies heavily on the closely knit inner circle of Muslim leaders. Foremost of these is his chief aide, Minister Malcolm X Shabazz, minister of the powerful Temple No. 7 in Harlem and one of the few ministers granted an "original" (that is, an Arabic) surname.[14] One recent observer has described Malcolm as "the best thing that ever happened to Muhammad."[15]

Malcolm is an indefatigable organizer and speaker. Whereas Muhammad speaks almost exclusively to the black masses, Malcolm frequently appears at colleges and universities, and he is a popular radio and television discussant. He also visits temples in every part of the country with the regular frequency of a salesman. He organizes new temples, pumps spirit and encouragement into the missions or newly founded cell groups, conducts rallies and fund-raising campaigns and serves as Muhammad's general trouble-shooter and spokesman.

The New York minister is a tall, powerfully built, light-skinned Negro. Much of his youth was spent on the streets of Harlem as "Big Red"—a nickname he earned during a career of petty hoodlumism, which he blandly attributes to his early training as a Christian and to the white man's habit of making it difficult for the so-called Negro to earn a decent living in a respectable way.

Like Muhammad, Malcolm has had his difficulties with the police, though for different reasons. He explains with great bitterness that, since his delinquency as a youth was caused by social conditions for which the white man is responsible, the white man should thank him for trying to change those conditions now. While in prison, he was attracted to the daring "disclosures" in Muhammad's teachings, became a Muslim and turned back from his criminal career. Malcolm credits his rehabilitation entirely to the "knowledge of self"—and its corollary, "the truth about the white man"—as taught him by Elijah Muhammad.

All I have learned has been from the Islamic influence of Mr. Muhammad. . . . I am what you would call an ex-convict. I am not ashamed of this because it was all done when I was a part of the white man's Christian world. As a Muslim, I would never have done these awful things that caused me to go to prison.[16]

Malcolm X was born Malcolm Little in Omaha, Nebraska, about 1925. He was one of eleven children and, like his acknowledged master, the son of a Baptist minister. While he was very young, the family moved to Lansing, Michigan, where the father —Malcolm calls him "a race man" and "a little too outspoken for Lansing"—soon incurred the hostility of the whites. When Malcolm was only six, the family home was burned by the Ku Klux Klan. "The firemen came and just sat there without making any effort to put one drop of water on the fire. The same fire that burned my father's home still burns my soul." But the worst was yet to come. "A typical Garveyite," the father "was making his first step toward economic independence by building his own store. At the time we were the only Negroes in the block." His initiative drew a swift reprisal—"my father was found with his head bashed and his body mangled under a streetcar." Malcolm is certain that this was a calculated murder.

The bitterness over his father's troubles with the white people of Lansing has never left Malcolm X. On the contrary, he seems to have nurtured and fed it, so that it now structures and orients most of his interpersonal and professional relations. "There is no white man a Muslim can trust." Yet, ironically, it was a white woman whose kindness Malcolm remembers most vividly.

After his father's death, the Little family fell upon evil days. His mother boiled dandelion greens every day to try to keep the children from starving to death. "We stayed dizzy and weak because we stayed hungry," Malcolm recalls. What he and his brothers could pilfer augmented the wild greens his mother picked along the roadsides. They fought desperately to remain together; but eventually the family broke up, and Malcolm was sent to an institution for boys. There, he recalls with a rare touch of tenderness, "when everybody else at that school was kicking me around, the housemother took up for me. She was good to me, and I followed her around like a puppy. I was a kind of mascot." Soon it was arranged for Malcolm to attend a nearby school. He was the only Negro at the school, and he stood first in his class often enough to incur resentment from teachers and pupils alike.

He was asked in the eighth grade what he wanted to become. He preferred law but was told that law was not a suitable profession for a Negro and that instead he should think of a trade such as carpentry.[17]

"This," said Malcolm, "was the turning point in my thinking." Eventually he left the school and moved East to what became a life of juvenile delinquency. "By his late teens, Malcolm was operating successfully on the fringes of the Harlem underworld."[18]

Admitted to the underworld's fringes, sixteen-year-old Malcolm absorbed all he heard and saw. He swiftly built up a reputation for honesty by turning over every dollar due his boss ("I have always been intensely loyal"). By the age of 18, Malcolm was versatile "Big Red." He hired from four to six men variously plying dope, numbers, bootleg whiskey and diverse forms of hustling. Malcolm personally squired well-heeled white thrill-seekers to Harlem sin dens, and Negroes to white sin downtown. "My best customers were preachers and social leaders, police and all kinds of big shots in the business of controlling other people's lives."[19]

Malcolm sometimes earned as much as $2,000 a month. He "paid off the law from a $1,000 roll from the pockets of his $200 suits." But eventually a less susceptible "law" caught up with him, and "Big Red" went to prison—not once, but several times.

In 1947, while in the maximum-security prison at Concord, Massachusetts, Malcolm was converted by one of his brothers who had become a member of the Detroit Temple. Since then, the Movement has claimed all his energies and all his loyalties. His personal loyalty to Muhammad, in particular, seems to be un-

shakable, despite his own popularity with Muslims across the
country and abroad. In 1959, for example, he visited several of
the Moslem states in the Middle East as Muhammad's emissary.
He was the guest of minor officials of several governments, but
refused the invitations of those of higher rank on the grounds that
such honors should be reserved for Muhammad himself. On the
other hand, Malcolm's impatience with some of the older ministers' "softness" towards the white man is seldom disguised.

The Big X is undeniably brilliant. His formal schooling
ended at the eighth grade, but experience has taught him since
then. He has more than held his own, in numerous radio and
television appearances, against men with far better formal educa-
tions. In the Massachusetts prison, the minister's son read "thousands of books because I wanted to know what made people the
way they are." He is clearly superior to Muhammad in intellect,
yet he credits Muhammad with "everything I know that's worthwhile." Whether he is addressing the masses on a Harlem street
corner, the Muslim faithful gathered in any one of the Messenger's
scattered temples or a university seminar, his important statements
are inevitably prefaced with "The Honorable Elijah Muhammad
teaches us. . . ." And there is pride and confidence in his voice.

The onetime hoodlum considers himself "completely reformed, for knowing the truth, I don't need the crutches I used to
think I had to have. When I was in the world of the Christians,
I behaved as they did; I did what the white man did because, like
everybody else, I thought this was the best thing possible to do."
His popularity in Harlem is such that in recent months he has
been mentioned as a possible candidate for Adam Clayton Powell's
seat in the United States Congress. To this suggestion Malcolm
replies: "Why should I oppose Powell? He is a Black Man.
There are plenty of devils up there whose seats we could use."

Near the Center

So far as is known, the Muslims do not have a rigid hier-
archical structure of administration. Muhammad is the "Messenger" by reason of having caught the mantle from Fard, founder
of the Movement. But apart from Muhammad, no one has an

inherent claim to any office. Malcolm serves as Muhammad's aide at the Messenger's pleasure; by the same token, Muhammad could summarily banish him to outer darkness. Presumably the same is true of Raymond Sharrieff, who is Muhammad's son-in-law and the Supreme Captain of the secret paramilitary organization, the Fruit of Islam. Sharrieff has long been a Muslim, but he is hardly known outside of the organization. Even the Muslims know little about him except that he is Muhammad's chief aide in managing the sect's commercial enterprises and overseeing the FOI. Some police authorities suggest that Sharrieff also collects tithes from delinquent members and, through a hand-picked corps of lieutenants, effectively silences any defectors from the Movement who may wish to cooperate with the police in exposing its secrets. The Muslims say only that Sharrieff "sees that the wishes of the Messenger are carried out."

Also near the power center of the Movement is Minister Louis X of the Boston Temple No. 11. He is closely associated with Malcolm X, having come into the Movement through Malcolm's New York Temple No. 7. Louis has produced and starred in his play *Orgena* in several of the major cities where the Muslims have temples; and in recent times he has appeared with Malcolm X as a principal speaker, on the same program with the Messenger himself. Like nearly all Muslim ministers, Louis seems indefatigable. On one occasion he returned home from a speaking engagement in New York to find that one of his five children was seriously ill. He took the child to the hospital and returned at once to his work. Asked how he could concentrate on his tasks without apparent concern, he explained, "Mr. Muhammad teaches us not to grieve over what we can do nothing about. I have prayed to Allah. If Allah takes my son, it is because Allah is wiser than I and he knows better than I whether he should continue to live. But whether or not my son lives, the Messenger's work must still be done." Louis (a former Episcopalian) and his wife (an ex-Catholic) have been Muslims for six years. He is in his late twenties, and his Boston temple is one of the fastest growing in the organization.

Of Muhammad's six sons, five are now close to the administrative center (though not necessarily to the power center) of the

Movement. Wallace D. Muhammad travels extensively in the interest of the Movement. Herbert is its public relations director, and Akbar is secretary of Temple No. 2. Elijah, Jr., is second in command of the FOI. Wallace D. is the minister of the Philadelphia temple; in 1960 he was sentenced to serve three years in prison for refusing to bear arms in the service of the United States, but was freed pending appeal.

Others near the center of the Movement are ministers Lucius X of Washington, D. C.; Isaiah Karriem of Baltimore; and one of Malcolm's brothers, Wilfred X of the Detroit Temple No. 1. (Another of the Big X's brothers, Philbert X, is minister of the temple in Lansing, Michigan.)

Lucius X was previously an elder in the Seventh Day Adventist Church and had the oversight of several churches of that denomination in the Chicago area. He went to Muhammad's temple to challenge the Muslim teachings and stayed on to become a member of the Black Nation of Islam. His experience in the Christian ministry undoubtedly makes him one of the better prepared leaders in the Movement. From Chicago, Lucius was sent to the strategic Temple No. 4 in Washington, where he recently built a $150,000 temple—the first new-from-the-ground-up mosque in the Movement. (All other temples meet in older buildings, such as churches and halls, which have been converted into mosques.) Lucius' neighbor, Isaiah Karriem, is now building a $60,000 community center adjoining his Baltimore temple "to get black children off the street."

Perhaps the most important woman in the sect is Lottie X of Chicago, who, as head of the Muslim Girls Training Class (MGT), is the counterpart of Raymond Sharrieff. Sisters Thelma X and Tynetta X write for various Muslim publications.

Trouble on the Horizon

Elijah Muhammad is a hale, energetic and mentally vigorous man, capable of sustaining a grueling workday under very nearly spartan self-discipline. He celebrated his sixty-third birthday in 1960 and seems likely to remain in firm control of his Black Nation for many years to come. While he does so, any aspirant to power within the Movement must be immensely cautious and far-sighted, for rivalry—or even open disagreement—with the Messenger is not tolerated.

Muhammad does not proclaim himself divine, but he is invested with quasi-divinity as one who knew Allah (W. D. Fard) and has carried Allah's revelation down the years and across the continent. Muhammad's people know well that he has raised them from a small cult, nearly shattered by police harrassment and factional in-fighting, to a powerful force in America's social and political economy. Their unquestioning devotion to Muhammad is further intensified by the unique emotional cathexis of the true believer. And Muhammad himself does not discourage this triple flow of gratitude and adoration. In the early years after Fard's death, he asserted his claim as the sole Messenger of Allah, in whom the Movement must thenceforth be concentered. There is no evidence that he has ever seen reason to abate that claim.

Yet flesh is mortal; and even to the Messenger of Allah, death must one day come. So far as is known, Muhammad has not yet named his successor, and we may assume that a struggle for that honor is already under way. The two leading contenders would logically be Malcolm X and Raymond Sharrieff (though one of Muhammad's sons, Wallace D., is also mentioned as a possible heir-apparent). Malcolm is Muhammad's chief lieutenant in the open affairs of the Movement and his emissary to the Islamic nations of Africa and Asia. He is its most articulate spokesman and its most indefatigable organizer, infused with the Messenger's authority and admired by the ministers and the laity alike. Raymond, on the other hand, is Muhammad's son-in-law and his chief lieutenant in the secret affairs of the Movement, manager of its business enterprises and Supreme Captain of the secret army, the Fruit of Islam. Malcolm is undeniably the more popular contender: he would certainly win a resounding mandate in an election by the Muslim faithful. But Muslim affairs are not settled by elections.

At the moment, few observers doubt that Malcolm X will be Muhammad's successor and that he will bring quick intelligence and vision to the post. For Malcolm, the Movement has not yet begun to realize its potential, either as a local movement or as a

unit of international Islam. Under his leadership, it would
doubtless continue to expand its membership base, and it would
probably soon adopt many of the ritualistic requirements of
orthodox Islam, so that it might be officially and universally
recognized as Moslem. But Malcolm has never seen Allah; like
Rozier before him, his revelation is second-hand. Even if he
accedes smoothly to the throne—even if he is chosen for that
honor by Muhammad himself—he will not be considered quasi-
divine, and he will not reign unchallenged. On the day that the
Messenger "returns to Allah," the now capped volcano of rivalry
and dissension is likely to erupt.

By the time of Muhammad's death, the Black Muslim Movement will presumably have increased to some hundreds of thousands of members. What with active tithing and the establishment
of Muslim commercial enterprises, there will be a wealthy empire
at stake. The political force of the Movement will also be a rich
prize—not to mention the immense personal prestige and sense of
command that will be inherent in the position of leadership of so
potent and monolithic an organization.

During the intervening years, at least two large factions are
almost certain to have appeared. As the Movement gains vested
interests—real estate and commercial enterprises, as well as economic and political weight in the Negro and white communities—
one bloc of the Muslim leadership will become increasingly conservative. It will urge the case for maintaining a stable status quo,
rather than risk the loss of so much that will have been so ardu-
ously gained. This bloc will very quickly realize that the Muslim
gains can be protected only while there is a fairly stable white
society in America. Racial separation—and especially an economic or political weakening of the dominant white community—
would place severe strains on the Muslims' dependent economy
and would render meaningless their political balance of power.
This bloc will probably also tend to seek a status quo in revelation, asserting that Fard's original divine knowledge has been
given its perfect and ultimate expression by his Messenger, Elijah
Muhammad.

A successful Movement, however, is certain to have attracted
more and more true believers, and a second bloc within the leader-

ship will inevitably share their fiery, aggressive spirit. This second bloc will be scornful of mere material and negotiable gains. Clinging to the spirit of the original revelation and holding it capable of continual renewal in each generation, it will demand a relentless war on the detested status quo, with its entrenched white domination. Given sufficient time and numbers, this bloc may split further into purists, who abide by Muhammad's injunction to shun violence, and radicals, who demand war and victory at any cost. To both these sub-blocs, however, the conservative position will be equally abhorrent.

A ruler who is not considered divine. A rich prize for anyone who succeeds in wresting the position of command away from the incumbent. And built-in tensions that *must* create conflicting blocs, each of which will feel morally impelled to control the course of the Movement. . . . How can there help but be bitter and vicious struggles for power? Even the sense of a common enemy will not rule out such struggles, as the history of the Russian Communist movement shows all too well.

Indeed, the struggle for succession that will erupt at the Messenger's death is already in progress. Evidence is sparse and at times ambiguous, for the Muslims' central organizational problems are closely guarded secrets. (Even the few ex-Muslims who can be found are *very* reluctant to discuss this aspect of Muslim affairs.) But occasionally a development becomes known which casts a penetrating light into the darkness in which these rivalries and power-plays are wrapped. One such development, which occurred in Atlanta within the last few years, is doubly significant. It suggests (1) the pivotal power that Malcolm X now holds in the ministerial organization and (2) the fact that he feels constrained to use that power to strengthen his own position in the Movement as a whole.

This revealing development is the banishment from the Atlanta Temple No. 15 of the popular Minister James and his replacement by Jeremiah X, hand-picked for this new assignment by Malcolm X. No one outside the Movement knows what sin James committed to incur the displeasure of his superiors; he simply disappeared suddenly from Atlanta, and his name became taboo throughout the Muslim brotherhood. He was no longer even mentioned by anyone in the Movement; any reference to him was (and still is) met with stony silence or an adroit shifting of the conversation to some other subject. At last report, James was living quietly in Houston, either under lengthy suspension or actually expelled from the Black Nation.

One can speculate that James' popularity with non-Muslims in Atlanta, and the failure of the Atlanta temple to develop as rapidly as so large a concentration of Negroes would seem to augur, got him into serious difficulties. Then, too, James was possibly the best educated Muslim in the Movement until very recent times. He was fluent in several languages, played several musical instruments and was highly articulate. Was he a potential challenge to Malcolm's lieutenancy? Did he spend too much time fraternizing with Protestant clergy and the college crowd in Atlanta? Or was he set on building a personal empire at Temple No. 15? No one can be certain, but it is worth noticing that the hard-driving Jeremiah, who was brought in to replace him, is his opposite number in almost every respect. Under Jeremiah, temple membership has increased, and he has categorically ignored all but the most depressed elements in Atlanta's Negro community. The temple no longer rents quarters in the heart of the Negro business district on Auburn Avenue. Instead, it has moved into a "walk-up" hall on the edge of the slums. James and some of his aides had maintained living quarters in an Atlanta hotel; Jeremiah lives in a modest apartment on the edge of a redevelopment area, scarcely two blocks from some of the worst slums to be found in the South.

Minister Jeremiah works hard—and he gets results. Already he has been made organizer and overseer for the entire Southeast, in which capacity he reports to Malcolm X. Jeremiah is also an important anchor-man in the East Coast chain of temples. The nerve center of the East Coast is Malcolm X's own Temple 7 in New York. Louis X of Boston, trained and placed by Malcolm, anchors the New England end of the line. Jeremiah, another protege of Malcolm's, now controls Atlanta and directs the Movement in Jacksonville, Miami, Birmingham, Chattanooga and the other large cities in the Southeast. Only the temple in Washington, D. C., is headed by a potential counterforce—Lucius X, whom many of his colleagues believe to have ambitious of his own. Could it then be accidental that Wallace D. Muhammad, one of the Messenger's ablest sons, was sent out from Chicago to man the nearby Philadelphia temple? It would hardly seem so!

II. THE SECRET ARMY

The Black Muslim leadership is uncompromising in its attitude toward the white community. It is waging an economic and ideological war that will not end, it insists, until the white race has disappeared. There has as yet been no physical conflict (except for one flare-up in a Chicago courtroom and another in Detroit in the early 1930s, before Muhammad's command of the Movement was consolidated), and Muhammad urges his followers never to initiate a battle. But every Muslim is expected to fight if attacked and to lay down his life, if necessary, for the Black Nation. The entire Movement is, in short, a kind of reserve fighting corps—a potential phalanx of Black Men ready to wage open war against the entire white community in case of white provocation.

The nucleus of this force—its vanguard or officer cadre—is the secret army known as the Fruit of Islam, which was established as a protective unit in the early years of the Movement. Beynon reported laconically in 1937:

Fear of trouble with the unbelievers, especially with the police, led to the founding of the Fruit of Islam—a military organization for the men who were drilled by captains in military tactics and the use of firearms.[20]

Since then, the FOI has flexed its muscles and become probably the most powerful single organization within the Movement. It now has a "section" in every temple, and its local officers report not to the minister but to the Supreme Captain of the FOI, Raymond Sharrieff, at the Movement's headquarters in Chicago. This virtually autonomous body is an elite group, carefully chosen, rigorously trained, aware of its own distinction and responsibilities, admired (and very likely feared) by the rest of the Muslim brotherhood. It is entrusted with top security assignments and remains on constant alert. Most ominous of all, it shrouds its activities in nearly absolute secrecy—a tactic that has aroused the deepest suspicions of observers as experienced and sophisticated as the FBI.

The most significant change in the role of the Fruit of Islam, however, has recently become known. Its functions have not only expanded outward but have also doubled back upon the Movement itself. The FOI no longer dedicates itself solely to guarding the Black Nation against "trouble with the unbelievers, especially with the police." It now acts also as a police force and judiciary —or, more exactly, a constabulary and court-martial—to root out and punish any hint of heterodoxy or any slackening of obedience among the Muslims themselves. Whether this enforcement of internal discipline has become the FOI's *primary* function, no observer is yet able to say.

The Fruit of Islam is comprised of the best physically and psychologically conditioned males in the Black Muslim Movement, though the criteria for admission vary slightly to meet local conditions. In some of the larger temples, only the best qualified men under the age of thirty are admitted. In some small temples, every male Muslim is considered eligible. (Obviously each section is urged to reach a specified minimum size, even at a possible sacrifice in quality.) A few temples have as many as three distinct FOI groups: a Junior FOI for youths up to sixteen, a prime group for men sixteen to thirty-five, and a third group for men over thirty-five. No reliable estimate of the total membership of the FOI is available.

The chain of command is simple and strictly maintained. The FOI sections are divided into squads, each of which is under the command of a lieutenant. The lieutenants of each section report to a captain, who heads the section and reports (according to informants) "directly to Muhammad." In practice, the captains undoubtedly report to Muhammad's deputy in this area, the Supreme Captain of the FOI, Raymond Sharrieff. One of Muhammad's sons, Elijah, Jr., is second in command and serves as captain of the FOI section in Temple No. 2, the Chicago headquarters temple, from which Muhammad's personal security force, or honor guard, is drawn.

As part of their tactic of respectability, the Muslim leaders present the FOI as an ordinary physical training program, like those of "the YMCA, CYO, Masons or Boy Scouts." Its members do, indeed, engage in "body-building and physical hygiene" activities. Unlike most Boy Scout troops, however, they also receive training in judo, military drill and the use of knives and blackjacks. There is no evidence that the FOI sections still receive small-arms training—as Beynon reported in 1937—or that the FOI high command is gathering an armory for emergency use. Such activities are not unlikely, however, for the FOI looks forward to playing an heroic role in the impending "Battle of Armageddon."

The FOI's present-day duties fall under two broad headings, *security* and *discipline*. As a security force, the FOI stands guard in the temples, checks visitors at all Muslim meetings and provides a personal guard for all ministers and traveling officials, including the Messenger and Malcolm X. As a disciplinary force, it supervises the "trials" of Muslims charged with such offenses as adultery, the use of narcotics, misuse of temple funds, not attending meetings, sleeping during meetings, failing to bring "Lost-Founds" (visitors) to meetings, reporting temple activities to outsiders, using unbecoming language before female Muslims, eating or selling pork, failing to pay extra dues for being overweight, allowing anyone to enter the temple under the influence of liquor or stating an unwillingness to die for Allah.

At the "trial," the offending Muslim is placed in the custody of the temple's FOI. The proceedings are conducted jointly by the FOI captain and the minister, with the entire FOI section in attendance. (In the case of lesser infractions, all regular members of the temple may be admitted.) The defendant is not allowed to offer any defense: the charges against him are read, and the verdict is thereupon pronounced—by the minister in case a religious issue is involved, by the FOI captain in all other cases. This verdict is final; there is no appeal.

At least three types of sentence are known to be imposed as the result of these FOI trials. For minor violations there is a "Class C" sentence, under which the convicted Muslim is required to perform labor at the temple or some other designated place for a period of time. A more serious but not infrequent punishment is the "Class F" sentence, or suspension, under which the convict is isolated from all Muslim contacts for a period of time ranging from ninety days to five years. During this time he is barred from all Muslim temples, enterprises and businesses; and other Muslims are forbidden to talk with, visit or otherwise associate with him. The most serious sentence—and it is apparently rarely invoked—is formal and permanent expulsion from the Movement.

Recruits to the FOI are carefully screened before admission, for they are expected to set the highest possible standards of character and dedication. Each candidate is required to pass oral examinations on certain levels of "knowledge" about the Movement and its history—examinations in which the candidate must recite long memorized passages verbatim, without a single error. Candidates are also required to take a secret oath on admission.

From that point on, the men and officers are held rigorously to the most demanding Muslim ideals, for the Fruit of Islam are considered the living exemplars of the Black Nation. They must be "absolutely independent in every respect"—a grandiose phrase which actually means only that they must be self-reliant and able to protect themselves against any form of attack. They must be perfectly obedient to all constituted authority, black or white, and they must promote complete unity and harmony within the group. They must respect and protect black womanhood; there can be no deviation, for the "era of disgrace" for the black woman has come to an end, "even if it costs her life and the lives of her defenders." They must reassume the position of leadership and guidance in their own homes. And they must examine and question everything they see and hear, accepting nothing as sacred or certain except on its intrinsic merits—another Muslim ideal that in practice means somewhat less than it says.

As a result of its power and secrecy, its high standards and strict discipline, the FOI has drawn about itself an especially glamorous aura. Its military aspect appeals directly to the pent-up militancy of the true believer; and many Muslims who may not join the FOI act out their militancy by adulating it. To these true believers, the FOI is the vanguard of Muslim destiny, the glorious army of the Black Man's revolution that is now gathering its strength. But the FOI also has a certain mystical status. "Fruit," the Muslims explain, is the "final product of any tree"; it is the purpose for which the tree exists. Yet in the fruit is the seed: the beginning of a new tree. The Black Muslims see themselves as the fruit of the American system of slavery and oppression, bearing within themselves the seed of the coming Black Nation. The Fruit of Islam, therefore, symbolizes the inner meaning of the Movement as a whole.

Yet the structure and role of the FOI—indeed, its very existence—suggest that it may soon become the focus of profound tensions inside the Movement. For example, when a struggle for succession breaks out at Muhammad's death, as it inevitably must, to whom will the FOI throw its support? And if the FOI is recognized as a key weapon in that struggle, will there not be increasingly tense intrigues among the leadership for control of the secret army? Surely it is no accident that Muhammad has appointed, as the two chief officers of the FOI, his son-in-law and his son.

Again, the FOI trials reveal clearly that discipline in the Muslim ranks is less than perfect. The Muslim leadership has chosen to notice even minor infractions and to punish them through the FOI. But if "loyalty" and "obedience" are so narrowly defined, they *cannot* be maintained; and if the inevitable infractions are punished highhandedly, the Muslims' spontaneous loyalty and obedience to the Movement must eventually give way to resentment and rebellion. In that case, the FOI might easily degenerate into a strong-arm elite keeping a restive people in line. Such a development would mean trouble not only within the Movement but also between the Muslims and the white community.

Above all, there is the curious paradox that a divine Black Nation, outraged by the injustices of a class-structured white society, has now deliberately created an elite of its own. How will the mass of Muslims react as they come to realize that, after all the bright promises, they are second-class citizens again, even in the Black Nation of Islam?

III. THE SEARCH FOR RESPECTABILITY

Violence and the Christian Tradition

The private image of the Movement has changed considerably since the days of Wallace Fard, and it continues to be modified as the Muslims search for respectability and acceptance.

The Detroit Muslims of the 1930s had a number of bizarre
excesses charged against them, including, as we have seen, human
sacrifice.

On November 21, 1932, the people of Detroit became conscious of
the presence of the cult through its first widely publicized human sacrifice. A prominent member, Robert Harris, renamed Robert Karriem,
erected an altar in his home at 1249 Dubois Street and invited his
roomer, John J. Smith, to present himself as a human sacrifice, so that
he might become, as Harris said, "the Savior of the World." Smith
agreed, and at the hour appointed for the sacrifice—9:30 a.m.—Harris
plunged a knife into Smith's heart.[21]

Other reports of sacrifices or attempted sacrifices were current in
Detroit as late as 1937.

In Chicago in 1935, two hundred Muslims rioted in a courtroom and attempted to storm the bench while one of their members was on trial. Before the melee was over, one policeman was
dead and eleven had been injured. Two of the Muslims were shot
in the clash, and forty were sent to prison.[22] As recently as 1958,
Muhammad made a special trip to Detroit to quiet his followers,
who were having trouble with the police.[23]

In 1960, in a case involving Muslims in New York City, the
presiding judge cleared the courtroom before the jury's verdict
was read, fearing that "the Muslim followers who packed the hall
every day of the seven-day trial might demonstrate if a verdict of
guilty were issued."[24] The Muslim defendants had been charged
with assaulting two policemen who entered their homes without a
warrant; they were found not guilty, and the anticipated trouble
did not develop. The *Los Angeles Herald-Dispatch* reported, however, that fifty Muslims, "led by Minister Malcolm X, silently
patrolled the corridor of the court building while the jury carried
on its deliberations" and that "outside the court building in a

small park across the street, some 400 male followers of the Muslim faith were gathered. They were silent, well-disciplined, ominous." Malcolm X was described as "a disturbingly intent figure as he sat on a corridor bench munching dried raisins . . . pondering the explosive factors largely in his command."[25]

Such incidents are isolated, however, for Muhammad prefers to disassociate his Movement from violent activity of any kind. His followers are forbidden to carry weapons, and they are cautioned not to carry any instrument that might conceivably be considered even a potential weapon, should they be searched by an over zealous police officer. But the Muslim leader is caught on the horns of a dilemma, for he has taught his followers not only to avoid precipitating violence but also to defend themselves and each other if they are assaulted.

We must take things into our own hands. We must return to the Mosaic law of an eye for an eye, and a tooth for a tooth. What does it matter if 10 million of us die? There will be 7 million of us left, and they will enjoy justice and freedom.[26]

The constant threat of violence is implicit in the basic doctrines of the Movement, and this fearlessness before the white man is one of the Movement's strongest appeals.

Much is made of the "Battle of Armageddon" that is expected to take place in North America. But this battle—until recently a prominent feature in Muslim literature and teachings—is carefully relegated to the realm of the eschatological, where such battles usually are fought. It belongs to a future in which the present believers are not likely to participate. *Unanticipated* violence, on the other hand, may occur at any moment. The Muslims display a kind of contained aggressiveness, which may occasionally provoke violence without actually initiating it.

Muhammad does not wish to alter the self-image of the Muslims as "men among men." Yet he does wish his followers to be accepted as peaceful, law-abiding, religious individuals. There may be no logical inconsistency here, but there are serious emotional obstacles which prevent the Negro community at large from accepting him and his Movement on the terms of his stated proposals. First of all, American Negroes have known no religion other than Christianity, and the Christian faith—with its emphasis on charity and long-suffering—has perhaps been more meaningful to them than to many who have not been the victims of social rejection. Consequently, *any* new religion not strongly interlaced with at least lip-service to the Christian traditions of meekness and love may expect to find the Negro masses generally unreceptive.

Again, Muhammad's peculiar brand of Islam at once snatches away the comforts of heaven, which have been earned at so great a price on earth, and substitutes a Supreme Black Man for the sure and comforting presence of an omnipotent Father. Those educated in the Christian spirit believe that patience and loving-kindness on earth will earn the sweetest of all rewards: eternal life in a kingdom where all men love their brothers and live as equals in the nearness of God. In exchange for this gentle faith, the Muslims offer the Negro Christian only the taste of violence—the chance to vent his most acrid hostilities here on earth and then to die forever. This exchange is not generally palatable to even the most humiliated and resentful Negro Christians.

In an attempt to bridge the gap, Muhammad has recently modified and hushed some of the Movement's most strident assaults on Christianity itself. The "debunking" of the virgin birth of Jesus, for example, was a standard dramatic feature of every temple lecture a few years ago. Today it is seldom mentioned unless the issue is raised by a non-Muslim. The Muslim denunciation of the Bible as a "poison book" has been radically reinterpreted. The Bible, the ministers now say, is both true and accurate when "correctly interpreted." It was "poisoned" by the white man, who wished to use it to justify his wicked behavior. Finally, Negroes are cordially invited to attend lectures—and even formally to join the Movement—while remaining active members of the Christian church.

The Muslims have thus softened their derision of Christian *symbols* but not their contempt for the Christian *faith*. They are clearly gambling that the symbols have become empty of meaning, that the Negro clings to them only because they are familiar and comfortable and a badge of religious respectability. The Muslims are willing to let the Negro cherish these meaningless symbols, at least for a while, if he will become a Black Muslim at heart. And many recent developments in the Negro Christian community seem to be nurturing this prospect. The earthly rewards of meekness and a gentle faith are slow in coming, perhaps too slow for the prevailing mood of urgency. Negro Christians, like white ones, are rapidly learning to modify their faith wherever secular advantage is at stake. Even among the devoted cadres of the new nonviolence movement, Christian love may at times become a technique rather than a way of life.

A new aggressive spirit is undeniably taking possession of America's Negro youth. But the Muslims have erred badly in mistaking this aggressive spirit for a spirit of aggression. Starting from his present ground of oppression and enforced humility, the Negro can go a long, long way toward asserting himself without crossing the border into violence. There are inescapable signs that the Negro is abandoning Christian love as an effective agent of social change. But his purpose is still to enlighten the white man, not to annihilate him. Moreover, the goal of this new aggressive spirit is flatly opposed to Muslim separatism. Negro youth do not want a Black Nation. They want their fair share of what *this* society has to offer, and they are convinced that it can be had without a resort to violence.

The young Negroes who are now flocking to the Black Muslims are dissidents who know only how to hate because they have been surrounded by the symbols of hatred all their lives long. They are of serious concern to our society, which has created them, but they are far from representing a sizable portion of the Negro community as a whole.

The open bid for respectability which has tended to characterize the Black Muslim Movement in recent years is largely traceable to Malcolm X, and it is he who may be hung on the horns of the dilemma. In order to broaden the scope of the Movement, to facilitate its appeal to the entire Negro community, he has been willing to make a superficial peace with the conservative Negro leadership and to make room in the Muslim mythology and services for Christian symbols. But to achieve the respectability he desires, he must compromise still further. Until the Muslims at least *talk* in terms of peace and love, they will generally be considered unrespectable, and a firm ceiling will remain on the Movement's potential for growth. If he leads the Muslims down this path, however, he will weaken—perhaps irreparably—the dynamic of hatred which is the Movement's vital force.

In the long run, therefore, Malcolm must abandon either the purity of Muslim dogma or his dream of respectability and massive expansion. He must either remain a Muslim in the tradition of Muhammad or become, in the eyes of his followers, just another of the "Uncle Toms" he has so long denounced.

The Race Issue

The Black Muslim leadership's search for respectability—a concomitant of its desire for rapid growth—may also force an internal showdown on the vehemence and bitterness with which the race issue is to be pressed. At the moment, Muhammad still openly denounces the white man—the entire white race, without exception—in the most scathing language ever heard in the white-dominated nations of the world. These denunciations attract and delight the true believer, but they repel most Negroes, who themselves are daily victims of extreme and irrational racial generalizations. The average Negro feels that anyone who publicly participates in the categorical denunciation of any race must be either insane or a troublemaker or both.

Yet Muhammad is aware of the paradox that the less respectable he is, the more he is *respected*. His boldness in "saying for millions what millions fear to say for themselves" may elevate him to a recognized position of leadership in the Negro community. Even more important, he feels, it may earn him the respect of the white man, who admires solidarity and determination. And the *respect* of the white man is the key to *respectability* among American Negroes, for "whom the white man respects, the Negro hastens to embrace." Thus, ironically, Muhammad may win by demagogy a seal of approval that he could never win by moderation.

In playing this gamble, Muhammad risks incurring the fate that befell Marcus Garvey: tagged as a hate-monger, Garvey could not consolidate the Negro masses under his standard and so was easily toppled by a combined action of white and Negro leaders. Perhaps for this reason, Muhammad is especially distressed by charges that he is hate-mongering. He asserts that hate would be morally justified, for "the white man has hated the Negroes . . . ever since they have been on this planet earth,"[27] and that hate is given divine approval in the Christians' own Bible:

God, Himself, hates: see Malachi 1:2-3: "Was not Esau Jacob's brother? saith the Lord: yet I loved Jacob and I hated Esau. . . ." St. Luke 14:26, no man could be the disciple of Jesus unless he hated his father, mother, wife, children. . . .[28]

Yet his own racial teachings, he insists, are not hate but the simple truth.

I am here with the truth for you to accept or be the losers. I am not afraid to speak the truth regardless. . . . Let those who accuse me of teaching hate point out that portion of my teaching which constitutes hate. . . . Is it hate to call upon you to unite?[29]

Muhammad presents himself as a man who is dispassionately revealing the truth about an enemy—an absolutely ruthless enemy, who has skillfully camouflaged his character by distorting the facts of history and intimidating all who are unwilling to accept the distortion. The Messenger claims to preach not hate but simply "the truth which is capable of setting the Black Man free."

If this gamble pays off, Muhammad may gain respectability for his Movement without retreating an inch on the race issue and without internal dissensions. If it fails, the result may be a tug-of-war between those who cling to respectability and those who cling to hatred. In either case, the Messenger has made his own position clear: "I will never, after having knowledge, love nor befriend the enemies of . . . my Black Nation, whether my people believe as I do or not."[30]

8 The Black Muslims and Orthodox Islam

A major goal of the present Muslim leadership is to achieve general acceptance of the Movement as a legitimate religion—specifically, as a legitimate sect of orthodox Islam. This is not an internal necessity: the Muslims' self-respect does not hinge on such acceptance. Muhammad has stated that the Muslims *are* legitimate and Islamic, and so far as the Muslims themselves are concerned, this settles the matter. Nor is it an expedient directed at the Negro community, for the aegis of orthodox Islam means nothing in America's black ghettos. So long as the Movement keeps its color identity with the rising "black" peoples of Africa and Asia, it could discard all its Islamic attributes—its name, its prayers to Allah, its citations from the Quran, *everything*—without risking in the smallest degree its appeal to the black masses.

In pressing their demand for complete acceptance as a legitimate religion and a Moslem sect, the Muslims have their eye primarily on the white community. In many ways, America does live up to its surpassing democratic ideal, pre-eminently in the elaborate safeguards it provides for freedom of worship. Religious groups in America are unfettered; only in the most extreme cases is certain quasi-secular behavior in the name of religion construed as against public policy and, as such, prohibited.[1] The Black Muslims know well that, as they prosper, they will encounter in the white community a pressure for the most stringent repressions and reprisals. The more swiftly and securely they can become acknowledged as a legitimate religion, the more securely they can rely upon the counterpressures of democratic toleration and constitutional immunity.

The Muslims have generally been given the benefit of the doubt thus far. They have been treated, if only provisionally, as a legitimate religion. Except in prisons, their meetings have never

210

been barred by any agency of the government. The Universities of Islam are legally approved as parochial schools. And the temples and school properties are tax-exempt in all states where they exist, under the same regulations that govern the church properties of all other religious bodies.

Even this provisional acceptance, however, is far from complete. The FBI, for example, keeps the Movement under as close surveillance as it would a political terrorist organization. And in some instances, the Muslims' status as a religion has been flatly denied by government officials. Perhaps the most significant of these denials to date have occurred in prisons, which are among the Muslims' most fertile recruiting grounds. In some prisons, the Muslims are permitted to hold services, but in others they are denied the right of assembly. A case in point is Clinton State Prison at Utica, New York, where four Negro inmates were allegedly placed in solitary confinement when they sought to practice their new faith. (The warden described three of the prisoners as "Protestants a year ago"; the fourth had been a Catholic.) Prison officials did not dispute that discipline improves markedly among those converted to Islam, but they protested that the Muslims have "ulterior motives," aimed at "forcing supremacy over whites, although they do not express it."[2]

To defend themselves against such harassments, now and in the future, the Muslims are pressing hard for complete recognition as a legitimate religion, on equal terms with the reigning triumvirate of Protestants, Catholics and Jews. At Utica, for example, a suit was entered on behalf of the four converts, and a federal court judge granted service of a summons on the prison warden as defendant.

Muhammad's insistence on his Movement's Islamic identity has much the same immediate purpose. Complete acceptance as a legitimate religion would give the Muslims a degree of security but, in view of the antagonism they will arouse, perhaps not enough. As a mere private cult, they would still be vulnerable to unofficial but damaging molestation. If they can entrench themselves as a Moslem sect, however, they will be very nearly immune to overt white hostility, for the international political implications of the suppression or harassment of Moslems in the United States would be extremely grave. Muhammad craves this immunity and the resultant freedom of maneuver, and except for his crucial doctrine—denunciation of the white race "and all that race goes for"—he seems ready to moderate his program to achieve this end.

At the moment, orthodox Islamic groups in the United States do not acknowledge the Black Muslims as in any way related to world-wide Islam. The response from Arab and other Moslem nations is more ambiguous. There seems good reason to believe that the Black Muslims will soon be officially sheltered in the community of international Islam.

A Legitimate Religion?

The line that separates a purely social organization from a purely religious communion is seldom well defined. Religion is, in part, a facet of man's social life; and social concerns are at times invested with an almost religious aura. Some great religious movements developed originally out of social concerns (Methodism is a well-known example), and social movements ranging from communism to the Townsend Plan have exhibited marked religious overtones.[3] An incipient mass movement such as the Black Muslims, therefore, may be *both* "social" and "religious," though its emphasis will be weighted in one direction or the other.

America has always been wary of definitions which claim to draw a precise line between the religious and the secular. Such definitions tend to be either too nebulous or too subjective; in either case, they are unreliable guides for a democracy intent on safeguarding an absolute freedom of worship. The American public, as a result, eschews all rigid criteria of orthodoxy and maintains an historically unique tolerance of religious deviation. Americans may reject and even combat an organization which claims to be a religion, but they are not likely to deny that it *is* a religion.

Within the American tradition, then, it is not necessary for the Black Muslims to prove that they are a valid religious communion. The question is whether it can be proved that they are *not*. If the negative cannot be proved, a general acceptance of the Movement as a legitimate religion is assured.

Emile Durkheim, one of the most critical observers and students of the sociology of religion, insists that any attempt at a definition of religion must derive from the existential phenomenon, from "the reality itself . . . for religion cannot be defined except by the characteristics which are found wherever religion itself is found."[4] At an irreducible minimum, he suggests, these characteristics are *beliefs* and *rites*.

Religious phenomena are naturally arranged in two fundamental categories: beliefs and rites. The first are states of opinion, and consist in representations; the second are determined modes of action.[5]

A religious rite is distinguished from its secular counterpart by the sacred nature of its object. A moral rule or a legal statute, for example, may prescribe behavior identical to that of a religious rite; but the religious prescription refers to a different *class of objects*. The religious object is "sacred"; the secular object, even when of the highest social value, is "profane." There is no necessary relationship, however, between the sacred and either "deity" or the "supernatural." Neither the divine nor the supernatural is necessary to a religion.

The circle of sacred objects cannot be determined . . . once for all. Its extent varies infinitely, according to the different religions. That is how Buddhism is a religion: in default of gods, it admits the existence of sacred things, namely, the four noble truths and the practices derived from them.[6]

Indeed, the "circle of sacred objects" cannot be rationally defined at all. That is sacred which the believers of a particular faith *feel* is sacred. And this feeling is at once the most subjective and most widespread, the most familiar and most elusive of phenomena. It evades definition, yet its presence is the identifying mark of a legitimate religion. In pragmatic terms, wherever a body of men shares the feeling that a specific group of objects is sacred and has elaborated this feeling into specific beliefs and rites, there a religion must be said to exist.

It must be granted, then, that the Black Muslim Movement constitutes a legitimate religion within the definition of the sociology of religion.[7] But there are many kinds of religion; and while all enjoy a nearly unrestricted freedom of worship in America, they are not all granted equal deference and respect by the community at large. Mere cults, for example, like the followers of Father Divine and "Daddy Grace," are not taken as seriously as Presbyterians, say, or as Jews. But the Black Muslims want and are determined to achieve the respect of all Americans, even of the doomed "blue-eyed devils." Their success will depend, in large part, on the *kind* of religion they are—that is, on the degree of religious stability and respectability they can be said to have achieved.

Perhaps the best known analysis of religious groups into broad categories is that developed by Ernst Troeltsch and refined by J. Milton Yinger. This system of categories, like all others familiar to Americans, is based on Christian groups, and there is no real assurance that it is valid when applied to non-Christian religions such as the Black Muslims. It is, nevertheless, the system by which the Muslims will be evaluated by most Americans; it is the scale against which the Muslims will actually be measured in their demand for deference and respect.

Troeltsch divides religious groups into two types: the *church* and the *sect*. The leader of a church is characteristically a "priest"; the leader of a sect is characteristically a "prophet." In broader terms:

The Church is that type of organization which is overwhelmingly conservative, which to a certain extent accepts the secular order, and dominates the masses; in principle, therefore, it is universal; i.e., it desires to cover the whole life of humanity. The sects, on the other hand, are comparatively small groups; they aspire after personal inward perfection, and they aim at a direct personal fellowship between the members of each group. . . . Their attitude towards the world, the State, and Society may be indifferent, tolerant, or hostile since they have no desire to control and incorporate these forms of social life; on the contrary, they tend to avoid them; their aim is usually either to tolerate their presence alongside of their own body, or even to replace these social institutions by their own society.[8]

The church, in short, attempts to include the whole society in its outlook and thus inevitably becomes an integral part of the social order. It may even become a determining force, providing stability and sanction; but to the same extent it becomes a captive of the upper classes and dependent on them. The church may thus defeat its own ends, for as the lower classes find themselves abandoned, schisms will occur, and the social order will again be threatened. New religious groups, or sects, will then coalesce in response to various middle- and lower-class needs not met by the church—needs which center at times on theological or ritual disagreements but more often on questions of economic or political enfranchisement, racial or ethnic status, social mobility or social change. The church, to the extent that it is a balance wheel of the status quo, is impotent to cope with such revolutionary tensions.

The sect, by contrast, draws primarily upon the disinherited, the unchampioned and those opposed to the existing social order. It repudiates the compromises the church has made with secular institutions, and it resents the church's failure to assert itself against social abuses. The sect may respond to worldly evil by withdrawing from society, hoping to avoid present injustice and ultimate perdition, or by embracing a radicalism intended to establish in the social order its own ideals and sense of justice.

Not all sects (as Yinger points out) originate in the lower classes. The Methodist movement, for example, "remained throughout its history in the control of men who had been born and bred in the middle class,"[9] although it was substantially a lower-class movement until recent times. The Bahais, Christian Scientists, Theosophists and numerous other familiar sects have been predominantly middle-class from their inception. Middle-class sects are not characteristically in protest against the social order, for they have usually been favored by it. They are more often disenchanted with the institutionalized churches, which seem to them to be neglecting essential human values.

Lower-class sects, on the other hand, are most often spawned in poverty, disprivilege, depression and despair. They are the refuge of those who are without power and who lack even an effective advocate in the circles where power resides. The existing society has been unjust to them, so they will reorganize the social order—usually along lines that those in power construe as "radical." But sects of this type tend to elicit concerted opposition and are thus predisposed to failure. They incur the hostility not only of the power elite but also of the less radical sects, which are potentially more mobile and which stand to suffer if the power structure, feeling threatened, becomes more rigidly exclusive. The usual history of a radical sect is therefore short.

The Black Muslim Movement is clearly a sect, in Troeltsch's broad definition of that term. Appealing to an almost exclusively Christian Negro community, the Movement repudiates the Christian church not only in particulars but *in toto*. It insists upon the separation of Black Men from white society, leaving that corrupt edifice to crumble under the weight of its own iniquity. And where the Movement is forced into contact with the white community, it reacts with a radicalism which is—from the Muslim point of view, at least—idealistic and just. But to categorize the Muslims as a sect is not quite so simple as Troeltsch's terms suggest, for Yinger's modification introduces a new element that must be carefully reckoned with.

As part of his refinement of Troeltsch's categories,[10] Yinger points to the existence of a third type of religious group which, while it somewhat resembles the sect, is in fact quite dissimilar. This type is the *cult,* a small group of people unrelated to any other religious institution and "tied together only by common religious emotions and needs."[11] Yinger seems to consider the Black Muslims a cult, pure and simple:

Pure cult types are not common in Western society; most groups that might be called cults are fairly close to the sect type. Perhaps the best examples are the various Spiritualist groups and some of the "Moslem" cults among American Negroes.[12]

The cult, as Yinger defines it, is characteristically organized around a charismatic leader (such as Muhammad), in whom are centered the loyalties of the rank and file. As a result, the cult usually is confined to a small area and dies with its founder: problems of succession are not effectively anticipated, and the bereaved cult disintegrates into splinter groups, which eventually fade into oblivion. But while it exists, the cult deviates even more sharply than the sect from the dominant church and the established social order, and its "implications for anarchy are even stronger."[13] It takes individual problems, especially the "search for a mystic experience,"[14] as its total concern and shows little or no interest in problems of social justice. Cult members are typically indifferent to their status and prospects in the enveloping society.

On the surface, the Black Muslim Movement might seem to merit Yinger's designation of it as a cult. It is (1) a relatively small group of people (2) under strong charismatic leadership, (3) deviating sharply from the established social order and (4) diverging absolutely from the dominant church of its society. But on close inspection, a number of significant differences appear. (These differences were perhaps not familiar to Yinger when he wrote in 1957, for there has been no serious published study of the Black Muslims in almost twenty-five years.)

The Muslims originated as a small, local group, but in recent years their membership has spiraled to at least 100,000—some estimates would triple that figure—with more than fifty temples in major cities from Boston and Miami to San Diego. While still relatively small compared to the nation's major religious bodies, they are larger than *most* American denominations, sects and cults. More than fifty Protestant denominations, for example, have fewer than ten congregations each, and more than half the sects in the nation have only 7,000 members or less.[15]

The impressive cohesion of the Black Muslim Movement today is certainly due to the charismatic leadership of Elijah Muhammad. True, he is not the founder of the Movement but only the Messenger of Allah; the Muslims passed through their first crisis of succession when, under extremely divisive conditions, the mantle was passed down from Wallace Fard to Muhammad. Yet the Muslims' absolute loyalty to Muhammad and their uncritical faith in his wisdom and leadership suggest a simple continuity of charisma, which has postponed the problem of succession without really solving it. On the other hand—and perhaps of decisive importance—the Movement is rapidly developing a firm organizational structure. Under the direction of an aggressive clergy and inner council, the Movement continues to expand vigorously in all parts of the country without the immediate charismatic presence of the Messenger.

The Muslims do deviate sharply from the established social order, and their call for separation in some ways resembles the withdrawal characteristic of the cult. The Muslims consider futile any attempt to reform American society; they plan simply to retire from it, cultivate the Black Nation and wait. The white devils, lacking black victims, will then presumably turn on each other and destroy themselves, and the Black Man will inherit the earth. Yet the driving force of the Movement is not separatism but hatred; and the torrent of racial condemnation which fills its sermons and publications is undeniably social protest, all the more so for its bitter rejection of any hope for reform. There is no trace among the Muslims of that mystical absorption and indifference to social injustice which mark a cult.

Finally, the Muslims are unequivocal in their repudiation of the dominant church in American society. Their beliefs and rites are almost totally deviant from those of the Christian tradition, and within this frame of reference a case might be made for labeling them a cult. But the Muslims do not claim to be a Christian sect. They have declared themselves an integral part of Islam, which they consider the church of the Black Nation. Muslim leaders are now working skillfully and hard to establish the Movement's authenticity as a legitimate Moslem sect. If they succeed—and it seems virtually certain that they will—the last realistic argument that would relegate the Movement to the status of a cult will have been answered.

The massive weight of all available evidence, in short, suggests that the Black Muslim Movement is not a cult but a sect.[16] It is not local, ephemeral or isolated; it will not collapse at Muhammad's death, and it may soon be able to draw upon the vast prestige and power of international Islam to defend it in case of harassment by the white community. To shrug it off, in the manner of some observers, as "just another cult" would be a tragic error. The Muslims today are powerless children of despair and poverty in revolt against a social order they have found unjust. But they will not remain powerless, and it is likely that they will be with us for a long time to come.

A Moslem Sect?

The Muslim dream is to have a solid Black Muslim community in the United States, recognized and supported by Moslems throughout the world as an integral part of Islam. This is not sheer expediency: from the earliest days of the Movement, the Black Muslims have considered themselves devout adherents of the Moslem faith. They recognize Allah as the one true God (though they see Him not as a unique deity but as the Supreme Black Man among Black Men, all of whom are divine). They base their services on both the Quran and the Bible, and they are learning Arabic so as to be able to rely entirely on the original Quran. They observe the classic Moslem prayer ritual and dietary laws, and they hold in high esteem the traditional pilgrimage to Mecca.

On certain fundamental points of doctrine, however, the Black Muslims have departed widely from the orthodox Moslem tradition. Partly for this reason, and partly from an instinctive militancy toward newcomers, the official representatives of orthodox Islam in the United States have refused any recognition of the Black Muslims. The Movement has not been admitted as an affiliate of the official Federation of Islamic Associations in the United States and Canada, nor has it been recognized as legitimate by any affiliate of the federation. It has, in fact, been vigorously denounced by several Moslem groups, including the rival Muslim Brotherhood of America.

Muhammad readily admits that some of the teachings and practices of his Movement are at variance with those of other Moslem groups, but he presents these as differences of *interpretation* within a unity of belief. American Negroes, he argues, have been the victims of a harsh and cynical oppression, and the Islamic faith in its pure orthodox form is not appropriate to their needs:

My brothers in the East were never subjected to the conditions of slavery and systematic brainwashing by the Slavemasters for as long a period as my people here were subjected. I cannot, therefore, blame them if they differ with me in certain interpretations of the message of Islam.[17]

He is not troubled by the rejection of the handful of orthodox Moslems in the United States; his hopes are staked on recognition by the more important (and more flexible) officials in the Moslem nations of Africa and Asia.

Two of the Black Muslims' basic doctrines are at the heart of the controversy: their insistence that the Black Man must separate himself from the abhorrent and doomed white race, and their belief that it is the manifest destiny of the Black Nation to inherit the earth. These doctrines are in flagrant contrast to the orthodox Moslem ideal of an all-embracing brotherhood of man. Moslems have, throughout their history, shown a rare and admirable indifference to boundaries of race; and any tinge of racial bigotry in an acknowledged Moslem group would cause the orthodox acute embarrassment and anguish. The Black Muslims, however, refuse absolutely to moderate or compromise their racist doctrines. Muhammad is convinced that a belief in pan-racial brotherhood would leave his followers with no more dignity and hope than they can now find in the Christian church.

Are these contradictions so extreme that the Black Muslims must be said to have excluded themselves from Islam? The question will have to be answered, of course, by Moslem theologians, but it seems likely that they will find the Black Muslims to be within the pale—a legitimate if somewhat heretical Moslem sect. Every faith has its deviates, and every international faith makes broad allowances for interpretations of doctrine to fit local conditions. The fact that orthodox Moslems in America reject the Movement has no real significance: most Christian sects and denominations were likewise spurned by the orthodox in their founding years. And a clear precedent exists in Islam itself for the ultimate recognition of heretics as a sect despite major doctrinal differences. This precedent is the Ahmadiyah movement, a small Moslem group in India and Pakistan.[18]

The "prophet" of the movement was the pious Mirzā Ghulām Ahmad (1839-1908), . . . [who] was accepted by many, including orthodox religious, as a great [Moslem] reformer. Suddenly, in 1889, his popularity gave place to extreme denunciation, when he announced that he had received a revelation authorizing him to receive men's allegiance as the promised Messiah and *Imām Mahdī;* that is, Jesus returned to earth and the apocalyptic saviour who [Moslem] tradition has held will appear at the last day. The general [Moslem] community, and particularly the divines, outraged by this blasphemy, attacked him relentlessly. . . . Despite intense persecution, the community grew, in numbers and in faith.[19]

There are still intermittent quarrels between the Ahmadiyah and the orthodox, but the Ahmadiyah are now generally accepted as a legitimate sect of Islam.

The open assertion by the Black Muslims that it is their destiny to inherit the earth and that the present rulers of this world will soon fall upon evil days is certainly not unique in the history of religions. Such a religious philosophy is at least as old as the ancient Hebrews and at least as recent as the newest adventist Christian sect. (The characteristic orientation of all religions has been the expectation that God's first pleasure is His own elect, the elect being those who are pure in doctrine, correct in ritual and, oftentimes, racially select.) The multiple fractures within the Catholic and Protestant communions respectively, and the sects which elaborate every other major religion, provide ample if disheartening evidence of this universal assumption.

Islam itself, although it has no significant racial bias, does share this pronounced intolerance for the nonbeliever. To this extent, the ground is prepared for orthodox Moslem acceptance, under certain conditions, of the Black Muslims' racial hatred. One Christian writer, while praising Islam's record of racial inclusiveness, has suggested that racial lines might be drawn and held even by orthodox Islam, "if it got a foothold in Europe or America, where the deeper racial prejudices seem most to flourish." He cites the case of a Moslem missionary in this country meeting separately with white and Negro faithful "because of the Christian background of the white people." [20]

Racial hatred, wherever it is taught or practiced, reflects a social depravity. It debases the hater, alienates the hated and usually impairs the creative capacities of both. Yet history offers almost no instance of a religious sub-group being expelled from the parent communion because it teaches hatred of the outsider. The Christian church, for example, was divided in its early years over the issue of whether to admit gentiles; today it is in controversy over the status of its Negro members. Yet never, in all its turbulent history, has the church developed a tradition of excluding those whose racial views are repugnant to the mainstream of Christian thought. Instead, the church has sought to preserve its ties, hoping that time and circumstance, interpreted through the spiritual emphases of the church, might work reform.

The most pertinent example, perhaps, is the split within American Protestantism over the question of slavery. The Southern churches taught—and many still teach—that some races are superior to others and that men's social destinies are divinely predetermined by race. These churches formally withdrew from communion with the Northern churches when they could reach no agreement on the slavery issue, yet their status as Christian churches was never in dispute. Even today, a number of Southern Protestant churches proclaim the inferiority of the Negro, whose role as a "hewer of wood and drawer of water" is said to be pre-ordained by God Himself; and in the Mormon Church, racial bias categorically excludes the Negro from full membership. Yet these churches have not been expelled from the Christian communion, nor are they even held in suspicion of heresy by their brothers in Christ. Shall we expect any other religion, even Islam, to be more insistent on brotherly love than we are ourselves?

In 1959, Malcolm X made a special trip to Egypt and other Moslem countries to test the acceptability of the Black Muslim Movement abroad. He was received cordially as a "Moslem brother." Later that year, Muhammad and two of his sons made a tour of several Moslem countries. The Messenger was recognized as an important leader and was permitted to make the traditional Moslem pilgrimage to Mecca. He wrote to his followers in the United States:

On my arrival in Jeddah, Arabia, December 23, 1959, it was almost a necessity that I go to Mecca. The next day . . . the authorities made ready a car to take me and my two sons over the forty-mile distance from Jeddah to that ancient city which is the glory of the Muslim world of Islam.[21]

In Cairo, Muhammad reported that:

Here . . . I met the Great Imam. He invited me to visit him, and I have experienced great happiness . . . with him. He is over all the Imams in . . . Egypt. He placed a kiss upon my head, and I placed a kiss on his hand.[22]

Back in the United States, the Muslim leader described his Islamic tour to some ninety-five hundred Negroes who gathered to hear him in Los Angeles. In Boston and New York, meanwhile, Malcolm X announced that the question of the Muslims' orthodoxy is "a closed issue," because "those who are not orthodox do not go to Mecca."

The Political Implications

Like Christianity and Judaism, Islam is more than a religion: it has served also as a political force, drawing together coalitions of states for various purposes at various times. Today it is dynamically important in shaping political alignments among Moslem nations from Morocco to Indonesia—that is to say, across the entire span of the African-Asian land mass. If these states could establish a large and influential Moslem bloc in the United States, their coalition would circle the earth.

Apart from the followers of Muhammad, there are scarcely 33,000 Moslems in the whole of North America—compared with 345,000 in South America, 12½ million in Europe and more than 400 million in Africa and Asia. This disproportion is due not so much to the vitality of the Christian church as to America's immigration policies, which discriminate against Africans and Asians. To build an effective bloc in the United States, therefore, the Moslem states would have to convert large numbers of American citizens to Islam—and this the Black Muslims are doing with amazing success. The orthodox Moslem bodies in America are rapidly being dwarfed, and their cries of protest are likely to fall upon apathetic ears in the important Islamic capitals of the East.

Much has been made of an alleged link between the Black Muslims and the United Arab Republic. The Muslims are accused of accepting financial support from the Egyptians and of being "pro-Nasser." There is no evidence to support the allegation of financial support, and Muhammad has vigorously denied these allegations:

Now it has been charged that I am receiving aid from some alien government or ideology. These charges, of course, come from those who resent the progress we have made toward enlightening our people. I want to say here and now that these charges are absolutely false. I do not receive any aid from the United Arab Republic; I do not receive aid from the Communist party; there is not one dime that comes to us from any source other than our own followers.[23]

But political favors do not always turn on money. The UAR has shown little public recognition of the Movement, but Muslim leaders have been welcomed enthusiastically abroad, and the Movement has received important encouragement and advice from Egyptian nationals in this country. The Muslims have responded by considering themselves specifically "anti-Zionist" rather than "anti-Semitic," and they are proud to identify themselves with President Nasser, whose picture graces the walls of many Muslim homes and temples.

Malcolm X has made a frank bid for UAR support, offering the growth-potential of the Movement as a prime incentive. "The Arabs," he asserts, "as a colored people, should make more effort to reach the millions of colored people in America who are related to the Arabs by blood." The Arab leaders' response to this appeal is not known. But Malcolm's pledge that "these millions of colored peoples would be completely in sympathy with the Arab cause" was undoubtedly received with quiet appreciation.

In January 1958, Muhammad sent the following cablegram to President Nasser, who was then host to the Afro-Asian Conference:

Lt. President Gamal Abdel Nasser
President of the Egyptian Republic, and
Host to the Afro-Asian Conference

In the name of Allah, The Beneficent, The Merciful.
Beloved Brothers of Africa and Asia:

As-Salaam-Alaikum. Your long lost Muslim Brothers here in America pray that Allah's divine presence will be felt at this historic African-Asian Conference, and give unity to our efforts for peace and brotherhood.

Freedom, justice and equality for all Africans and Asians is of far-reaching importance, not only to you of the East, but also to over 17,000,000 of your long-lost brothers of African-Asian descent here in the West. . . . May our sincere desire for universal peace which is being manifested at this great conference by all Africans and

Asians, bring about the unity and brotherhood among all our people which we all so eagerly desire.

All success is from Allah.

As-Salaam-Alaikum:

> *Your Long-Lost Brothers of the West*
> *Elijah Muhammad*
> *Leader, Teacher and Spiritual Head of*
> *The Nation of Islam in the West. . . .*[24]

The *Pittsburgh Courier* carried President Nasser's purported reply:

Mr. Elijah Muhammad:

Leader, teacher and spiritual head of the Nation of Islam in the West.

I have received your kind message expressing your good wishes on the occasion of the African-Asian Conference. I thank you most heartily for these noble sentiments.

May Allah always grant us help to work for the maintenance of peace, which is the desire of all peoples. I extend my best wishes to our brothers of Africa and Asia living in the West.

> *(Signed) Gamal Abdel Nasser*[25]

In the summer of 1959 came Malcolm X's visit to the United Arab Republic. The invitation was originally extended to Muhammad, who then appointed Malcolm to make a preliminary tour as his emissary. Malcolm was warmly received in Cairo and Saudi Arabia by Arab officialdom, and he met all of the important people in the Moslem Congress, thus insuring Muhammad's impending visit against embarrassment. The Black Muslims were taken as Moslems, and the Egyptians were delighted by the throngs of black worshipers they saw on the 11″ x 20″ photographs Malcolm carried in his briefcase. They were also properly appalled at his descriptions of the oppression of the Black Man in America.

During his tour, Malcolm found that:

The people of Arabia are just like our people in America . . . ranging from regal black to rich brown. But none are white. It is safe to say that 99 per cent of them would be jim-crowed in the United States of America.[26]

From Africa, he wrote:

Africa is the land of the future . . . definitely the land of tomorrow, and the African is the man of tomorrow. . . . Africa is the New World, a world with a future . . . in which the so-called American Negroes are destined to play a key role. . . . Like the Asians, all Africans consider America's treatment of Negro Americans the best yardstick by which to measure the sincerity of America's offers on this continent. . . . The veil of diplomatic art does not obscure the vision of African thinkers when abuse of black Americans still obtains.[27]

A few months later, Elijah Muhammad went to Cairo and thence to the Holy City. (Strangely enough, Muhammad is not fluent in Arabic. On the counsel of his advisors, he learned the various Moslem prayers and creedal affirmations before setting out on his trip.) On his return to America, he declared: "The whole world of Islam is behind me. I was received as a brother and a leader. I did not have to ask for a visa to make the Hajj [pilgrimage] to Mecca, the Holy City. They asked me to go."[28]

That these visits of top Muslim leaders to the Islamic countries have political implications is taken for granted by most observers. The precise weight of these implications remains open to speculation. However, it is reasonable to conclude that the controversial Muslim leader could hardly have been admitted to Mecca in the face of the opposition of American Moslems unless he had powerful friends abroad to sponsor and receive him. Because of his heterodoxy, that sponsorship is unlikely to have been primarily religious. It seems possible that some Moslem leaders, at least, found the political possibilities sufficiently impressive to overbalance the religious risk.

9 The Meaning for America

The American conscience is like a Georgia mule drowsing under a mulberry tree: it will twitch where the fly bites, now here, now there, and so to sleep again.

This lethargy is the problem of America. She is neither more evil nor more immoral than any other nation, but she has a jaded social consciousness that has not been truly alerted since the time of the abolitionists. The 1954 school desegregation decisions and the student sit-ins have troubled her sleep, but they have not yet awakened her. She has not been stung in a tender enough spot in recent times. Perhaps the Black Muslims will find such a spot; if they do, and if they sting hard enough, we may all be benefited by the smarting.

I. THE SPECTRUM OF NEGRO PROTEST

A Vestige of Faith

The American Negro does not truly hate the white man. Not yet. For a long time, Negroes have tried to convince themselves that the white man's resistance to social change derives not from a sense of racial superiority but from a twisted nationalism. Some Negroes, at least, are still willing to believe that the white man behaves as he does because he is *American*.

For most of us, there is no value quite so exalted as that implicit in being "American." All other values are subsidiary— religion, political affiliation, even moral consciousness. To be an American means to be associated with a great civilization, a unique civilization. We may share certain values with the rest of the world—values of religion and art, for example—but only *we* are Americans. We are the founders and developers of and heirs to the mightiest nation on earth, with a heritage unduplicated

227

anywhere else in the world. But "American" also has an implication of color. Few of us have really lost the feeling that this is a "white man's country" and that all other races enjoy it by the white man's sufferance. We do not say this bluntly: it is considered in poor taste and, if quoted abroad, not in the national interest. But we act as if we were certain of its truth and validity. Our textbooks, mass media and community behavior confirm this white nationalism everywhere.

A diminishing number of Negroes, therefore, believe that the Negro is rejected in America not primarily because of his race but because he is "not truly American." The Negro, they believe, is considered an alien, an outsider, for whom special adjustments must be made in law and custom. His color merely identifies him and serves to warn "real Americans" of his presence. The immediate result, of course, is the same: the Negro is barred from full participation in the values of citizenship. But the long-range prospect for a solution would be vastly different. If discrimination is based on pure racial antagonism, the white man will have to change his prejudice, for the Negro cannot change his skin. But if discrimination is based on national sentiment, the white man need not revise his thinking so drastically. He can still draw the comforting, sharp line between "American" and "not American"; he need only realize that his Negro neighbors are on the "American" side of the line. From there it would be a short step to accepting the Negro as an equal.

Sophistry? Perhaps—a sophistry encouraged by the Negro's desperate wish for a peaceful way out of his second-class prison. And like his more naive, more pathetic trust in the white man's ultimate "good intentions," it has been all but completely shattered. A vestige of faith remains—but for how long? If the white man's conscience remains drugged, the flood of disillusion will soon sweep even this last frail hope away.

From time to time, the trusting Negro has sought to prod the white man's moral sense indirectly—through the churches, the labor unions and various interracial organizations—and by personal appeal. Always there has been a willingness to give the white man the benefit of every doubt. But nothing changed; and after a hundred years of waiting and hoping, the Negro finally

went to court. Where he had been willing to accept "consideration," he now began demanding his rights—his rights to work,
vote, buy a home, eat a meal, see a movie, worship in a church,
ride a bus, sit in a public park and send his children to school on
the same terms as all of America's other first-class citizens. But
the courts are slow; litigation is expensive; and the implementation
of court rulings seems to be peculiarly uncertain in the area of
civil rights.

So there has developed, in the last decade, a wide and dramatic spectrum of extralegal Negro protest. The passive Negro,
who trusts that God and the NAACP will salvage his dignity while
he concentrates on avoiding trouble, is rapidly becoming extinct.
Those Negroes (most of them young) who still believe in the
possibility of peaceful change have developed a bold but gentle
technique to quicken the white man's conscience. They simply
ignore restrictive laws and go wherever they know they have a
moral right to be—on trains and busses, in restaurants and stores,
public beaches and houses of God. These are not "angry young
men"; they are not "bitter." They are just tired of waiting.

At the opposite end of the spectrum are the Black Muslims.
They *are* angry; they *are* bitter; and they are also tired of waiting.
Their response to white nationalism is extreme, and their militancy
is barely restrained. But America can benefit from the lesson they
seem intent upon teaching.

Group Identification: The Corporate Response

In Chapter II, we noted three types of response to pressure
and discrimination: avoidance, acceptance and aggression. These
represented the attempts on the part of individuals to adjust to
social hostilities directed against them. These same channels of
response may also find a corporate expression.

People organize in the face of a persistent threat. The plan-
tation "folk Negro" is adjusting to social hostility when he goes
out alone to steal the white boss's corn or potatoes on Saturday
night. He is no less adjusting when he loses himself "beyond the
Jordan" in company with his neighbors on Sunday morning. One
response is a personal expression of resentment and aggression;

the other is a corporate escape. Each kind of response, personal
and corporate, has its special advantages in relation to the situation that excites it.

Minorities are created by pressures exerted by the majority.
If the majority did not choose to exclude a group, the group
would not be a minority; it would be an indistinguishable part of
the whole social body. In the same way, the sense of unity and
cohesion which we call group identification develops in response
to outside pressures. It is a way of ensuring not identity (the
majority has seen to that) but the survival of the members and
their most cherished values.

Professor Arnold Rose believes that "group identification is
the minority's major defense against discrimination and prejudice
from the majority."[1] This major defense seems to be clearly
effective. Wherever men have exhibited a corporate unity in the
face of social oppression, they have had respect and ofttimes an
abatement of persecution. The recent desegregation of eating
facilities in the South is a classic example. In six months of concerted effort, Negro students (supported by some whites) caused
the desegregation of lunch counters in about seventy Southern
communities.[2] To be sure, organized resistance seldom maintains
the "good will" of the prejudiced majority; but only a diseased
good will is linked with discrimination for its very existence.
Indeed, the very presence of social abuse is *de facto* evidence of
the absence of a healthy good will. What the minority group
loses by organization is not so much "good will" as an artificially
maintained rapprochement.

But group identification also has its hazards.

Group identification . . . may create foolhardiness and a tendency
to martyrdom without securing the gain that risk-taking can secure.
It creates a group pride that may become satisfied with mediocrity.
It frequently promotes chauvinism and nationalism, which volun-
tarily separates the group from the broader opportunities and contacts
that it presumably is fighting to secure.[3]

It may, in short, militate against the very aims it seeks to achieve.
A group which becomes enamoured of its own achievements, real
or mythological, or which blinds itself to the accomplishments of
other groups closes the door to its own improvement And the

image it presents to others may be so threatening as to increase tensions or cause outright alarm.

Most ethnic minorities in the United States can look forward to eventual assimilation, for their distinguishing characteristics are cultural rather than biological.[4] Consequently, their organizations tend to exist primarily for sociability rather than for defense or protest. Such organizations came into being as temporary expedients, until the organizational life of the majority is opened to their members, and the least severely excluded minorities show the least incidence of in-group associations. European immigrants, for example, have a very low incidence of such associations (except those related to their churches), while American Negroes probably have more in-group organizations than all other minorities combined. A few years ago the Common Council for American Unity estimated that there are only 155 fraternal organizations, with fewer than 3 million members, for all the different nationality groups in the United States.[5] But this figure did not include racial groups. It would probably have been *doubled* by the inclusion of Negro fraternal groups alone, not to mention the Negro defense and protest organizations, which span the entire spectrum from the ultra-radicalism of the Black Muslims to the ultra-conservatism of the National Urban League.

Jews, like Negroes, have developed a large number of voluntary associations, though most Jews do not belong to them.[6] "When Jews find themselves unwanted in fraternities, country clubs, and other sociable organizations, they form their own in great numbers to 'demonstrate' that they can enjoy themselves without benefit of admission to the majority's sociable groups."[7] Neither group does so without resentment; but the Jew, who has a unique, well-defined and clearly remembered cultural heritage to sustain him, probably suffers less from exclusion from the common life of the majority group than does the Negro, who has adopted the cultural heritage of the group which excludes him.

Moreover, some Jews can and do pass into the dominant white group, often through the simple expedient of changing their names. Like Negroes, some may pass temporarily in order to enjoy advantages or avoid discrimination in business or social life. In a New York suburb, for example, there is a Jew whose legal name is John Smith; and as Dr. John Smith he has a good dental practice. How he would fare if he practiced as Jacob Goldstein is problematic. Dr. Smith himself has no doubt but that, in the community where he lives, there is a considerably larger practice available to Dr. Smith than there would be to, say, Dr. Goldstein.

America has never been a land of unlimited opportunity for Jews. As soon as they arrived on our shores, they found themselves confronted with the same bigotry and hatred that had driven them from Spain, from Russia, from every corner of the globe. But the Jews fought back. They organized for the protection of the group. First, the Independent Order B'nai B'rith, or "Sons of the Covenant," was founded in New York City in 1843. Three quarters of a century later, in 1913, the Anti-Defamation League was organized as a unit of B'nai B'rith specifically for the purpose of combating anti-Semitism. It does so primarily by investigating and exposing anti-Semitic groups.

The American Jewish Committee, the American Jewish Congress (which uses legal action, educational propaganda and social research as weapons against bigotry), the Jewish War Veterans, the Jewish Labor Committee—these and a substantial number of other national, state and local organizations serve the Jewish community in two ways. They stand guard against prejudice and discrimination, keeping a watchful eye on such areas as civil rights, immigration laws, American foreign policy in the Middle East, politics and interfaith relations. And they caution the Jewish community itself against yielding blindly to a false acceptance. In many communities, Jews can be accepted warmly by the majority if they will simply give up their Jewish identity and cultural values. This is, of course, an indirect anti-Semitism, and the organizations seek to meet it by acting as rallying points for the preservation of Jewish values.

Except for these Jewish groups and the comparable Negro groups, there are in America few widely known minority protest or protective organizations. Perhaps the only such organizations exist among the Japanese-Americans, who, like Negroes, suffer from high social visibility. Most Japanese-American groups are social and mutual aid societies (such as the *kenjinkai,* or organizations of families originating in the same *ken,* or prefecture).

For many years, however, the Japanese Association of North America sought to protect Japanese-Americans from discrimination and was active in many legal cases on their behalf. Unfortunately, unlike its counterpart, the NAACP, the JANA was neither broadly based nor successful: all its members were Japanese, most of them alien, and the group lost nearly every case it entered. Eventually it confined its activities to promoting social welfare and Americanization among its members.

A far more effective social action group, the Japanese-Americans Citizenship League, developed out of the old JANA. Unlike the parent organization, the JACL admits only American citizens to membership. It has an able and energetic leadership, and like many Negro organizations, it has the support of some liberal whites. The JACL is both a political and a community service organization; it has entered the courts in a number of cases with conspicuous success.

Spanish-speaking Americans, the second largest unassimilated ethnic group in the country,[8] have organized a number of local or regional groups which concern themselves with problems arising from discrimination. The largest of these is the United League of Latin American Citizens, commonly known as ULLAC.[9] Most of the 3½ million Spanish-speaking minority, however, is concentrated in the Southwest (almost a third of them in Texas),[10] and ULLAC necessarily confines its major activities to state and regional problems.

It is the Negroes, then, more than any other minority, who find a corporate release in social, protective and protest organizations. It is the Negroes who give decidedly the most emphasis to protest organizations and whose protest finds the widest range of corporate expression. But all Negro protest groups, across the entire spectrum, have one thing in common: a new sense of *urgency,* which sets them sharply apart from the comparable groups of other minorities.

Every Negro protest organization today is, in its own way, impatient. Each is learning to seize the moral initiative. Each is preparing to force America to a showdown. And sooner or later, America will have to yield—if not to the soft-spoken, reasonable demands of the conservative organizations, then to the strident, extreme and vengeful demands of the black nationalists. For the moment—a brief and fateful moment—the choice is still in our hands.

II. SEPARATIST ORGANIZATIONS

Most Negro organizations are restricted in membership to Negroes alone. This is not entirely a matter of choice: white separatism rules out any realistic alternative, except in organizations whose sole interest is civil rights. A few white men are willing to work with the Negro on strictly racial matters; almost none are willing to relax with him, pray with him or work with him on issues other than civil rights. On the other hand, Negro organizations of a separatist nature—that is, of deliberate in-group membership—are seriously hampered by their very exclusiveness in such civil-rights activities as they do undertake.

Making a virtue of necessity, the Negro turns to these organizations primarily for a sense of group identification, which serves him as an important bastion against feelings of inferiority and helplessness. In such groups he discovers (in Lloyd Warner's words) "a focal point of organization and . . . the necessary feelings of strength and security."

Until fairly recent times, the Negro's church was the most important organization standing between him and the unremitting pressures of our caste-oriented society. To a great extent, the church was escapist. E. Franklin Frazier observes that it "has two roots: one in the efforts of the free Negroes in the North to escape from their inferior position in white churches and assert their independence, and the other in what has been aptly called the 'invisible' institution on the plantations during slavery."[11] Benjamin Mays concludes that "if the Negro had had greater freedom in the social, economic, and political spheres, fewer Negroes would have been 'called' to preach, and there would have been fewer Negro churches."[12]

Indeed, in one large biracial denomination today, the Negro leadership is said not merely to tolerate but to endorse the continuance of separate congregations, with the "inferiority" of the Negro membership accepted in exchange for the "equality" of the

Negro clergy and other church officials. A national news magazine reports:

Racial segregation should be continued in the Methodist Church for the foreseeable future . . . a Methodist Commission reported last week. There was no minority dissent to the report. . . . Moreover, leaders of the 360,000 Methodist Negroes . . . agreed with the decision. The reason for this extraordinary state of affairs [is that] . . . this segregation [has] brought some advantages for Negro Methodist in terms of representation and influence in the Church. . . . There are four Negro Methodist bishops in the [all Negro] Central Jurisdiction, for instance, while the theoretically non-segregated Protestant Episcopal Church in the U.S.A. has none at all in the continental U.S.[13]

The participants to this arrangement do not wholly agree with the popular interpretation of it, but that interpretation suggests a widespread feeling in the Negro community that the church has withdrawn from any effective interest in social action.

The Negro church has not, of course, been entirely escapist:

The [Negro] churches have sometimes been charged with providing an escapist philosophy and so diverting the Negro protest. There is, no doubt, considerable truth in this charge, especially with respect to the revivalist churches to which many lower-class Negroes belong. But the all-Negro church was probably the very first protest organization under slavery, and . . . many Negro ministers [today] take their texts from those sections of the Bible which favor equality and fraternity.[14]

It remains true, nevertheless, that the Negro church has never been a significant instrument of effective protest. Furthermore, the Negro clergy has yielded a considerable amount of its influence in recent years to business and to other professions. Only lately are there some indications of a renaissance in clerical leadership; and even now, the most significant social leadership is offered by those denominations that lack institutionalized hierarchy. "For the most part, Negro churches have contributed to the perpetuation of the American racial system through the reinforcement of the extant mores."[15] In spite of its estimated 10 million members,[16] the Negro church has sponsored comparatively few programs against the discrimination it exemplifies.[17]

The Negro has traditionally relied upon various types of fraternal organizations to assure him comfort and companionship while he lives and often to bury him (or at least to dignify his funeral) when he dies. His lodges and orders have frequently been the only arena in which he could exercise his political interests; and in many communities, except for his churches, they have been the only social and recreational outlets available to him. In recent years the fraternal orders have diminished in importance, yet even today one rarely encounters a Negro community without at last an order of Masons or Elks. The latter organization, under the leadership of such astute politicians as Republican George W. Lee of Memphis, has long been an important factor in national politics. As a general rule, however, neither politics nor social protest has been a prime concern of the fraternal orders, and they have had little influence on the lightening of the Negro's racial burdens.

Negro fraternal organizations date back to 1775, at least, for on March 6 of that year, fifteen Negroes were initiated into a British lodge of Freemasons at Boston. After the Revolution, the white American Masons refused their Negro brothers permission to set up a lodge, but the Negroes applied directly to the Grand Lodge of England and were immediately granted a charter. The first Negro lodge was established in Boston in 1787. Through much the same procedure, the Odd Fellows were chartered in New York City in 1843 under direct warrant from England.

The Colored Knights of Pythias was probably unique in its origin. In 1870, a group of Negro citizens petitioned the Supreme Lodge for membership. When the petition was denied, several fair-skinned Negroes, passing as white, infiltrated the order and learned its ritual. They then set up a Supreme Council and organized a lodge of their own in Vicksburg, Mississippi. It is ironic that the order from which they were excluded had itself been created "to extend friendship, charity, and benevolence among men." Negro lodges were soon organized throughout the country.

Perhaps the most important of the older fraternal and benevolent associations is the Improved Benevolent and Protective Order of Elks, founded in Cincinnati in 1898. By 1946 the Elks had a half million members and owned property and U. S. War Bonds worth more than $50 million. The Order had given

$500,000 in scholarships to Negro college students through its Grand Commissioner of Education and had contributed important equipment to Meharry and Howard University medical schools. Its Civil Liberties Department has been active in civil rights litigation on behalf of Negroes.

Eight college-based Greek letter societies for Negroes represent a membership of almost 135,000 men and women.[18] These societies, like the older fraternal organizations, grew out of the exclusion of Negroes from participation in the normal social life of the community to which education and status would have normally entitled them.

The first Negro fraternity—not a college society—was organized by a group of men of similar interests and social status in Philadelphia in 1904. Sigma Pi Phi, now more commonly referred to as "the *Boulé*," has traditionally conceived itself as an "aristocracy of talent" and has, in fact, included among its members some of America's most distinguished Negroes. E. Franklin Frazier describes it as apparently "governed still by that [outlook] of the 'isolated aristocracy of talent' which comprised its membership 40 or more years ago. . . . But the spirit of social exclusiveness has persisted while the emphasis on intellectual and professional attainment has disappeared."[19] In recent years, the *Boulé* has waned in prestige and membership, for the college fraternities are more attractive to the "talent" that used to embellish its rolls.

The first Negro college fraternity, Alpha Phi Alpha, was organized at Cornell University in 1906, when, "because of race prejudice these students were not eligible for membership in white fraternities and were excluded from general participation in the social activities of the University."[20] Five years later, the same experience gave birth to a second fraternity, Kappa Alpha Psi. Two others followed at Negro colleges in 1911 (Omega Psi Phi) and 1914 (Phi Beta Sigma), as did four sororities during the same general period.

Unlike the *Boulé,* the college fraternities (mainly through their graduate chapters) have participated vigorously in the fight for full citizenship and have shown a constructive over-all concern for the welfare of the Negro community. For several years, these organizations jointly supported the American Council on Human

Rights (ACHR), a Washington-based organization concerned with minority-group protection. One sorority, Alpha Kappa Alpha, maintained a lobby in Washington to influence legislation affecting Negroes; it has also spent thousands of dollars sponsoring an extended Health Project to provide medical and dental care for Negroes in several Mississippi counties. Another, Delta Sigma Theta, has a comprehensive program including support of child welfare and aid to delinquent girls. The fraternity Kappa Alpha Psi has an extensive "Guide Right" program for counseling Negro high school youths and encouraging them to prepare themselves for creative participation in American vocational and professional life. All the Greek letter societies have contributed important financial support to the NAACP.

In the Negro community, these societies have a community-wide responsibility that is not paralleled by their white counterparts. They began as social clubs, and they remain so; but their very existence is a sobering reminder of the unusual responsibilities that devolve upon educated Negroes in terms of leadership and example. The societies are controlled by Negro intellectual and professional leaders, rather than being centered on the college campuses; and while they represent a certain exclusiveness (only college men and women of acceptable academic performance may become members), they are dedicated to a creative concern for the entire racial group.

III. INTEGRATIVE ORGANIZATIONS

Most Negro organizations are separatist in membership; only a few find it advisable or necessary to invite white participation. There are two main reasons. First, a biracial invitation involves, for the Negro, the risk of a humiliating rebuff. Second, each member of a biracial group must forego the sense of strength and security—a counterbalance to his individual weakness—that comes with racial solidarity. This is true even though the massive proportion of the membership might be, in fact, of the same race. No organization would expose its members to such risks if it did not consider integration itself an issue of extreme importance. It is not surprising, therefore, that the few integrative (not racially exclusive) organizations which do exist in the Negro community have integration as their fundamental purpose for being.

Since the term "integration" produces, in many people, an excruciating anxiety,[21] a few definitions may be in order. *Integration,* for our present purposes, refers to the freedom of a minority to participate in the total life of the community without necessarily merging with the majority group. In an integrated society, each minority is assured of this freedom by specific laws, a tradition of justice and a prevailing sense of respect for human dignity and aspiration. It is also free, however, to retain its own identity and cultural values. *Assimilation,* on the other hand, refers to the merging of a minority into the general community and the gradual disappearance of its identity and its unique cultural values. In an assimilated society, a minority group does not cling—and is not forced to cling—together. Its members flow into the general community, accepted and fully mobile in every area of social and cultural intercourse.[22]

Unlike the Jew, the Negro need not be troubled by the possibility of assimilation into the mainstream of American life. Even those Negroes who consider it desirable know that it is not soon to be achieved. "Assimilation," Gunnar Myrdal has warned, "is likely to occur only when the majority accepts the idea." Other observers are more specific: "When the combined cultural and biological traits are highly divergent from those of the host society, the subordination of the group will be very great, their subsystem strong, the period of assimilation long, and the process slow and painful."[23] The American Negro does not seriously address either his efforts or his hopes to such a goal.

But if he is unexcited about assimilation, he is intensely serious about integration, and an increasing number of his organizations are devoting themselves energetically to that end.

Probably the best-known organization commonly associated with Negroes is the National Association for the Advancement of Colored People. The NAACP was created by liberal whites and militant Negroes, largely in response to the increasing outrages against Negroes in the South early in this century. J. Saunders Redding reports that:

In the first decade of the [present] century, nearly a thousand of them [Negroes] were lynched in public spectacles that outmatched the Roman circus for savagery and obscenity. No appeal to conscience was effective. Civil, legal, and moral rights meant nothing.[24]

White supremacy and a white disposition to violence followed the Negroes as, in terror and despair, they migrated north and west. In the summer of 1908, a race riot—precipitated by a false accusation of rape, and led by a white woman, who was already under indictment as a criminal and out of jail on bond—focused the attention of the nation on Springfield, Illinois. "Here in the home of Abraham Lincoln, a mob containing many of the town's best citizens raged for two days, killed and wounded scores of Negroes, and drove thousands from the city."[25] In the wake of the riot, the city of Springfield discharged more than fifty Negro employees, although their efficiency and fidelity were not in doubt. The state of Illinois dismissed still others. A thousand disheartened Negroes, "many of them substantial and respected citizens, left the city for parts unknown."

It was against this background that the NAACP came into being. In an article in the *Independent,* the prominent Southern journalist William English Walling declared:

Either the spirit of the abolitionists, of Lincoln and Lovejoy, must be revived and we must come to treat the Negro on a plane of absolute political and social equality, or [Southern demagogues] will soon have transferred the race war to the North.[26]

Walling was moved not so much by the riot itself as by the implications of such terror for the national welfare. If unchecked, such behavior could destroy the political democracy and the unity of a nation only two generations emerged from civil strife. "Who realizes the seriousness of the situation," he appealed, "and what large and powerful body of citizens is ready . . . to aid?"

As a result of Walling's article—and through the good offices of Mary White Ovington, a wealthy white social worker in New York City—a call "for a national conference on the Negro question" was issued on Lincoln's birthday of the following year. The response was indicative of the concern of men and women of stature over the unhappy state of affairs. To the meeting came such notables as W. E. B. DuBois, Jane Addams, John Dewey, Moorefield Storey, Oswald Garrison Villard, Rabbi Stephen Wise,

William Lloyd Garrison and J. G. Phelps Stokes. Fifty-three persons signed the statement, and the NAACP was formally incorporated in 1910, committed to an uncompromising policy of racial equality.

The NAACP today "is a large membership organization, with some 350,000 members located in almost every state. . . . More than 50 percent of the members are in the 17 southern and border states. Both the membership and the national staff of 90 persons are multiracial, with an estimated 8 to 12 percent of whites among the members."[27] All presidents of the NAACP have been white, as are twelve of the forty-eight members of the present board of directors. The executive secretary, Roy Wilkins, and the chief legal counsel, Thurgood Marshall, are Negroes. The treasurer is Allan Knight Chalmers, a white professor at the Boston University School of Theology.

The Board of Directors has included such well known persons as Walter Reuther, Ralph Bunche, Mrs. Eleanor Roosevelt, Benjamin Mays, Herbert H. Lehman and Judge William H. Hastie. Among the vice presidents (the association has twenty-one) have been Norman Cousins, Senator Wayne Morse, Rabbi Judah Cohn, Oscar Hammerstein II, Bishop W. J. Walls, Eric Johnston and A. Philip Randolph.

In the fifty years of its existence, the NAACP has done much to loosen the collar of caste that has chafed the Negro's neck for so long. It has made a triple-threat attack—legal, legislative and educational—against disprivilege and discrimination. Its legal efforts have included forty-six appeals to the United States Supreme Court; it has won all but four. Among the victories have been court rulings that racial segregation is unconstitutional in public schools and colleges, in public parks and playgrounds, in intrastate busses and in interstate travel accommodations of all kinds. The NAACP has won Supreme Court decisions invalidating the enforcement of racially restrictive covenants in housing; it has more firmly established the Negro's right and opportunity to vote; it has enabled him to escape the indignity of eating in segregated dining rooms or waiting in segregated waiting rooms when he travels beyond the borders of his state. It has been a major factor in the passage of fair employment legislation in fifteen states and has been successful in its efforts to eliminate discrimination in public housing in at least eight states. It has championed the student sit-in movement and provided expert counsel for students who have been jailed in the course of such demonstrations.

The effectiveness of the NAACP can perhaps be seen most clearly through the attempts that have been made to destroy it. In 1956 alone, Louisiana, Alabama and Texas banned the organization by court decree, and the Virginia legislature moved to halt its activities in that state. Several Southern states have laws which make it impossible for public servants such as teachers to belong to the organization and still retain their jobs. The list goes on and on, for the NAACP has made more important enemies than any other organization with which Negroes have ever been associated in their journey along "the lonesome road." This could well be the best index of its success.

Like the NAACP, the Urban League is meticulously bi-racial. Of its executive board of fifteen members, eight are white and seven are Negroes. The league has always had a white president and a Negro executive secretary. And like the NAACP, the league looks to the combined efforts of Negroes and whites to find some workable solutions for the country's racial problems. The Reverend J. A. McDaniel, executive secretary of the Memphis Urban League, interprets the philosophy of the national organization as follows:

The Urban League is an interracial organization, and it strives to work within the framework of interracial cooperation. We [Negroes and whites] are interdependent—one upon the other. We of the Urban League do not believe that the Negro can resolve his problems alone; nor can the white man [resolve his] alone. But working together in the American philosophy of teamwork, we can resolve our differences and our problems.[28]

But here the similarity between these organizations ends.

"If the NAACP was too radical to merit the support of the philanthropists who gave to Negro causes," observes J. Saunders Redding, "the National Urban League was not."[29] In this distinction lies the answer to much of the present confusion about the roles of these organizations. The NAACP receives the greater part of its financing from membership fees, individual contributions and foundation grants. The Urban League is dependent almost entirely upon local resources, such as community chests. The league's program and philosophy, therefore, must remain within certain conservative limits; it must remain acceptable to its local sources of support. Yet the league is governed by national policies; its program emphases vary according to local needs and conditions, but even in the South it hews closely to its founding commitments.

The league was born as a coalition of three social agencies in New York City in 1910. Around 1905 or 1906 two interracial groups—the Committee for Improving the Industrial Conditions of Negroes in New York City and the League for the Protection of Colored Women—were organized by certain white philanthropists in an attempt to ameliorate social conditions among Negroes in New York. In 1910 a similar group, the Committee on Urban Conditions Among Negroes, made its debut. In 1911 these three organizations merged to become the National League of Urban Conditions Among Negroes (later abbreviated to National Urban League), espousing the theme that the Negro needs "not alms but opportunity—opportunity to work at the job for which the Negro [is] best fitted, with equal pay for equal work, and equal opportunity for advancement." This has remained the league's controlling philosophy, and "jobs for Negroes" has received its major program emphasis, although other services are frequently made available.

The league today maintains fifty-eight branches in twenty-nine states, with twelve affiliates in the South. (Its executive offices, like those of the NAACP, are in New York City.) Along with screening, training and selling of Negro labor, most local affiliates offer a multitude of other services. They may operate day nurseries and baby clinics, promote health weeks, find homes for wayward girls, provide individual testing and counseling services, serve as clearinghouses for information about Negroes or advise government or municipal agencies on matters affecting the Negro community. But the primary concern of every local Urban League is to find jobs, more jobs and better jobs for Negro citizens.

Like the NAACP, the National Urban League has been criticized by members of both races as being "too radical" or "too conservative." It is probably fairer to say that each local league moves as rapidly as local conditions warrant. Sometimes it moves slightly in advance of the community it has undertaken to serve, but it never moves so far ahead as to isolate itself and its program from the good will and financial support of its interracial supporters. In contrast to the NAACP, the National Urban League pioneers without being adventurous, and the type of interracial rapport it seeks to establish could hardly be accomplished in any other way. Its services and methods, though unspectacular, are very important, for through its program the conditions that produce potential Black Muslims are being quietly—though slowly— eliminated.

As Gunnar Myrdal has suggested, no single organization can be effective alone in combating racial prejudice, for no single organization can work simultaneously through speed and gradualness, through assertiveness and compromise. A variety of specialized groups concentrating on limited and particular problems is far more successful than any multifaceted, monolithic organization could be—far more capable of exciting the imagination and eliciting the support of major segments of the general population.

For this reason, a number of Negro (or Negro-oriented) antisegregation organizations have come into being or become prominent since 1954, when the Supreme Court rejected the "separate but equal" doctrine for public schools. Perhaps the most famous of these groups is the Montgomery Improvement Association, organized in 1955 by Dr. Martin Luther King and his associates in Montgomery, Alabama. The MIA grew out of a protest against segregated seating on the Montgomery city busses. It eventually won the support of most of the 50,000 Negroes in that city and of thousands of people of every race throughout the world. For more than a year, the Negroes of Montgomery walked to their jobs, to school and to church, rather than submit any longer to the indignities and abuse of segregated seating on public busses. Eventually, segregation on the busses was outlawed, as it has been in many another city since. Dr. King moved to Atlanta to continue his work as president of a new organization, the Southern Christian Leadership Conference, which stresses nonviolent action as a technique for effecting social change. But the MIA remains as an organ of protest and a symbol of the Montgomery Negroes' determination to be "first class."

For a number of years, the Atlanta-based Southern Regional Council has worked quietly behind the scenes to keep open the channels of communication between Negroes and whites in the South. The biracial council does not consider itself a "race-relations" organization in the strictest sense of that word; it works toward equal opportunities for both races as a means to a higher standard of well-being for all men. The council operates in twelve Southern states. It compiles data and statistics, provides information on racial frictions and interracial achievements, and strives to reduce conflict while producing equality of opportunity. Its several agencies are professionally staffed with social scientists and experts in human relations.

The student sit-in movement has introduced more direct action, though it has pledged itself to techniques of nonviolence. This movement began as a spontaneous rejection of segregation on February 1, 1960, when four Negro students who had been shopping at a Woolworth store in Greensboro, North Carolina, sat down at the lunch counter and requested service. They were refused but continued to wait patiently—a gesture that fired the popular imagination and was quickly imitated elsewhere. The movement spread rapidly throughout the South; and in less than a year, some eating facilities in about a hundred cities had been desegregated. In Atlanta, the sit-ins crystallized into a structured organization with a permanent headquarters.[30] Scores of students have been arrested and jailed, but there is no sign of abatement in the protests of the Negro students and their white allies. They remain undaunted, even in the face of repeated demonstrations by the once-dreaded Ku Klux Klan.

Numerous other direct-action groups have also appeared, some in specific localities and others—such as the Committee on Racial Equality (CORE)—with nationwide interests. As the crisis becomes more acute, new groups will doubtless arise and take their places beside them. For the widespread fear and intimidation, which characterized the illiterate Negroes of another age, is gone forever. Today's generation of Negro youth are not afraid. They are determined to change the Negro's status *now*—by nonviolent action, if nonviolence will work. So long as they have a vestige of faith in the white man's latent decency, their strength will be exerted through integrative organizations to shape an integrated society. But if that flickering faith is allowed to perish, black nationalism may feed sumptuously on their despair.

IV. THE BLACK MUSLIM MOVEMENT

The Black Muslims constitute a unique movement: a dynamic social protest that moves upon a religious vehicle. The Movement's main emphases are upon social action. Yet it is none the less essentially a religion—a religion of protest.

Religion addresses itself to the ultimate problems of human life. "It is the refusal to capitulate to death, to give up in the face of frustration, to allow hostility to tear apart one's human associations."[31] It gives meaning and depth to life in the face of experiences that appear meaningless and shallow. But it may also concentrate the strength of the individual or community for an immediate challenge to intolerable injustice or repression.

The beliefs and rites that make up a religion are the expressions of those who have felt the problems most intensively, who have been most acutely sensitive to the tragedies of death, the burdens of frustration, the sense of failure, the disruptive effects of hostility. Powered by the strength of their feelings, . . . religious innovators have created "solutions" appropriate to the enormity of the problems . . . [which] have brought their adherents some relief. Thus religions are built to carry the "peak load" of human emotional need. . . .

In this sense, religion can be thought of as a kind of residual means of response and adjustment. It is an attempt to explain what cannot otherwise be explained; to achieve power, all other powers having failed us; to establish poise and serenity in the face of evil and suffering that other efforts have failed to eliminate.[32]

It is within this frame of reference that the Black Muslim Movement must be evaluated.

The Edge of the Spectrum

The spectrum of Negro protest organizations covers a wide span, from the most reticent separatist groups to the most determined integrative movements. At what point on this span are the Black Muslims to be found?

On the surface, the Movement seems to be unequivocally separatist, with a restricted membership and an overwhelming dedication to group identification, racial solidarity and mutual aid. But the membership is not restricted to Negroes; it is restricted to Black Men, who comprise all mankind except the white race. The Movement is thus highly integrative in intent. Yet whites and Negroes account for very nearly the entire population of America, so the Movement is clearly separatist in effect.

As a separatist group, the Muslims might be expected to show a strong awareness of group solidarity, backed by a generous program of mutual aid. And so they do. Like other Negro separatist groups, they might also be expected to pay only casual attention to racial tensions and the prospect of integration in America. The Muslims, however, are obsessed with this issue. They reject and detest the very idea of integration, but discussion of it dominates all their preachings and publications. In this focus of attention they seem to range themselves as an integrative group —turned inside out.

Indeed, in their whole sphere of social concerns, the Black Muslims are a paradox. They are obsessed with the humiliation of white supremacy, yet they scorn any gesture toward civil rights. And they respond to racial tensions in *all three* basic ways: by aggression, avoidance and acceptance. Their aggression is extreme; their vilification of the white man is impassioned and caustic, with its cardinal tenet the white man's imminent doom. This aggression has thus far fallen short of physical violence; but few observers doubt that the Muslims, if they were physically harassed, would hesitate to retaliate in kind. At the same time, the Muslim doctrines of religious and economic separation are a model of avoidance. And the Muslim dogma of absolute hostility between the Black Man and the white "devil" is simply an acceptance of the dogma of the white supremacists, made palatable by reversing the values held to be inherent in "black" and "white." The Muslim dogma is thus, in great part, a lightly disguised rationalization of things as they are, though the Muslims declare that their destiny is to change the social order rather than to accept and reinforce it.

As a religion, the Movement is also a paradox. It is a legitimate Islamic sect; yet it teaches from the Bible, and it rejects certain of the cardinal Moslem doctrines, notably those of pan-racial brotherhood and the unique divinity of Allah. The Movement is vauntedly anti-Christian, yet it taunts the white man by measuring him against his own high Christian principles—a tactic that implies a strong, though disillusioned, Muslim respect for Christian ideals. Finally, the Movement is a religion with no distinct God, no afterlife and no heaven. It is a religion of the here-and-now. In this, of course, it somewhat resembles Buddhism; but whereas Buddhism is motivated by love, the Black Muslim Movement is powered and energized by hate.

Yet, for all its paradoxes, the Movement's position on the spectrum of Negro protest is clear. Whether separatist or integrative, whether aggressive or avoiding or accepting, the Movement is temperamentally extremist. It is balanced precariously at the very edge of the spectrum, at the farthest extreme from the serene near-docility of the Negro Church. If the Movement becomes significantly more extreme—and this is a possibility that must be reckoned with—it will no longer be expressing simple protest. It will have crossed the line to open and violent rebellion.

Function and Dysfunction

The Black Muslims, though they scrupulously obey all the laws which govern American citizens, do not consider themselves Americans at heart. They are a separate people, citizens of the Black Nation, joyously obedient to the laws of Allah as interpreted by his Messenger, Elijah Muhammad. To affirm and support the functional structure of American society—the fabric of mutual interrelationships that holds our many groups and subgroups together—is the furthest thing from their mind. Yet it is essential for us to evaluate the Movement, at least tentatively, in terms of its impact upon the organic unity of our society. Only in this way can we begin to understand what challenge we are facing and how we must respond.

Such an evaluation can never be definitive or precise. For example, America is not perfect, and attempts to cure its imperfections may take the form of serious intergroup conflict. Is this social conflict functional? Robert K. Merton holds that it is, so long as it aims at adaptation and adjustment *within the system*, not apart from it. This seems to be reasonable, but other observers disagree;[33] and in any case, the line between functional and dysfunctional social conflict remains hazy. Nor is this the only difficulty. The same social phenomenon may often be seen as both functional and dysfunctional (that is, as tending to shatter the organic unity of the society). To identify it as functional or dysfunctional, one must try to estimate its *ultimate* impact on the social fabric. Such a judgment is hazardous at best. Moreover, every broad evaluation of a group in these terms is inescapably subjective, since the benchmark is the observer's own perception of the nature and limits of our society as an organic whole.

For all these reasons and more, the functional and dysfunctional aspects of the Black Muslim Movement are not always easy to assess. But an attempt must be made. The Muslims are growing daily in size and power, and they are determined to have an impact on our entire way of life.

The Black Muslim Movement is functional for its membership, for the entire Negro community and for the society as a whole in its insistence upon high standards of personal and group morality. It encourages thrift, cleanliness, honesty, sexual morality, diet control and abstinence from intoxicating liquors, and it effectively reestablishes a center of authority in the home. Muslims are expected to hold steady jobs, to give a full day's work for their pay and to respect all constituted authority. As a result, the Movement reduces adult and juvenile delinquency and strengthens its members' sense of independence and self-respect.

At a deeper level, the Movement provides outlets, short of physical violence, for the aggressive feelings roused in its members by the callous and hostile white society. Muslims tend to be Negroes for whom the pressures of racial prejudice and discrimination were intolerable, whose increasing resentment and hatred of the white man demanded release. Unable to rationalize their deprivations (as Negro intellectuals do) and unable to find relief in the Christian church or any secular institution, they might well have followed the downward paths open to the despairing everywhere—the paths of crime, drunkenness, dope addiction, prostitution and wanton violence, directed indiscriminately against their oppressors or displaced senselessly against others of the oppressed. As Muslims, however, they find a "safe" outlet for their tensions in verbal attacks on the white man and in powerful demonstrations of group solidarity. Indeed, the Movement is most clearly functional in its regeneration of men and women who, having despaired of more creative possibilities, found themselves enslaved to destructive habits and lost to social usefulness.

The religious awakening which the Movement brings to its adherents is also functional for the entire society. Many Muslims had previously been affiliated with no religion; others had been Christians but found their needs unmet by the characteristic expressions of the contemporary church. On the whole, it is better for society for its dissatisfied elements to be associated with some religion rather than with none. (The specific religious doctrines of the Movement are, of course, irrelevant here. The organic unity of American society is not threatened by such articles of faith as the Muslims' respect for the Quran as the word of Allah or their belief in Fard as divine.)

In several important ways, the Muslims tend to strengthen the dignity and self-reliance of the Negro community. They are proving dramatically that a new, positive leadership cadre can emerge among American Negroes at the grass-roots level. The Muslim schools are emphasizing Negro history, Negro achievements and the contributions of Negroes to the world's great cultures and to the development of the American nation. These facts are rarely taught in public schools, and the Muslims may be alone in trying to bring the Negro community to an awareness of its racial heritage. Again, the Muslims' "buy black" policy is creating some new opportunities for Negro business and professional men—opportunities which are almost universally denied them in the wider community.

The Black Muslims do not, of course, want the Negro community to share its new-found skills and creative energies with the despised white man. But their drive to make the Negro aware of his own potential is nevertheless functional. Despite the Muslims' appeal for separation, a Negro community awakened at last to dignity and self-reliance will be ready to insist upon its status as an equal partner in the American democratic enterprise.

Finally, the very existence of the Muslims—their extreme black nationalism and their astonishing growth and vitality—is functional to the extent that it forces the larger, Christian community to face the reality of racial tensions, to acknowledge its own malfeasance and to begin a spiritual and moral reform. The Muslims' dramatic expression of racial solidarity may shock the white man into a realization that Negroes will no longer permit their just demands to be casually shrugged aside. Indeed, Muslim extremism may even rebound and actively assist the forces of integration. It may, for example, force a white reappraisal of other protest organizations, such as the NAACP, which are now widely resisted as "too pushy" or "radical." If these groups come to be seen as relatively conservative, if they gain increasing white support, and if the great surge of Negro protest is constructively channeled as a result, the Muslims will have proved integrative despite themselves. But this possibility hangs upon a slender thread—the hope that America will take the warning and act to save itself in time.

The Black Muslims' virulent attacks on the white man may prove to be a useful warning, but they are deeply dysfunctional in the most immediate sense. They threaten the security of the white majority and may lead those in power to tighten the barriers which already divide America. The attacks create guilt and defensiveness among both Negroes and whites, and offer to extremist elements on both sides a cover for antisocial behavior. Above all, the attacks promote a general increase in tension and mutual mistrust. Calm heads might see the Muslims as a timely warning; jittery and frightened men are more likely to lash back in an unreasoning and potentially explosive panic.

These attacks on the white man may also have tragic consequences for international relations. Americans tend to take for granted that the rising nations of Afro-Asia are Moslem, but few of us have a clear knowledge of even the major tenets of the Moslem faith. If the Black Muslims become accepted here as a legitimate Moslem sect, their doctrines—including their hatred of the white man—may well be mistaken for orthodox Moslem doctrines, at least by the rank and file. In that case, the true Moslem ideal of panracial brotherhood would either remain generally unknown or else be considered an all-too-familiar hypocrisy. Such a misunderstanding might contribute disastrously to the triggering of political tensions as the Western and Afro-Asian worlds meet.

Muslim attacks on Christianity, its clergy and its believers are also immediately dysfunctional. The Muslims' refusal to distinguish the offenses of individuals from the principles of the Christian religion is inescapably divisive. The abuse of Negro women and the lynching of Negro men are not *Christian* acts. By identifying them as such, the Muslims are intensifying social discord and raising still higher the barriers to creative social interaction.

But these overt attacks on the white man and his prevailing religion are, at least, on the surface. They can be watched carefully and, to some extent, counteracted. A more insidious dysfunction is implicit in the very premise of the Movement and is furthered by every Muslim activity, even by those activities whose functional value must also command respect. This dysfunction is the deliberate attempt to break all contacts between the Negro and the white man in America.

Segregation is not, of course, a Muslim innovation. It was begun and enforced in America by the white man; the Muslims have added only a black seal of approval. But a deliberate policy of segregation is always dysfunctional, regardless of its source.

To the extent that the Negroes develop peculiar and exclusive institutions, they are to that degree isolated from the only culture they may hope to acquire. The creation of a distinctive Negro culture in the midst of an advanced and highly complex civilization is manifestly impossible. If, because of distinctive temperamental traits, the Negro group has the capacity to enrich modern culture by a distinctive racial contribution, it can be done by the incorporation of the group rather than by their exclusion.[34]

A functional group is one that reinforces not the status quo, whatever that happens to be, but the organic unity of the society. Segregation is a dysfunctional part of America's status quo, though our irresistible trend is toward integration. In siding with the disease against the cure, the Muslims are profoundly and decisively dysfunctional, both to the Negro community and to the society as a whole.

V. THE DEEPER CAUSE

"Minorities," Gordon Allport has written with wisdom and insight, "are damned if they seek assimilation, damned if they don't. . . . What is needed is freedom for both assimilation and pluralism to occur according to the needs and desires of the minority group itself."[35]

The American Negro has chosen to be "American" rather than "Black," and all his energies have been marshaled to achieve this goal. He does not want segregation or separation; he wants only to be an American citizen, with the rights and privileges of every other citizen. He is not shaken in this determination, even though he is receiving no significant support from any powerful factor of the white community. His prolonged and baffling failure to secure his rights does, however, leave him prey to frustration and anxiety; and this anxiety is compounded by the emergence of the "backward" Negroes of Africa into political independence. American Negroes are horrified to know that they may soon be the only victims of racial subordination left in the civilized world.

There is general agreement among American Negroes that the white man has failed to demonstrate any real capacity for genuine brotherhood and equal justice. There is a widespread belief that the white man will *never* of his own accord accept non-whites as his equals in status and opportunity, in America or elsewhere. There is a surprisingly broad conviction that—as the Muslims insist—the white man has deliberately "written the Negro out of history," refusing to recognize the Black Man's contribution to the great Afro-Asian civilizations and, especially, to the development of America. The educated Negro is aware that little popular recognition is given to his forefathers in the stories of "the men who made America." Of this cultural snub, whether intentional or not, he is increasingly resentful. He has contributed to the making of America, first as a slave and then as a citizen, and he wants the recognition and unrestricted citizenship that are his due.

The Negro community is not willing to repudiate the Christian faith, as the Muslims demand. But there is a significant if silent reservoir of sympathy for the Muslims' racial doctrines. There is among American Negroes an increasing hostility for the white man—a hostility born of despair. The world around us is in cataclysm. It is hard to wait until tomorrow for what everyone else has today, especially in an atomic age, when tomorrow may never arrive. The Black Muslim Movement represents one attempt to break out of this bondage of discrimination and despair, which now threatens the peace and casts a dark shadow over the happiness and prosperity of all America.

Very many people believe with Harry Ashmore that "the Muslims are not themselves going anywhere."[36] Many others take comfort in a belief that the Movement has reached the zenith of its membership and influence. Perhaps it has. But the Muslims are embarrassing to both the white and the Negro communities: they call attention to a situation so irrational and so ugly that neither side wants to face it squarely. It is, therefore, only to be expected that many people wish the Muslims would simply fold their tents and go away, and that they will try to hex them away by refusing to admit that they really exist.

But the Muslims do exist. They do attract the support of the masses and of a small but increasing number of intellectuals. And they will continue to expand as long as racial tension is permitted to flourish in America. True, the Movement in its present form may be crushed by an embarrassed and apprehensive citizenry, white or black. It can be stopped today—and it should be, if it seriously threatens the peace and security of the nation. But in shattering the Movement we shall not eliminate the tension and the need which created and catapulted it to its present momentum. Out of the ashes of the Black Muslims, another "black" specter will inevitably rise to challenge us, for we can destroy the Muslim organization but not the Negro's will to freedom. The essence of the Black Muslim Movement will endure—an extreme expression of the American Negro's rising dissatisfaction with the way things are, and his deepening conviction that this is not the way things have to be.

The meaning for America is clear. We must attack the disease, not its symptoms. We must confront the issue of racism and discrimination. When we have done so with the determination and moral conviction so brutal a problem deserves, there will be no Black Muslims. There will be no need for them. And America will be a better place for us all.

Notes

Preface

1. See Erdmann D. Benyon, "The Voodoo Cult Among Negro Migrants in Detroit," *The American Journal of Sociology,* XLIII, No. 6 (May 1938), 894.

Chapter 1

1. Mike Wallace and Louis Lomax, "The Hate that Hate Produced," *Newsbeat.* New York: WNTA–TV, July 10, 1959. This excerpt is from the unpublished typescript of the television documentary.
2. The author of *The Trial* is Louis X, a talented and versatile young Bostonian. Before joining the Muslims, Louis (whose Christian name was Gene Walcott) had been a popular calypso singer and musician, and had attended college in North Carolina. He is now Minister of the Boston Temple of Islam. He and his family were previously Episcopalians; his wife is a former Roman Catholic.
3. A companion piece, also by Louis X, is *Orgena,* which seems to be "A Negro" spelled backwards. *Orgena* satirizes "Americanized" Negroes in such stereotyped roles as dope addicts, alcoholics, flashily dressed businessmen, educators and the "400 set." This is what the white man has made of them since "kidnapping them from their ancient cultures three hundred years ago." Near the end of the play, the Muslim faith and the teachings of Elijah Muhammad restore to the Black Man the traditional dignity and intelligence he once enjoyed in his own great civilization. *Orgena* and *The Trial* are usually staged on a single bill.
4. Malcolm X, "The Truth About the Black Muslims." An address at the Boston University School of Theology, May 24, 1960. Italics supplied.
5. *Time,* August 10, 1959.
6. From a series of street interviews by the author.
7. Nat Hentoff, *The Reporter,* August 4, 1960, p. 40.
8. Arnold J. Toynbee, *A Study of History* (2d ed.; London: Oxford University Press, 1935), I, 224.
9. W. Lloyd Warner and Leo Srole, *The Social Systems of American Ethnic Groups* (New Haven: Yale University Press, 1945), p. 285.
10. Mike Wallace and Lou Lomax. "The Hate that Hate Produced" *Newsbeat.* New York: WNTA–TV, July 10, 1959. [Typescript of a television documentary.]
11. See George E. Simpson, "Recent Political Developments in Race Relations," *The Phylon,* Second Quarter (Summer 1958), p. 209. Cf. Liston Pope, *The Kingdom Beyond Caste* (New York: Friendship Press, 1957), pp. 64-68.
12. The rejoicing at the Supreme Court's overturning of legalized segregation in American schools was not quite universal. Says Liston Pope, "Even the Afrikaans-language press in the Union of South Africa gave

extensive attention to it, while generally denying that the situation in the Union permitted movement in any similar direction." *Op. cit.*, p. 11.

13. "Every part of the United States comes under federal executive orders that forbid discrimination on *some* jobs. Fifteen states have laws against discrimination on *most* jobs. Thirty-seven cities, many of them outside these fifteen states, have city ordinances against discrimination on *most* jobs." Quoted from *Your Rights Under State and Local Fair Employment Practice Laws* (American Federation of Labor and Congress of Industrial Organizations Publication No. 23 [Washington: 1956]), p. 2.

14. See William Peters, *The Southern Temper* (New York: Doubleday & Co., 1959), pp. 225-227. Quoting from the *Harvard Business Review* (1957), Peters points out *inter alia* that "The median income of all United States Negro families is 56 percent of the income of white families—$2,410 a year as opposed to $4,339. In the South, where conditions are worse, the median income of Negro families is only about 49 percent of what white families take in." See also Mr. Peters' discussion on the dearth of Negroes in federal employment in the South, pp. 241-266. In spite of federal safeguards against discrimination, Peters finds that ". . . with rare exceptions, Negroes are not employed above the level of janitorial and labor services by federal agencies in the South." Cf. *The New York Times,* November 16, 1959, p. 1: "A Presidential committee has made what it considers 'significant breakthroughs' in obtaining skilled jobs for Negroes in the South. . . . Instead of asking contractors for a generalized and practically unenforceable commitment not to discriminate, the committee is now seeking a specific promise to hire Negroes for new jobs immediately. . . . The committee's new policy has also had results in Border and Northern areas where Negroes had had a hard time breaking out of menial factory work. . . . [But] no one on the committee suggests that these [cited] cases are enough to make a fundamental change in job opportunities for large numbers of Negroes."

15. See *Ebony,* Sept. 1960.

16. For several years, the reported number of lynchings has declined. However, the infamous lynching of Emmett Till, a Negro boy visiting in Mississippi in 1955, and the lynching of Mack Parker, another Negro in Mississippi, in April 1959 have again focused international attention upon the continuing tenuousness of civil security for Negroes in parts of this country. The Federal Bureau of Investigation, called into the Parker case at the request of the Mississippi governor, spent $80,000 in an extended investigation of the lynching. The U. S. Attorney General described the case as "one of the most complete investigations I've ever seen conducted." The FBI report was turned over to a Mississippi grand jury, which declined to call a single FBI witness and adjourned without returning any indictment whatever. See *The New York Times,* November 18, 1959, p. 1. Many Negroes consider the Parker lynching to be little more than "official murder." Parker was left in an unguarded, small-town jail under circumstances which seemed to invite his abduction and murder. However, killings in this category are often at the hands of the arresting or detention officials themselves, who find it necessary to shoot their unarmed prisoners "in self-defense" or "to prevent escape." See Peters, *The Southern Temper,* pp. 214-218, for a description of a double "self-defense" killing by a Southern sheriff.

17. "The campaign of the whites for 'white supremacy' has, on the whole, been successful. That is, the Negro has been put and kept in a subordinate status. The actual story of the Negro since slavery is the story of this attitude in practice." Abram Kardiner and Lionel Ovesey, *The Mark of Oppression* (New York: W. W. Norton & Co., 1951), p. 61.

18. *The Christian Science Monitor* (Boston), January 27, 1960, p. 4.

19. *Ibid.*

20. E. D. Beynon, "The Voodoo Cult Among Negro Migrants in Detroit," *The American Journal of Sociology*, XLIII (July, 1937—May, 1938), 896. Nadim Makdisi, editor of the Voice of America's Arabic service, points out that the second largest Moslem community in America is concentrated in the Detroit-Dearborn area.

21. Beynon, *op. cit.*, p. 895. From an interview with Sister Denke Majied, formerly Mrs. Lawrence Adams.

22. *Ibid.*

23. *Ibid.*, p. 895.

24. *Ibid.*, p. 896. From an interview with Brother Challar Sharrieff.

25. *Ibid.* From an interview with Sister Carrie Mohammad.

26. *Ibid.*

27. *Ibid.*, p. 897.

28. *The New Crusader* (Chicago), August 15, 1959, p. 1.

29. Beynon, *op. cit.*, p. 899.

30. *Ibid.*, p. 902

31. *Ibid.*, p. 901.

32. *Ibid.*, p. 897.

33. *Ibid.*, p. 904.

34. "The Truth about the Black Muslims." An address at the Boston University School of Theology, May 24, 1960.

35. *New York Courier*, August 6, 1960.

36. See Beynon, *op. cit.*, p. 897.

37. *Ibid.*, p. 898.

38. Temples or missions have also been reported in Cuba, Hawaii and Jamaica, but the report is unconfirmed.

39. As indicated, this sampling may not be a completely reliable index. In the first place, it is too small, and the ecological distribution of the respondents (Atlanta, 34; Chicago, 111; Boston, 183; New York, 133) does not present an adequate relation to the distribution of the Muslim membership. Secondly, the sampling was done piecemeal over an extended period; and since names or other positive identification could not be used, it is possible that some persons responded more than once.

40. Beynon (*op. cit.*, 898), asserts that "practically none of them [the Muslims] had been in the North prior to the collapse of the Marcus Garvey movement." But there are certainly a number of ex-Garveyites in the movement today, perhaps as many as 10,000-15,000.

41. Beynon, *op. cit.*, p. 905.

42. *Ibid.*

43. *Ibid.*

44. *Ibid.*

45. E. Franklin Frazier, *Black Bourgeoisie* (Glencoe, Ill.; The Free Press, 1957), p. 120.

46. *The Chicago Sun*, October 24, 1942.

47. From a series of interviews with Muslim leaders in Chicago and New York.

48. *Color and Conscience* (New York: Harper and Brothers, 1946), p. 191.

49. Malcolm X, "The Truth About the Black Muslims" (*Supra* 34).

50. Malcolm X at Boston University Human Relations Center, February 15, 1960.

51. James Hicks, editor of the New York *Amsterdam News* and a close observer of the movement, says: "They have high regard for their women and fight like hell for each other." *The Reporter*, August 4, 1960, p. 39.

52. Malcolm X at Boston University Human Relations Center, February 15, 1960.

Chapter 2

1. Edmund D. Cronon, *Black Moses* (Madison: The University of Wisconsin Press, 1955), p. 66.

2. Arnold Rose, *The Negro in America* (Boston: Beacon Press, 1948), pp. 17-18.

3. *Ibid.*, p. 16.

4. *Ibid.*, pp. 11-12.

5. E. Franklin Frazier, *The Negro in the United States* (New York: The Macmillan Co., 1949), p. 88. Quoting Lionel Kennedy and Thomas Parker, *An Official Report of the Trials of Sundry Negroes Charged with an Attempt to Raise an Insurrection in the State of South Carolina*.

6. W. Lloyd Warner and Leo Srole, *The Social Systems of American Ethnic Groups* (New Haven: Yale University Press, 1945), p. 295.

7. Abram Kardiner and Lionel Ovesey, *The Mark of Oppression* (New York: W. W. Norton & Co., 1951), p. 39. But see a somewhat broader concept of ethnocentrism in Brewton Berry, *Race and Ethnic Relations* (Houghton, 1951), p. 77. Says Berry, "The ethnic group is a human group bound together by ties of cultural homogeneity. . . . Above all, there is a consciousness of kind, a we-feeling. The ethnic group may even regard itself as a race, but the fact of such common descent is of much less importance than the *assumption* that there is a blood relationship, and the myths of the group develop to substantiate such an assumption."

8. For discussion on race, see the following: Ethel Alpenfels, *Sense and Nonsense About Race* (New York: Friendship Press, 1957); Ruth Benedict, Race: *Science and Politics* (New York: Viking Press, 1950); Franz Boas, *Anthropology and Modern Life* (New York: W. W. Norton & Co., 1928); J. Deniker, *The Races of Man* (London: Walter Scott Publishers, 1913); Oscar Handlin, *Race and Nationality in American Life* (New York: Doubleday & Co., 1957); F. H. Hankins, *The Racial Basis of Civilization* (New York: Alfred Knopf, 1926); Ben J. Marais, *Colour, the Unsolved Problem of the West* (Capetown: Howard B. Timmins, 1952); Simpson, George E., and Yinger, J. Milton, *Racial and Cultural Minorities in the United States,* 1st ed. rev. (New York: Harper and Brothers, 1958); W. Ashley Montague, *Man's Most Dangerous Myth* (New York: Columbia University Press, 1942); Gordon Allport, *The Nature of Prejudice* (New York: Doubleday, 1958).

9. "A 'stock' may be defined as the descendants of a large group of people who once lived in the same geographical area and shared certain physical traits that are inherited. These traits set them apart from other groups who have other combinations of physical characteristics." Alpenfels, *Sense and Nonsense About Race,* p. 19.

10. See Gunnar Myrdal, "Race and Ancestry," *An American Dilemma* (New York: Harper & Bros., 1944), pp. 113-136. See also John Hope Franklin, *From Slavery to Freedom* (New York: Alfred A. Knopf, 1956); E. Franklin Frazier, *Negro in the U.S.,* n6.

11. W. E. B. Dubois, "Three Centuries of Discrimination," *The Crisis,* LIV (December 1947), 362-363. Cf. Melville J. Herskovits: "The word 'Negro,' as employed in the United States has no biological meaning. . . . a social definition takes precedence over the biological reality." *Man and His Works,* (New York: Alfred A. Knopf, 1950), p. 144.

12. Melvin Conant, *Race Issues on the World Scene* (Honolulu: University of Hawaii Press, 1955), p. 119.

13. See Michael Clark's comprehensive article on the "Rise in Racial Extremism," *The New York Times,* January 25, 1960, p. 1.

Chapter 3

1. Drew was born in 1866. For a description of his movement, see Arthur H. Fauset, "Moorish Science Temple of America" in J. Milton Yinger, *Religion, Society, and the Individual* (New York: The Macmillan Co., 1957), pp. 498-507; or see E. Franklin Frazier, *The Negro in the U.S.,* pp. 358-359.

2. For an enlightening discussion of this 19th-century doctrine, recently resurrected by some American Christians, see Everett Tilson, *Segregation and the Bible* (Nashville: The Abingdon Press, 1958), pp. 23-26.

3. Arthur H. Fauset. Quoted in Yinger, *Religion, Society, and the Individual,* p. 498.

4. Yinger, *op. cit.,* p. 500.

5. *Ibid.,* p. 504.

6. *Ibid.*

7. Dr. George W. Bagnall in a discourse entitled, "The Madness of Marcus Garvey," quoted in Edmund Cronon, *Black Moses* (Madison: University of Wisconsin Press, 1948), p. 107. Cronon's book is probably the best recent study of the Garvey Movement.

8. J. Saunders Redding, *They Came in Chains* (Philadelphia: J. B. Lippincott Co., 1950), p. 261.

9. John Hope Franklin, *From Slavery to Freedom* (New York: Alfred A. Knopf, 1956), p. 472.

10. *Ibid.,* pp. 473-474.

11. *Ibid.,* p. 471.

12. Cronon, *Black Moses,* p. 16.

13. *Ibid.,* p. 17.

14. Redding, *They Came in Chains,* p. 259.

15. Cronon, *Black Moses,* p. 41.

16. Garvey's understanding of the American caste system was probably faulty. In his native Jamaica, the mulattoes formed a more or less distinct class between the whites and the unmixed blacks. In America, a Negro is commonly identified as anyone having any Negro ancestry whatever; and all Negroes of whatever color are relegated to a common caste.

17. Cronon, *op. cit.,* p. 44.

18. *Ibid.,* p. 47.

19. *Ibid.*

20. Quoted in *ibid.,* p. 65

21. *Ibid.,* p. 67.

22. *Ibid.,* p. 70.

23. *Ibid.,* p. 185.

24. *Ibid.,* p. 187.

25. *Ibid.,* p. 184.

26. *Ibid.,* pp. 124-125.

27. Elmer T. Clark, *The Small Sects in America,* p. 172.

28. Cronon, *op. cit.,* p. 178.

29. *Ibid.,* p. 179.

30. *Ibid.,* pp. 129-132.

31. See E. Franklin Frazier, *Black Bourgeoisie* (Glencoe, Ill.: The Free Press, 1957), p. 123. These Negroes "who were acquiring middle-class status," Frazier says, "did not only regard his program as fantastic, but they did not want to associate with his illiterate poor black followers, especially

since West Indians were prominent in the movement." See also, J. Saunders Redding, *op. cit.*, pp. 260-261.

32. See John Hope Franklin, *op. cit.*, p. 482.
33. Frazier, *Black Bourgeoisie*, p. 260.
34. Cronon, *op. cit.*, pp. 113 ff.
35. *Ibid.*, p. 111.
36. *Ibid.*

Chapter 4

1. The basic doctrines of the Muslims are laid down in a booklet written by Muhammad and called *The Supreme Wisdom*. This is the primary source book for all that is peculiar to the Muslims and for Muhammad's teachings as they appear in the Negro press.
2. Malcolm X at the Boston University Human Relations Center, February 15, 1960.
3. *Supreme Wisdom* (2d ed.), pp. 6-7.
4. *Ibid.*, p. 17.
5. *Ibid.*
6. *Ibid.*, p. 19.
7. *Ibid.*, p. 21.
8. *Ibid.*, p. 27.
9. *Ibid.*
10. "Mr. Muhammad Speaks," Pittsburgh *Courier*, August 15, 1959.
11. Malcolm X at Boston University Human Relations Center, February 15, 1960.
12. *Ibid.*
13. *Supreme Wisdom* (2d ed.), p. 33.
14. From a typescript of "The Hate that Hate Produced," a television documentary on the rise of Black Racism by Mike Wallace and Louis Lomax. *Newsbeat* (New York: WNTA–TV, July 10, 1959).
15. *Ibid.*
16. "Mr. Muhammad Speaks," *Pittsburgh Courier*, June 16, 1959. Unless otherwise noted, all excerpts from "Mr. Muhammad Speaks" appeared in his column by that title in the *Pittsburgh Courier*.
17. *Ibid.*, May 2, 1959.
18. *Ibid.*
19. *The Supreme Wisdom* (2d ed.), p. 39.
20. *Ibid.*, p. 33.
21. Malcolm X on *Newsbeat*.
22. *The Supreme Wisdom*, p. 38.
23. "Mr. Muhammad Speaks," July 4, 1959.
24. *Ibid.*, December 13, 1958.
25. *Ibid.*, July 18, 1959.
26. "Mr. Muhammad Speaks," December 13, 1958.
27. *The Supreme Wisdom*, p. 12.
28. *Ibid.*, p. 13.
29. *Ibid.*
30. *Ibid.*
31. *Ibid.*, p. 28.
32. *Ibid.*, p. 36.
33. "Mr. Muhammad Speaks," January 17, 1959.
34. *Ibid.*, August 9, 1958.
35. From an interview with Malcolm X.
36. "Mr. Muhammad Speaks," August 22, 1959.

37. Len Holt, "Norfolk News Beat," *Afro-American,* August 13, 1960.

38. See *The Supreme Wisdom,* pp. 21 and 42.

39. *Ibid.,* p. 22.

40. Malcolm X at the Boston University Human Relations Center, February 15, 1960.

41. Eric Hoffer, *The True Believer* (New York: New American Library, 1951), pp. 55-56.

42. "Mr. Muhammad Speaks," August 9, 1958.

43. From an interview with Elijah Muhammad, March 4, 1959.

44. *Los Angeles Herald-Dispatch,* February 6, 1958.

45. *Ibid.,* January 16, 1960.

46. *Ibid.,* January 30, 1960.

47. *Ibid.,* February 7, 1959.

48. *Ibid.,* August 8, 1959.

49. *Los Angeles Herald-Dispatch,* February 20, 1960.

50. *Ibid.*

51. *Pittsburgh Courier,* August 15, 1959, quoting *U.S. News and World Report* of August 3, 1959.

52. "Mr. Muhammad Speaks," August 9, 1958.

53. *Los Angeles Dispatch,* January 30, 1960.

54. *Afro-American,* February 20, 1960.

55. Malcolm X on *The Jerry Williams Show,* Boston: Radio Station WMEX, April 2, 1960. From a taped transcription. Italics supplied.

56. Beynon, pp. 905-906.

57. *Ibid.*

58. "Mr. Muhammad Speaks," August 16, 1958.

59. Beynon, *op. cit.,* p. 905.

60. *Los Angeles Herald-Dispatch,* January 16, 1960.

61. *The Islamic News,* July 6, 1959.

62. Chicago *Daily Defender,* March 5, 1960. In a radio interview over Boston's station WMEX on April 2, 1960, Malcolm X called for "nine or ten states."

63. "Mr. Muhammad Speaks," *Los Angeles Herald-Dispatch,* July 16, 1960.

64. "Mr. Muhammad Speaks," *Pittsburgh Courier,* August 2, 1958.

65. *Ibid.,* October 11, 1958.

66. At the Boston University Human Relations Center, February 15, 1960.

67. "Mr. Muhammad Speaks," August 2, 1958.

68. *Ibid.,* May 3, 1958.

69. *Ibid.,* September 6, 1958.

Chapter 5

1. See Richard T. La Piere, *Collective Behavior* (New York: McGraw-Hill Book Co., 1938), pp. 504-510. La Piere describes a mass movement as a spatial movement of a considerable portion of the social population to some new, promised land. A movement built around some person or idea (which need not involve spatial relocation) is termed a "messianic movement." The messianic movement is built around a "miracle man" or a "miracle cure" or upon the idea of a "political messiah." "The messianic movement [is] . . . a collective flight from reality . . . following a new form of leadership which will bring health, wealth or happiness. The

movement begins with the idea that some person . . . is a messiah who has come to deliver the faithful from whatever it is that ails them."

2. I am indebted to Eric Hoffer, *The True Believer* (New York: New American Library, 1951), for many of the concepts discussed in this and the following sections.

3. Hoffer, pp. 52-53.

4. *Ibid.,* pp. 105-106.

5. *Ibid.,* p. 107.

6. *Ibid.,* p. 104. Hoffer quotes John Morley, *Notes on Politics and History* (New York: Macmillan Company, 1914), pp. 69-70.

7. *Ibid.,* p. 18.

8. *Ibid.,* pp. 85-86.

9. *Ibid.,* p. 86.

10. *Ibid.,* pp. 93-94.

11. "The Hate That Hate Produced," *Newsbeat* (New York: WNTA–TV, July 10-17, 1959).

12. *Time,* August 10, 1959.

13. James N. Rhea, *Providence Bulletin,* August 6, 1959.

14. From an interview with Malcolm X.

15. See "Mr. Muhammad Speaks," *The Reader's Digest,* March 1960.

16. From a series of Muslim interviews.

17. See, for example, Arna Bontemps, *Story of the Negro* (New York: Alfred A. Knopf, 1958).

18. From an interview with Minister Louis X.——The Muslim philosophy is limited, and the temple lectures are, without exception, re-phrasings of statements already made in printed materials, interviews or public lectures. For the sake of documentary accuracy, the quotations in this section are drawn from these other sources; but in content and range they faithfully represent the typical—one might almost say, the universal—temple lecture.

19. From an interview with Malcolm X.

20. "Mr. Muhammad Speaks," September 20, 1958.

21. "Mr. Muhammad Speaks," June 6, 1959.

22. *Ibid.,* April 18, 1959.

23. *Ibid.,* May 2, 1959.

24. *Ibid.*

25. *The Supreme Wisdom* (2d ed.), p. 19.

26. *Ibid.*

27. From a series of interviews with Muslims.

28. *The Supreme Wisdom,* p. 51.

29. A translation by Maulana Muhammed Ali and one by Allama Yusuf Ali are approved for the followers of Elijah Muhammad. Beynon says of Fard that he "used only the Arabic text which he translated and explained to the believers . . . [thereby making them] completely de-pendent upon his interpretation." However, Fard gave his followers texts he himself prepared which were memorized by all converts. (p. 900.)

30. *Los Angeles Herald-Dispatch,* February 20, 1960.

31. Beynon, *op. cit.,* p. 903.

32. *Detroit Free Press,* August 14, 1959.

33. *Ibid.*

34. *Mr. Muhammad Speaks,* May, 1960.

35. *Los Angeles Herald-Dispatch,* July 16, 1960.

36. *Los Angeles Herald-Dispatch,* February 13, 1960.

37. *Ibid.*

38. *Ibid.,* January 9, 1960.

39. *Ibid.,* July 30, 1960.

40. *Ibid.,* January 9, 1960.

Chapter 6

1. *New York Amsterdam News,* July 30, 1960. Reprinted from *The Saturday Review.*

2. An address: "The Truth About the Black Muslims." May 24, 1960.

3. *Denver Post,* August 13, 1959.

4. Malcolm X at the Boston University Human Relations Center, February 15, 1960.

5. See *Pittsburgh Courier,* July 19, 1958. Cf. *New York Amsterdam News,* July 12, 1958.

6. See *Time,* August 10, 1959.

7. Survey by the author; the results will be published later in an appropriate journal. A small percentage of business and professional men had clients or customers whom they knew to be Muslims. A very small percentage had Muslim friends. None had visited a Muslim temple.

8. *Sepia,* November, 1959, p. 22.

9. Vol. I, No. 1, 1959, pp. 20-21.

10. *Pittsburgh Courier,* September 12, 1959.

11. *Ibid.,* October 24, 1959.

12. *New York Amsterdam News,* March 5, 1960.

13. *The New Crusader,* August 1, 15, 22, 29; September 5, 19, 26; November 28 (all 1959).

14. *The New Crusader,* August 29, 1959.

15. Statement issued on August 5, 1959.

16. Quoted in *Pittsburgh Courier,* September 5, 1959.

17. Chicago *Daily Defender,* October 3, 1959.

18. *Los Angeles Herald-Dispatch,* January 30, 1960.

19. *Ibid.,* January 16, 1960.

20. *Ibid.*

21. *New Jersey Herald News,* January 2, 1960.

22. *The New York Times,* January 25, 1960.

23. Excerpt from a letter to the author, dated February 19, 1960.

24. *Columbus* (Ohio) *Dispatch,* August 10, 1959.

25. *Time,* August 10, 1959.

26. *Los Angeles Herald-Dispatch,* January 9, 1960.

27. *Ibid.*

28. Malcolm X at Boston University Human Relations Center, February 15, 1960.

29. *Ibid.*

30. *New York Courier,* July 22, 1960.

31. *Los Angeles Herald-Dispatch,* March 5, 1960.

32. *New York Amsterdam News,* July 16, 1960.

33. *Indianapolis Times,* August 10, 1959.

34. *Los Angeles Herald-Dispatch,* June 5, 1958.

35. *New York Amsterdam News,* April 26, 1958.

36. The churches involved were St. John's Congregational, Bethel AME and the Third Baptist Church. Police decided that there had been no breach of the peace, and no arrests were made. *The Springfield Daily News,* February 2, 1959.

37. *Chicago's American,* February 23, 1960.

38. *Pittsburgh Courier,* April 26, 1958.

39. *The New York Times,* January 25, 1960.

40. *Pittsburgh Courier,* March 3, 1958.

41. Observed personally by the author.

42. *Sepia,* November, 1959.

43. From an interview with Malcolm X.

44. *Detroit Jewish News,* August 21, 1959.
45. See Nadim Makdisi, "The Moslems of America," *The Christian Century,* August 26, 1959.
46. *The Muslim World,* Vol. L, No. 1, January, 1960.
47. *The* (Westchester, N.Y.) *Observer,* April 19, 1958. See also *The Moslem World and the U.S.A.,* August, September, 1956.
48. *New York Amsterdam News,* April 4, 1958.
49. *Ibid.* May 3, 1958.
50. Malcolm X at the Boston University Human Relations Center, February 15, 1960.
51. *Ibid.*
52. "The Truth about the Black Muslims," an address by Malcolm X.
53. *Ibid.*
54. *Time,* August 10, 1959, p. 25.
55. *The Christian Science Monitor,* May 16, 1960.
56. *Ibid.,* August 29, 1959.
57. *The Denver Post,* August 13, 1959.
58. *Providence Bulletin,* August 6, 1959.
59. *The Boston Herald,* February 8, 1960.
60. *The Detroit Free Press,* August 14, 1959.
61. *The Reporter,* August 4, 1960, p. 40.
62. *The Boston Globe,* May 12, 1960.

Chapter 7

1. 1950 population, 4,480.
2. Beynon, *op. cit.,* p. 903.
3. Elijah Muhammad, *The Supreme Wisdom: Solution to the So-called Negroes' Problem.* (2d ed.; Chicago: The University of Islam, 1957), p. 15. This booklet first appeared as "Volume I" in 1955 or 1956. The initial volume was revised and somewhat systematized in a "First Edition" printed in February 1957. An identical "Second Edition" was printed in April 1957.
4. *Mr. Muhammad Speaks,* May 1960.
5. *The Supreme Wisdom,* p. 43.
6. Nat Hentoff, "Elijah in the Wilderness," *The Reporter,* August 4, 1960.
7. *The Supreme Wisdom* (2d ed.), p. 21.
8. *The Islamic News,* July 6, 1959.
9. *Ibid.*
10. *Mr. Muhammad Speaks,* May 1960.
11. September 22, 1942, p. 9.
12. *Ibid.*
13. *The Chicago Sun,* October 24, 1942.
14. Malcolm explains that since all Black Men are from the tribe of Shabazz, his "Muslim" name is theoretically available to any member of the sect.
15. Alex Haley, *Reader's Digest,* March 1960.
16. *Sepia,* November 1959, p. 26.
17. Nat Hentoff, "Elijah in the Wilderness," *The Reporter,* August 4, 1960, p. 39.
18. *Ibid.*
19. From unpublished notes by Alex Haley.
20. Beynon, p. 902.
21. *Ibid.,* p. 903.

Notes

267

22. *Chicago's American,* January 18, 1958, and February 22, 1960.
23. *The Pittsburgh Courier,* January 18, 1958.
24. *Los Angeles Herald-Dispatch,* February 18, 1960.
25. *Ibid.*
26. *Chicago's American,* February 23, 1960.
27. *Los Angeles Herald-Dispatch,* February 18, 1960.
28. *Ibid.*
29. *Los Angeles Herald-Dispatch,* February 20, 1960.
30. *Ibid.,* February 18, 1960.

Chapter 8

1. Polygamy and snake-handling are common examples. Also, the courts will usually enforce the education of children up to age sixteen, and they have uniformly overridden religious objections to hospital care and such medical attention as blood transfusions, while prohibiting religious "healers" from claiming professional status.
2. See *New York Amsterdam News,* Nov. 7, 1959.
3. Cf. Hadley Contril, *The Psychology of Social Movements* (New York: John Wiley & Sons, Inc., 1941). pp. 169-210.
4. Emile Durkheim, *The Elementary Forms of the Religious Life,* trans. by Joseph Ward Swain (Glencoe, Ill.: The Free Press, 1947), p. 24.
5. *Ibid.,* p. 36.
6. *Ibid.,* p. 37. Cf. J. Milton Yinger, *Religion, Society and the Individual* (New York: The Macmillan Company, 1957), p. 14.
7. See Durkheim, *op. cit.,* p. 47.
8. Ernst Troeltsch, *The Social Teaching of the Christian Churches,* trans. by Olive Wyon (London: George Allen & Unwin Ltd., 1931), 331.
9. H. Richard Niebuhr, *The Social Sources of Denominationalism* (New York: Henry Holt & Company, 1929), pp. 65-67. Cited in Yinger, *Religion, Society and the Individual,* p. 151.
10. Yinger modifies Troeltsch's dichotomy of church and sect into a six-fold typology: universal church, ecclesia, denomination, established sect, sect and cult. The first five are merely subdivisions of Troeltsch's categories and are not substantively significant in evaluating the Black Muslim Movement.
11. J. Milton Yinger, *Religion in the Struggle for Power* (Durham: Duke University Press, 1946), p. 22.
12. Yinger, *Religion, Society and the Individual,* p. 155.
13. *Ibid.*
14. *Ibid.,* p. 154.
15. See Elmer T. Clark, *The Small Sects in America* (New York: Abingdon Press, 1949), p. 14.
16. See also "The Legalistic or Objectivist Sects," *ibid.,* p. 23-24.
17. *The Supreme Wisdom,* p. 4. See also the Introduction to *The Supreme Wisdom,* in which a Pakistani Moslem defends Muhammad's brand of Islam as appropriate for racial circumstances in this country.
18. For a discussion of this Moslem "heresy," see Charles S. Braden, "Moslem Missions in America," *Religion in Life,* Summer 1959.
19. Wilfred Cantwell Smith, *Modern Islam in India* (London: Victor Gollancz Ltd., 1946), p. 299.
20. Braden, *op. cit., supra.*
21. There follows a lengthy description of the ritual and ceremony incident to entering the Holy City and of the Kaaba, or Black Stone. *Los Angeles Herald-Dispatch,* January 30, 1960.

22. *Ibid.,* January 2, 1960.
23. *The Islamic News,* July 6, 1959.
24. *Los Angeles Herald-Dispatch,* February 2, 1958.
25. *The Pittsburgh Courier,* April 15, 1958.
26. *Ibid.,* August 15, 1959.
27. *Ibid.*
28. *Los Angeles Herald-Dispatch,* February 20, 1960.

Chapter 9

1. Arnold and Caroline Rose, *America Divided* (New York: Alfred A. Knopf, 1948), p. 218.
2. *New York Courier,* August 20, 1960.
3. Arnold and Caroline Rose, p. 219.
4. See Carl Wittke, *We Who Built America* (New York: Prentice Hall, 1939), for a systematic cataloguing of various national groups in the United States, their newspapers and societies.
5. Arnold Rose, *America Divided* (New York: Alfred A. Knopf, Inc., 1948), p. 233.
6. *Ibid.*
7. *Ibid.,* p. 234.
8. Paul A. Walter, Jr., *Race and Culture Relations* (New York: McGraw-Hill Book Co., Inc., 1952), p. 325.
9. *Ibid.,* p. 338.
10. *Ibid.,* p. 328.
11. *Black Bourgeoisie,* p. 87.
12. Mays and Nicholson, *The Negro's Church.* Quoted in Simpson and Yinger, *Racial and Cultural Minorities in the United States,* p. 583.
13. "Relative Route to Absolute," *Time,* January 18, 1960, p. 48. Cf. Liston Pope, *The Kingdom Beyond Caste* (New York: Friendship Press, 1957), p. 117.
14. Arnold M. Rose, *The Negro's Morale* (Minneapolis: The University of Minnesota Press, 1949), p. 98.
15. Simpson and Yinger, *Racial and Cultural Minorities in the United States,* p. 582.
16. Frazier, *Black Bourgeoisie,* p. 88.
17. Simpson and Yinger, *op. cit.*
18. Alpha Phi Alpha, 27,000; Kappa Alpha Psi, 20,000; Omega Psi Phi, 20,000; Phi Beta Sigma, 11,605; Alpha Kappa Alpha, 20,000; Delta Sigma Theta, 21,000. Harry Hansen (ed.), *The World Almanac* (New York: New York World Telegram, 1960), pp. 489-490. Figures for Zeta Phi Beta and Sigma Gamma Rho were not included in the data offered by this source. The writer offers 15,000 as a minimum estimate based on information from members of these sororities.
19. Frazier, *The Negro in the United States,* p. 382.
20. *Ibid.*
21. See C. Eric Lincoln, "Anxiety, Fear and Integration," *Phylon: Journal of Race and Culture,* September 1960.
22. Whether assimilation presupposed amalgamation is, I believe, purely academic. Amalgamation is a biological phenomenon, and in the United States it is also a well documented social fact. Further, amalgamation is cognizant of neither "integration" nor "assimilation"; it is oblivious of both.
23. W. L. Warner and P. S. Lunt, *Status System of a Modern Community* (New Haven: Yale University Press, 1942), pp. 285-286.

24. J. Saunders Redding, *They Came in Chains* (New York: J. B. Lippincott, 1950), p. 225.

25. National Council of Churches *Information Service,* February 23, 1957, quoting the Independent, p. 2.

26. Redding, *op. cit.,* p. 255.

27. "What is the NAACP?" *Information Service* (New York: The National Council of the Churches of Christ in the United States of America, February 23, 1957), p. 1.

28. Interview with the Reverend Mr. McDaniel.

29. Redding, *op. cit.,* p. 229.

30. See C. Eric Lincoln, "The Strategy of a Sit-In," *The Reporter,* January 6, 1961, pp. 20-23.

31. Yinger, *Religion, Society and the Individual,* p. 9.

32. *Ibid.,* p. 10.

33. For an informative discussion of the functional properties of conflict, see Raymond Mack and Richard Snyder, "The Analysis of Social Conflict," *Conflict Resolution,* Vol. I (June 1957), pp. 212-247. See also Robin M. Williams, Jr., *The Reduction of Intergroup Tensions* (New York: Social Science Research Council), 1947; and Son J. Hager, "Religious Conflict," and Robin M. Williams, Jr., "Religion, Value-Orientations, and Intergroup Conflict," *The Journal of Social Issues,* Vol. XII, No. 3 (1955).

34. E. B. Reuter, *The American Race Problem* (New York: Thomas Y. Crowell, 1927), p. 410.

35. *The Nature of Prejudice,* pp. 233-234.

36. *The Boston Globe,* May 12, 1960.

Index

Abdul-Hamid, Soufi, 169
Acceptance, 38-39, 71, 229, 247
Africa, emergence of new nations in, 9-10, 126, 147, 253
African Legion, 60
African Motor Corps, 60
African Orthodox Church, 62, 65
Aggression, 39-40, 41, 229, 247; inverted, 40; misdirected, 40, 250; outlets for, 249-50
Ahmad, Mirzā Ghulām; Ahmadiyah movement, 220-21
Alexander, Sanford, 130
Allah, belief in, 70, 219; Fard identified with, 16, 21, 72-74, 182, 195
Allport, Gordon, 253
Alpha Kappa Alpha, 238, 268
Alpha Phi Alpha, 237, 268
American Council on Human Rights (ACHR), 237-38
American Jewish Committee; American Jewish Congress, 232
"American," concept of, 227-28
Amsterdam News (New York), 142, 143-44
Anglo-Saxon Clubs, 60
Anti-Defamation League, 232
Antisegregation organizations, 244-45; *see also* Integration
Anti-Semitism, 168-69, 232
Anti-Zionism, 148-49, 166, 224
Arabic, learning of, 125, 127, 219
Asceticism, 29, 91
Ashmore, Harry, 178, 254
Asian-African Drums, 171
Assimilation, 239
Austin, Noel, 138
Avoidance, 35-38, 229, 247

Bahai, 29, 215
Barclay, Edwin, 61
Bates, Mrs. Daisy, 149, 150
Bell, Derrick, 148

Berry, Edwin C., 152
Beynon, Erdman, 23, 24, 199, 201
Bible, 11, 13, 206, 219, 248
Biological distinctiveness, 46, 47
Biological re-purification, 89-90
Biracial organizations, 145-52, 238-46
Black Cross Nurses, 60
Black Eagle Flying Corps, 60
Black Muslim Movement, 4-6; aims of, 27, 84-97, 98, 210; attraction of, 27-32, 108-9, 113; beginnings of, 10-17, 66, 72-74; black nationalism and, 34, 66; commercial enterprises of, 24, 60, 63, 64, 93; doctrines and mythology of, 68-80, 104, 220, 247; economic and political power of, 17-20, 196; factionalism in, 15-16, 179-209; foreign contacts of, 26, 171-72; functional and dysfunctional aspects of, 248-53; and international politics, 223-26; and Jewish community, 165-69; as a mass movement, 106-34; media of communication of, 129-34; membership of, 21-27, 85, 98-101, 106, 108, 111-15, 126; money problems of, 17-18, 20, 88, 90-93, 119, 123-24, 130; morality of, 55, 67, 80-83, 164; and the Negro community, 135-64; "open" rallies of, 175; and orthodox Islam, 169-72, 196, 210-26; schools of, 14, 26, 32, 126-28, 250; as social and religious movement, 212-23, 246-53; temples of, 11, 22, 24, 26, 81-82, 107, 115-26, 181, 184, 185-186, 194, 197, 198; and white community, 172-78
Black nationalism, 23, 33, 43-46, 251; characteristics of, 50; and social class, 46-49; *see also* Moor-

ish Science movement *and* Garvey, Marcus

Black Star Steamship Line, 60, 64

Black supremacy, 49, 76, 145, 147, 153, 177

B'nai B'rith, 232

Boston, Black Muslims in, 129, 134, 185; passing in, 36; Temple 11 in, 193

Boston Globe, 178

Boston Herald, 176, 177

Boule, the, 237

Brotherhood, as a tenet of Islam, 125, 220, 252

Brown, Earl, 138

Bunche, Ralph, 88, 131, 139, 241

Burley, Dan, 133

Bus strike, Montgomery, Ala., 137, 161, 244

Business, Negro, and Black Muslims, 140-41, 161, 162

"Buy black" policy, 20, 93, 250

Caste society, 38, 108

Castro, Fidel, 18

Chalmers, Allan Knight, 241

Chicago, commercial enterprises in, 93; Moorish Science movement in, 52; Muslim schools in, 26, 32; proposed Islamic Center in, 97, 128; race riot in, 56; Temple 2 in, 16, 17, 182

Chicago Daily Defender, 144

Christian Science Monitor, 140, 176, 177

Christianity, as counterpressure to black nationalism, 49; modification of attacks on, 206; and Moorish Science movement, 54; Negro believers in, 31, 67, 69-70, 123, 205-6 (*see also* Churches, Negro); Negro clergy and, 79-80; repudiation of, 26-27, 28-29, 121, 122-23, 132, 152, 248, 252; and white supremacy, 28, 78-80, 131

Church, description of, 214-15, 267

Churches, Negro, 33, 62, 155-59, 163, 207, 234-35; white, controversies in, 221-22; white, racial bias in, 28, 114, 158, 221, 234-35

Citizenship, limited, 174, 175, 228; unrestricted, desire for, 253

Clergy, Negro, 79-80, 153-54, 155-58, 234-35

Colonialism, 9, 28

Colored Knights of Pythias, 236

Committee on Racial Equality (CORE), 155, 245

Communist party, 16

Conduct, rules of, for Black Muslims, 29, 67, 80-83, 90-92, 105, 128, 132, 164; for the Moors, 55

Court cases, Muslims, 204-5

Cult, 216-17, 267; Black Muslims as, 106, 217; Ras Tafarian, 50, 58

Cultural heritage, Jewish, 231; Negro, 48, 58, 250

David X, 159

Dawud, Talib Ahmad, 144, 170-71

Death, contempt for, 103

Declaration of the Rights of the Negro Peoples of the World, 59

Delinquency, absence of, 25, 32, 115

Delta Sigma Theta, 238, 268

Denver Post, 176, 177

Depression, 12, 24

Desegregation. *See* Integration

Detroit, Fard in, 10-11, 72; migrants to, 21; Muslim schools in, 32

Detroit Free Press, 176, 177

Diab, Jamil, 26, 170

Dietary laws, 81, 91, 219

Discrimination, in employment and political affairs, 8, 88; in the North, 21; responses to, 35-40, 71, 229, 247

Divorce, 55, 82

"Double duty dollar," 43

Drew, Noble (Timothy), 13, 23, 50, 51, 52, 53, 54, 55, 66

DuBois, W. E. B., 45, 64, 240

Durkheim, Emile, 213

Eason, James W. H., 64-65

Economic program, Muslim, 17-18, 20, 88, 90-93, 119, 123-24, 130

Economic separation, 20, 88, 90-93, 247

Elks, Order of, 236-37

Equality, of ministers and "broth-

ers," 90; NAACP policy of, 241; of sexes, 31-32, 83
Ethiopia, 33-34; interest of, in Muslims, 16

Faith, Negro, in white decency, 227-29, 246; unity through, 103-4
Fard, Wallace D., 10-14, 15, 16, 66, 73, 106, 180, 181, 182, 183
Federal Bureau of Investigation, 94, 187, 211
Federation of Islamic Associations, 170, 219
"Folk Negroes," 38, 229
Fraternal organizations, 231, 235-37
Fraternities and sororities, 237-38
Frazier, E. Franklin, 234, 237
Freedom, will to, 161, 254
Freeman, Andrew G., 152
Freemasonry, 13, 236
Fruit of Islam, 14, 30, 82, 118, 184, 185, 193, 199-203
Fuller, S. B., 129

Gallagher, Buell, 27, 28
Garvey, Marcus; Garvey movement, 8, 23, 25, 42, 50, 56-66, 72, 94, 164, 208
Ghetto, Black, 25, 37, 90, 167; Jewish, 165
Granger, Lester B., 151, 152
Greek letter societies, 237
Group consciousness, 34-35; see also Race consciousness
Group identification, 229-34
Group solidarity, 247; see also Unity

Hajj Committee, 171
Harlem, 18, 143, 192
Harris, Robert, 13, 204
Hate groups, 151, 153, 177
Hatred, as basis of Muslim movement, 67, 112, 114, 147, 207, 208, 218, 221, 248; denial of teaching of, 186, 209; in a mass movement, 105-6; self, 35, 70
Hentoff, Nat, 134, 140
Herald-Dispatch (Los Angeles), 129-31, 142, 143, 148, 153, 204
History, Negro, emphasis on, 32,

120, 121, 126, 250; reconstruction of, 44, 58
Hoffer, Eric, 83, 105
Holy Koran, 53
Human sacrifice, 13, 204

Income, annual, 20, 258
Independent Episcopalian Church, 62
Indian ancestry, 46
In-group organizations, 231
Integration, of busses in Montgomery, 137, 161, 244; definition of, 239; of eating places in South, 230; importance of, to biracial organizations, 238-39; Muslim attacks on, 88-89, 124-25, 161; steps toward, 7-8
Integrative organizations, 145-52, 238-46, 247
Intellectuals, Negro, 29, 111, 139-40, 254
Intermarriage, rejection of, 47, 89
International interest in Muslims, 16
International relations, 223-26, 251-52
Islam, orthodox, 144, 223; in America, 169-72, 223; Black Muslims and, 210-26; confusion of doctrines of Black Muslims and, 251-52; international, 168, 171, 212; political issues and, 223-26; as religion of peace, 119-20, 125; see also Black Muslim Movement
Islamic Center, proposed, 97, 128
Islamic News, 133
Israel, 96, 166, 168

Jack, Hulan, 138
James, Minister, 197-98
James, William M., 158
Japan, interest of, in Black Muslims, 16, 26; Muhammad's sympathy for, 26, 188
Japanese-Americans, 232-33
Jeremiah X, 197, 198
Jesus, 54, 74-75, 78, 123; Black, 62
Jews, aggression against, 40, 168, 232; associations of, 231-232; and Black Muslims, 165-69; cultural heritage of, 231; in NAACP, 149,

167
Johnson, Gabriel, 59
Johnson, James Weldon, 64
Jones, Eugene Kinkle, 64
Judaism, attack on, 131, 131; *see also* Jews

Kappa Alpha Psi, 237, 238, 268
Karriem, Isaiah, 194
Karriem, Robert, 204
Keating, Kenneth B., 169
Kilroe, Edwin P., 62
King, Charles D. B., 63
King, Martin Luther, 138, 145, 152, 153, 154, 155, 244
Ku Klux Klan, 57, 60, 163, 190, 245

Lawson, James, 150
Leadership, individual Negro, 135-41, 163, 173; institutional Negro, 145-55; in a mass movement, 101-3, 105; Negro, Muslim attack on, 131, 139
Leavell, Balm L., Jr., 144
Liberia, 59, 61, 63
Little, Malcolm. *See* Malcom X
Lomax, Louis, 134
Los Angeles, 5; Black Muslim membership in, 178
Los Angeles Herald-Dispatch, 129-31, 142, 143, 148, 153, 204
Lottie X, 194
Louis X, 31, 71, 113, 193, 198
Love, in Buddhism, 248; as Christian principle, 152, 207; in Moorish Science movement, 54; in UNIA, 57
Lower class, Negro, 46, 67, 163-64; and black nationalism, 48-49; predominance of, among Black Muslims, 23-25, 85; sects of, 215
Lucius X, 194, 198-99
Lynchings, 56, 240, 258

McDaniel, J. A., 242
McGuire, George Alexander, 62
Malcolm X, 4, 7, 18, 19, 31, 67, 68, 69, 71, 82, 87, 94, 95, 96, 110, 112, 113, 115, 116, 130, 132, 134, 137, 138-39, 141, 148, 150, 151, 154,
157, 166, 169, 172, 173, 175, 178, 183, 189-92, 193, 195-96, 197, 198, 204, 205, 207-8, 222, 223, 224, 225
Males, predominance of, in Muslim membership, 23 31; role of, 31, 32, 55, 82, 83
Marshall, Thurgood, 138, 148, 241
Mass movement, 83, 98-106, 108, 212, 263-64; Black Muslims as, 106-34
Mays, Benjamin, 234, 241
Mecca, pilgrimage to, 219, 222, 226
Membership, Black Muslim, 21-27, 85, 98-101, 106, 108; application for, 109-10, 180; recruitment of, 111-15, 126
Memphis, desegration in, 159-60; passing in, 36
Merton, Robert K., 249
Messenger, 64, 132-33, 141
Methodist Church, 215, 234-35
Middle class, Negro, 46, 47-48, 64, 160-62, 215
Ming, Robert, 128
Ministers, Muslim, 14, 15, 118-26, 156
Minorities, 230, 253
Miscegenation, disdain for, 47, 89
Mr. Muhammad Speaks, 133, 134
Mohammad, Farrad. *See* Fard, Wallace D.
Montgomery Improvement Association, 244-45
Moorish Science movement, 26, 50, 41-55, 164
Morality, personal, 55, 67, 80-83, 164
Mormon Church, 222
Moslem World and the U.S.A., 172
Moslems, orthodox, 210-26; in America, 169-72, 223; *see also* Islam
Muhammad, Abdul, 15, 16
Muhammad, Akbar, 127, 194
Muhammad, Elijah, 4, 6, 14-15, 16-17, 21, 23, 55, 60, 71, 72, 75, 77, 84, 90, 93, 94, 97, 105, 126, 128, 137-38, 142, 145, 157, 163, 169, 175, 180-89, 192, 193, 194-95, 248; and Allah, 73; appear-

ance of, 183-84; arrests of, 94, 127, 143, 187-88; attitude of, to upper-class Negroes, 85, 111-12; denial of hate-mongering by, 186, 209; on eating pork, 81; and Fard, 180, 181, 182, 183; goals of, 86, 87, 92, 95, 96; at home, 25, 112; hostility of, to white man, 112, 122, 136, 161, 208; as leader, 106, 107, 108, 171, 179, 217; on NAACP, 146-47; and Nasser, 224-25; news column of, 129; on Original Man, 76; on orthodox Islam, 219, 220; pilgrimage of, to Mecca, 222, 226; political power of, 18-19; press reports on, 176, 177, 178; pro-Japanese sentiment of, in World War II, 26, 188; on regeneration, 82, 115; on self-reliance, 83, 89; on unity, 158-59, 162, 186

Muhammad, Elijah, Jr., 194, 200

Muhammad, Herbert, 194

Muhammad Speaks to the Blackman. 133, 145

Muhammad, Wallace D., 116, 149, 194, 195, 199

Muslim Brotherhood of America, 219

Muslim Girls Training Class, 14, 128, 194

Myrdal, Gunnar, 239, 244

Mythology, Muslim, 68-80

Naeem, Abdul Basit, 171-72

Name, changing of, by Jews, 231-32; by Muslims, 109-11, 121-22; "slave," 109, 110, 121

Nasser, Gamal Abdel, 172, 224, 225

National Association for the Advancement of Colored People (NAACP), 64, 65, 98, 130, 145-51, 160, 167, 238, 239-42, 251

National Movement for the Establishment of a Forty-Ninth State, 66

National Union of People of African Descent, 66

Nationalism, black, *see* Black nationalism; political, 56-66; religious, 51-55, 61-62; white, 228, 229

"Negritude," 45

Negro World, 58, 63

Negroes, churches of, 33, 62, 155-59, 163, 207, 234-35; concern over Black Muslims among, 135-64; "folk," 38, 229; fraternal organizations of, 231, 235-37; fraternities and sororities of, 237-38; heritage of, 48, 58, 250; increasing hostility of, to whites, 253-54 (*see also* Hatred); as integral part of American society, 136, 253; integrative organizations of, 238-46; the man in the street, 159-64; the moderate, 72; physical traits of, 6, 46, 47; range of protest of, 227-34, 246-48; separatist organizations of, 234-38; term "Negro" rejected by, 48, 68; will to freedom of, 161, 254

New Crusader (Chicago), 144-45

New York City, Garvey movement in, 58, 59; Negro organizations in, 33; Temple 7 in, 24, 198

Nkrumah, 69, 147

Nonviolence, 155; in Black Muslim Movement, 4, 114, 132, 199; in sit-in movement, 245, 246

Norris, Frank, 13

Odd Fellows, 236

Omega Psi Phi, 237, 268

Orgena, 113, 193

Original Man, 75-76, 121

Overton, L. Joseph, 150-51

Ovington, Mary White, 240

Owen, Chandler, 64

Pan-Islamic movement, 27-28

Parker, Mrs. Rosa, 159

Passing, 36

Passive resistance, 137; opposition to, 152, 155; *see also* Nonviolence

Pastors' organizations, 155-56

Peace Movement of Ethiopia, 66

Phi Beta Sigma, 237, 268

Philbert X, 194

Pittsburgh Courier, 106, 129, 142-43, 148

Political affairs, discrimination in, 8, 88
Political tensions, Western and Afro-Asian worlds, 251-52
Politicians, Black Muslims and, 138-39
Poole, Elijah. *See* Muhammad, Elijah
Powell, Adam Clayton, 18, 138, 139, 192
Prayer, 80, 118, 219
Press, Negro, 106, 107, 112, 129-31, 141-45; white, 106, 107-8, 140, 176-78
Protest organizations, 232-33, 235, 246-53
Providence Bulletin, 176, 177
"Psychological insulation," 139-40
Publications, Black Muslim, 132-34, 141, 145

Quran (Qur'an), 11, 13, 53, 125, 172, 219

Race consciousness, 9, 56, 62, 67, 93, 161, 208-9; lack of, in Oriental religion, 51, 252
Race pride, 43, 56, 57, 58, 161, 162
Race riots, 56, 240
Racial dichotomy, 6-7
Racial equality, NAACP policy of, 241; *see also* Integrative organizations
Racial heritage, Negro, 48, 58, 250
Racial purity, nonexistence of, 45
Racial solidarity. *See* Unity
Racism, 34, 39, 151, 158, 169, 221
Radio programs, 134, 177-78
Randolph, A. Philip, 64, 241
Ras Tafarian cult, 50, 58
Reader's Digest, 107, 140
"Red Summer" of 1919, 8, 56
Redding, J. Saunders, 239, 242
Rehabilitation, 29, 82, 111, 114-15, 190, 250
Religion, 246; in background of Muslims, 26; beliefs and rites of, 213; in Black Muslim Movement, 212-23, 250; freedom of, in America, 210, 212; nationalism in, 51-55, 61-62; types of groups

in, 214-17
Reporter magazine, 140, 176, 178
Respectability, search for, 200, 204-9, 214
Responsibility, emphasis on, 30, 32, 55; of Negro fraternities and sororities, 238
Ritual requirements, 80, 118, 219
Robinson, Jackie, 138, 155
Rogers, J. A., 138
Rose, Arnold, 230
Rozier, Theodore, 26, 182, 196
Rutherford, Joseph F., 13

Salaam, 133
"School case" decision, 7, 244, 257-58
Schools, Black Muslim, 14, 26, 32, 126-28, 211, 250
Schuyler, George S., 142
Sect, 214, 215, 267; Black Muslims as, 218-23, 248
Segregation, 41; directed at class, not individual, 47; as Black Muslim policy, 252; *see also* Integration
Self-assurance, 116
Self-discipline, 91, 104, 105, 137, 161, 194
Self-hatred, 35, 70
Self-image, 43, 48, 205
Self-improvement, 37, 57
Self-sacrifice, 103-4
Separation, economic, 20, 88, 90-93, 247; political, 4, 10, 46, 72, 88, 94-97, 129, 137; racial, 87-90, 196
Separatism, 154, 174, 247; white, 234
Separatist organizations, 234-38, 247
Sex roles, 31, 32, 55, 82, 83; *see also* Males *and* Women
Sharrieff, Raymond, 85, 130, 133, 184, 193, 195, 199, 200
Sherrill, William L., 65
Sit-in movement, 20, 79, 152, 154, 155, 159-60, 161, 245
Slave insurrections, 41, 43, 44
Slavery, mental, 69, 122, 180
Social class, black nationalism and, 24, 46-49
Social distinctiveness, 46, 47

Social protest, 218, 227-34, 235; Black Muslims as vehicle of, 246-53
Sociology, data of, 6-7
South, black nationalism in, 33; desegregation in, 159-60, 230; position of churches in, on slavery, 222; violation of etiquette rules in, 36, 40
Southern Christian Leadership Conference, 244
Southern Regional Council, 245
Spanish-speaking Americans, 233
Springfield, Ill., race riot in, 240
Staton, Dakota, 171
Steinbeck, John, 136
Stereotype, 41-42, 54, 119, 168
Stone, Chuck, 134
Stout, Bill, 177-78
Supreme Court, NAACP cases in, 241; "school case" decision of, 7, 244, 257-58
Supreme Wisdom, 124, 132, 180

Takahashi, Major, 16, 26
Television, 107, 134, 177-78
Temples, Black Muslim, 16, 17, 22, 24, 26, 81-82, 107, 181, 182, 184, 185-86, 194, 197, 198; visit to, 115-26
Thelma X, 194
Theosophists, 215
Time magazine, 107, 140, 142-43, 176
Tobacco, prohibition of, 81, 164
Touré, President and Mrs. Séku, 150
Toynbee, Arnold, 6
Trial, The, 113
"Trials" of Muslims, 201
Troeltsch, Ernst, 214, 216
Truman, Harry, 42
Tynetta X, 194

"Union-busting" interest in Muslims, 16
United African Nationalist Movement, 50, 66, 150
United Arab Republic, 223-25
United League of Latin American Citizens (ULLAC), 233
Unity, Black Muslim, 27, 30, 247; cultural, 45; instruments of, 103-6; of a mass movement, 99, 103-6; of a minority, 230; racial, 70, 84-87, 92, 146, 159, 160, 186, 238
Universal Negro Improvement Association, 50, 56-66; *see also* Garvey, Marcus
Universities of Islam, 14, 26, 127, 211
Up From Slavery, 57
Upper class, Negro, 46-47, 111-12, 156
Urban League, 64, 98, 151-52, 242-44

Vesey, Denmark, 43-44
Visibility, of Japanese-Americans, 232; of Jews, among Negroes, 167; of Negroes, 36, 46, 47
Vote, restrictions on, 8, 88
Voting behavior of Muslims, 18, 19

Wallace, Mike, 107, 134
Walling, William English, 240
Walters, Col., 138
Warner, W. Lloyd, 6, 44, 234
Washington, Booker T., 57
Washington, D. C., race riot in, 56; Temple 4 in, 194, 198
Weapons, prohibition of, 107, 117-18
White ancestry of Negroes, 46, 47
White men, and Black Muslims, 172-78, 210; enslavement of blacks by, 77-78; origin of, 76-77
White supremacy, 240, 258; and Christian church, 28, 78-80, 131
Wilfred X, 182, 194
Wilkins, Roy, 138, 147, 151, 155, 241
Williams, Jerry, 134
Women, forbidden contact with whites, 172; as leaders in Black Muslim Movement, 194; role of, 31, 32, 55, 83
World War II, 188

X as symbol in names, 110

Yakub, 76, 77
Yaslum, Gulam, 170
Yinger, J. Milton, 214, 215, 216, 217
Young, L. Masco, 133
"Young Blacks," 31

Zionism, 60, 148-49, 166